Consumer Culture
Second Edition

Consumer Culture

Second Edition

Celia Lury

polity

The right of Celia Lury to be identified as Author of this Work has been asserted in accordance with the UK Copyright, Designs and Patents Act 1988.

First edition published in 1996 by Polity Press
This edition first published in 2011 by Polity Press
Reprinted 2012

Polity Press
65 Bridge Street
Cambridge CB2 1UR, UK

Polity Press
350 Main Street
Malden, MA 02148, USA

ISBN-13: 978-0-7456-4329-8
ISBN-13: 978-0-7456-4330-4(pb)

A catalogue record for this book is available from the British Library.

Typeset in 10.5 on 12 pt Plantin
by Servis Filmsetting Ltd, Stockport, Cheshire
Printed and bound in Great Britain by MPG Books Group

The publisher has used its best endeavours to ensure that the URLs for external websites referred to in this book are correct and active at the time of going to press. However, the publisher has no responsibility for the websites and can make no guarantee that a site will remain live or that the content is or will remain appropriate.

Every effort has been made to trace all copyright holders, but if any have been inadvertently overlooked the publisher will be pleased to include any necessary credits in any subsequent reprint or edition.

For further information on Polity, visit our website: www.politybooks.com

Contents

Acknowledgement

I would like to dedicate this book to Eva Lash, and to thank her for permission to use the photographs included in the book. I would also like to thank my students and colleagues at Goldsmiths, readers and critics of the first edition of Consumer Culture, and Emma Longstaff from Polity, who encouraged me to embark on a second edition.

Introduction: What is Consumer Culture?

This chapter asks: 'What is consumer culture?', and in answer gives a list:

- The availability of a large and increasing number and range of types of goods for sale. There was, for example, a nearly tenfold increase in the number of new products introduced yearly in the

United States between the 1970s and the mid-1990s (Schor, 1999, quoted in Storper, 2001).

- The tendency for more and more aspects of human life to be made available through the market. One instance of this is the marketization of what were previously state or publicly provided services in the UK. Examples include health, housing and education – such that it is said that Britain is now a home-owning nation and that students are consumers of education.
- The expansion of shopping as a leisure pursuit – in the United States, shopping is the second most popular leisure pursuit – six hours per person a week – after watching television (Nicholson-Lord, 1992), while already in 1987 the country had more shopping malls than high schools. More recently, annual retail sales add up to more than $3 trillion a year, while consumer spending is thought to account for two thirds of US national economic growth (Zukin, 2004).

> Ikea's 2006 facts and figures report reckons that 458 million people visited its stores in 2006 – a figure approaching that of the entire population of the European Union. In France alone, Ikea was the second-largest supplier in all sectors of the furniture market in 2005, outdone only by the styleless, no-frills Conforama chain . . ., and, at this rate, may well be set to achieve first place by the end of 2007. Ikea's most popular product, the 'Billy' bookcase, has sold 28 million units world-wide since its inauguration in 1978, a figure slightly more than the population of Iraq. The Swedish superstore was generating an annual income of some 17.3 billion Euros by 2006, which has allowed farmer's son Ingvar Kamprad, who founded the business in 1943, to become one of the richest men in the world. (Hartman, 2007: 484)

- A proliferation of spaces, platforms and modes of consuming, including, for example, an increase in the range of different forums of shopping, from Internet shopping (including eBay and Amazon), retail tourism, mail-order, shopping malls, rummage sales, car-boot fairs, farmers' markets, vintage, pop-up and second-hand shops.
- An increase in sites for purchase and consumption, including the spread of shopping malls – between 1986 and 1990 almost 30 million square feet of shopping centre space was opened in the UK (Cowe, 1994) while the amount of retail space per person in the

USA has quadrupled over the last thirty years (Zukin, 2004) – and the emergence of so-called 'third spaces', in between home and work such as the Starbucks chain of coffee shops, but also gyms and clubs.
- The growth in size of retail chain stores, with stores in chains such as Walmart, Target, Home Depot and The Gap occupying up to 200,000 and even 300,000 square feet (Zukin, 2004); the growth in number of retail parks, leisure complexes, and consumption environments, from the increase in 'themed' pubs and restaurants to the setting up of Niketowns and Disneyworlds.

> Adidas . . . will have 5,000 shops in China by the end of the year [2008]. Its new store in Sanlitun – several miles away from the Bird's Nest Stadium – opened last month, and is the largest in the world, with 3,170 sq m of retail space over four floors. (Branigan, 2008: 23)

- The lifting in restrictions on borrowing money and the associated change in meaning of being in debt. During the last century, for example, there was a shift from the dubious respectability of the 'never-never', through the anxieties of hire purchase to the competitive display of credit cards – to a situation in which an Access card could be your 'flexible friend' and a Platinum American Express card is a symbol of elite exclusivity.
- The ethical and political organization of consumers by non-governmental organizations, companies and the state.

> A khakhi green café restaurant has quietly materialized in Hemel Hempstead. Under subdued lamplight, with the indie rock of the Editors playing in the background, a lunching doctor sits on a curvy chair modeled on Arne Jacobsen's modernist classic. He could have chosen Rainforest Alliance certified freshly ground coffee, with British organic milk, or a free-range egg, delivered by a lorry powered by biodiesel from recycled cooking oil, and a bag of carrot sticks or fresh fruit . . . But he has plumped for a Filet-o-Fish, fries and a fizzy drink. (Barkham, 2008: 7)

- The rise of brands, their increasing visibility inside and outside the economy.
- The pervasiveness of advertising in everyday life. It is said that a child today sees over 20,000 commercials annually (quoted in Yan, 2003: 200).

> In Japan, Mickey Mouse is being pursued by a cat. By many accounts she is an even more innocent, innocuous, and cute creature. She goes by the name of Hello Kitty. At the risk of sounding conspiratorial, Hello Kitty is not as innocent as she appears, and it is her very innocuousness that conceals her power. . .
>
> . . . Hello Kitty is the best known product of Sanrio, a Tokyo-based company founded in 1960 by Tsuji Shintarô. Sanrio's profits are enormous, totaling 120 million yen in 1998. In 1999, that equals approximately one billion US dollars. (McVeigh, 2000: 226)

> A Whitehall counter-terrorism unit is targeting the BBC and other media organizations as part of a new global propaganda push designed to 'taint the al-Qaida brand', according to a secret Home Office paper seen by the Guardian. (Travis, 2008: 1)

• The growing importance of packaging and promotion in the manufacture, display and purchase of consumer goods.

> [Bottled water] is now the fastest growing market in the global beverage industry with consumption highest in countries that have access to safe drinking water. It is the second largest beverage sold in the US with per capita consumption doubling between 1993–2003. In Canada bottled water outstrips coffee, tea, apple juice and milk. Markets are also growing in countries that are rapidly modernizing, and where water infrastructure is unsafe and/or underdeveloped. (Hawkins, 2009: 185)

• The rise of the use of the barcode – and more recently radio frequency ID (RFID) labels – to monitor and manage the sales of products: it is estimated that 5 billion barcodes are now scanned every day across the world (Sterling, 2005).
• The emergence of a range of so-called consumer crimes – credit card fraud, shoplifting and ram-raiding – and forms of retail therapy such as spas, health treatments and shopping itself.
• The difficulty of avoiding making choices in relation to goods and services, and the associated celebration of self-fashioning or self-transformation and the promotion of lifestyle as a way of life.
• The increasing visibility of so-called consumer illnesses linked to

what have been called 'maladies of agency' (Seltzer, 1993) and pathologies or 'maladies of the will' (Sedgwick, 1994) such as addiction, whether it be addiction to alcohol, sex, food or shopping, kleptomania, 'binge shopping' or compulsive buying.

One of the things that might strike you about this list is its length (and it would be easy to add more points), but another might be its heterogeneity. How are we to understand the diversity of things, processes, values, norms and practices that make up consumer culture? Most writers believe that there is not a single process at work in the emergence and growth of consumer culture, but a variety, pulling in different directions. Some of the most significant of these processes are:

1 The organized interpenetration of economic and everyday life.
2 The increasing importance of the exchange of commodities, that is, objects and services appropriated or produced for exchange on the market within an increasingly global capitalist division of labour, driven by the pursuit of profit.
3 The development of a series of ongoing relationships between different systems of exchange or regimes of value. These changes

have created a situation in which activities are linked through a whole set of interlinking cycles of production and consumption, associated with, but not necessarily determined by, the organization of commodity exchange.

4 The growth of a range of different forms of consumer politics, which seek to mobilize consumers to influence the state, producers and other consumers.

5 The active role of the state in organizing collective and individual forms of consumption.

6 The use of goods in contemporary societies by specific social groups or cultural intermediaries leading to forms of expertise and the creation of subcultures or lifestyles.

7 The political identification of freedom with individual choice.

Given the multiple histories and geographies of consumer cultures in different societies, this book cannot describe or explain the emergence and development of these processes in full. Indeed, it provides only very brief discussions of the history of consumer culture or the different forms it displays in different societies. Instead it aims to give you a series of perspectives to think about these processes. Chapter 1 outlines the significance of a material culture perspective, and stresses the importance of the distinction between the study of consumption and the study of consumer culture. Chapter 2 provides an account of different kinds of exchange, while chapter 3 explores the relations between objects and signs. In chapter 4 a number of explanations, understandings and descriptions of the history of the emergence of consumer culture will be introduced briefly, each of which gives a different emphasis to the processes just outlined here. This will lead into an account of the role of capital and class relations in the shaping of consumer culture in the UK in the second half of the twentieth century. In chapter 5, the importance of race and gender in the expansion of the circuits of consumption will be described by way of a number of case studies, giving a series of snapshots of the complex, dynamic and transnational relations of consumer culture. This will lead into a consideration of the mediatization of the economy, and the contemporary significance of branding in chapter 6. This is followed by an account of the ethics of consumer culture in chapter 7, which explores the complexities of making ethical consumer choices. Finally, chapter 8 addresses the implications of consumer culture for contemporary understandings of the self, social belonging and politics.

There is a double focus in each chapter and across the book as a whole. On the one hand, the aim is to provide an overview of key perspectives and studies relating to consumer culture, organized in relation to the themes of individual chapters as just described. On the other hand, across all the chapters, the book draws out the implications of these perspectives for understanding the significance of contemporary consumer culture for individual and collective identities. The exploration of the thesis that consumer culture is central to identity highlights the importance of recent transformations in the economy, foregrounding changes in the relationship between production and consumption, and focuses on issues of reflexivity, lifestyle and choice. The argument is that consumer culture has contributed to the emergence and growth of object worlds that encourage forms of reflexivity in individual and collective identity. In conclusion, the final chapter draws attention to debates that suggest that although personal and collective identity is still central to our participation in consumer culture, the terms of that identity are undergoing significant transformation.

1
Material Culture and Consumer Culture

Introduction

This chapter will start by introducing the view that consumer culture is a type of *material culture*, that is, *a culture of the use or appropriation of objects or things*. This is the starting point to the book as a whole since the argument that will be made is that consumer culture is a type of material culture in which the consumer emerges as an identity – as what Frank Trentmann calls a 'master category of collective and individual identity':

> Put simply, all human societies have been engaged in consumption and have purchased, exchanged, gifted or used objects and services, but it has only been in specific contexts in the nineteenth and twentieth centuries that some (not all) practices of consumption have been connected to a sense of being a 'consumer', as an identity, audience or category of analysis. (2006b: 2)

The book will argue that the emergence of the consumer as a master category of identity is a consequence of the growth of reflexive object worlds. But it begins with the term 'material culture' – and not simply consumer culture – for a number of reasons. The first half of the term – 'material' – points to the significance of *stuff*, of *things* in everyday practices, while the second half – 'culture' – indicates that this attention to the materials of everyday life is combined with a concern with the cultural, with norms, values and practices. The term 'material culture' is useful, then, because it implies that the material and the cultural are always combined together in specific relations and that these relations may be subject to study.

The term 'material culture' is also useful because it gives a critical distance on everyday uses of the term 'consumption'. The *Pocket Oxford Dictionary* defines 'consume' as 'make away with, use up, devour, eat or drink up', and there is a common conflation of consumption with the final use or destruction of something. The use of the term 'material culture' makes it clear that consumption as 'use' is *not* always a 'using up', although this confusion, and the use of the language of consumption in phrases such as 'being consumed' by envy, greed, desire, etc. is revealing of some of the anxieties that are attached to consumption in Euro-American societies (for a discussion of the etymology of the word 'consumption', consult Williams, 1983). Instead of interpreting this culture as destruction or using up, focusing on consumer culture as an example of material culture enables consumption to be seen in terms of *appropriation* and *transformation*.

There are two further things to be said about the notion of the material here. First, it refers not simply to objects of consumption, but also to the organization of objects in environments, object worlds and spaces of consumer experiences. Second, it includes what is sometimes called immaterial culture. This is not as paradoxical as it sounds: the term immaterial culture as used here does not refer to non-material entities such as ideas. Instead it refers to (material) products or services whose important characteristics are the outcome of intellectual – or immaterial – labour. In other words, the term 'material culture' will be used in this book to include objects and environments whose characteristics are the outcome of material or physical labour and intellectual or immaterial labour. It is thus a term that can be used to consider the changing balance between these forms of labour and their interrelationship in consumer culture.

As the following chapters will demonstrate, capitalism and mass production are commonly seen as the most important factors in the rise of mass consumption and consumer culture in Euro-American societies, but an account that focuses only on these factors as 'the cause' of consumer culture is too simple. It obscures the significance of systems of trade, imperialism, the shifting impact of particular social groups, the state (in both capitalist and non-capitalist societies), and the importance of other systems of exchange, such as those occurring in the household, the family and communities of one kind or another, as well as the significance of art and design, cultural intermediaries, and subcultures. In other words, while consumer culture has often been understood in relation to production, this couplet – production–consumption – is not sufficiently nuanced on its own.

It isolates and opposes production and consumption, and implies simple causal relations of determination. Different perspectives place a different emphasis on consumption as buying, consumption as having, consumption as being and consumption as doing.

In place of the oppositional couple production–consumption, a variety of different terms to address the complexity of relations between production and consumption are introduced during the course of the book, including the notion of a *cultural circuit* or *cycle*, *mediation* and that of *prosumption* and *the prosumer* (Ritzer and Jurgenson, 2010). These terms make it possible to situate consumption and consumer culture within wider movements of the economy and culture, but the move beyond a strict determination of production by consumption should not be taken to imply that power relations are absent from consumer culture. Rather, the aim is to allow the significance of more complex, iterative, and multidimensional power relations to be explored.

Consumption and consumer culture

Before going any further, it is important to make clear a point that may seem obvious: this book is about *consumer culture*, not *consumption*. As such, it is not concerned with consumption practices in and of themselves, but rather with the *significance and character of the values, norms and meanings produced in such practices*. This focus emphasizes the complexity of the relationship between ownership and use of material goods, economic status, inequality and meaning.

On the one hand, the literature on the growth of consumption is extremely important for understanding something of the context for consumer culture insofar as it shows that a significant proportion of the populations of highly industrialized and (post-)industrial Euro-American societies are *dispossessed* – that is, they are excluded from many forms of commodity consumption as they do not have access to the economic resources necessary for participation. As Zygmunt Bauman points out:

> All commodities have a price-tag attached to them. These tags select the pool of potential customers. They do not directly determine the decisions the consumers will eventually make; those remain free. But they draw the boundary between the realistic and the feasible; the boundary which a given consumer cannot overstep. Behind the ostensible equality of chances the market promotes and advertises hides the

practical inequality of consumers – that is, the sharply differentiated
degrees of practical freedom of choice. (1990: 211)

The picture becomes even more stark if a global analysis is introduced: 20 per cent of the world's population – those residing in the
rich nations – account for over 80 per cent of total consumer spending. Clearly, poverty places severe limits on the ability to participate
in consumption insofar as it is linked to the purchase of commodities:
economic status restricts the possible extent of an individual's participation in consumption or practical freedom – as Bauman puts it – to
exercise consumer 'choice'.

On the other hand, however, it is important not to jump to conclusions about the nature of the relationship between the economic
status and participation in consumer culture, or to assume that
there is a direct or straightforward relationship between poverty and
exclusion from consumer culture or wealth and inclusion. First, it is
important to stress that by no means all consumption is consumption of commodities, but also includes consumption of gifts, of self-
produced objects, of freely given services, and so on. Second, studies
on poverty have shown that the relationships between economic
wealth and participation in material culture are highly complex and
historically variable. There are no universal, direct relationships
between an individual's economic standing, ownership of goods, perception of what goods count as necessities and luxuries, understandings of needs or wants, tastes, and sense of style. So, for example,
Paul Gilroy (2010) notes that while the relative poverty of African
Americans and their lack of equality have resulted in lower overall
levels of car ownership than those found among white Americans,
those who do have a vehicle are more likely to have a luxury model
and to have spent a higher proportion of their income on purchasing
it. As Bauman puts it, consumer inequality is felt, 'as an oppression
and a stimulus at the same time. It generates the painful experience
of deprivation, with . . . morbid consequences for self-esteem . . . It
also triggers off zealous efforts to enhance one's consumer capacity
– efforts that secure an unabating demand for market offers' (1990:
211). In short, while poverty restricts the possibility of participating
in the consumption of commodities, it does not necessarily prevent –
indeed, it may incite – participation in consumer culture.

Such tensions may be even more acute not only when *absolute*
levels of poverty are taken into account but also when the *relative*
inequality between the rich and the poor increases. Indeed socio-
economic positionality is one of the most important factors in

shaping the dynamics of contemporary consumer culture, although once again not in a straightforward way. It is thus worth noting here that alongside the surprisingly high figures in relation to absolute poverty *income inequality* has increased in most of the major industrial countries of Western Europe and North America, as well as in most middle-income developing countries, over the last twenty or so years (Storper, 2001). The degree of relative inequality is highest in the United States and Britain, lower in most of the continental countries in Europe, and still lower in Scandinavia. The need to consider relative and absolute levels of poverty thus must be considered at both national and global levels to understand consumption patterns and consumer cultures.

At the same time, it is important to acknowledge that the practices of consumer culture cannot be reduced to direct responses to processes of production or to either absolute or relative socio-economic inequality. This means that while the study of capitalism may tell us how it is that particular goods are made available for a price, and how class and social inequalities are reproduced, this does not tell us directly about the uses and meanings of those or other goods for people. To understand this, we need to understand the values, meanings and practices of consumer culture and this is the principal aim of this book.

An important point in this regard is that the dominance of a culture in a society does not require all that society's members to be able to participate in the culture on the same terms. Indeed, a culture may be dominant even if most people can only aspire to participate in it: its dominance is felt to the extent that people's aspirations, their hopes and fears, vocabulary of motives and sense of identity are defined in its terms. All these points suggest that while it is important to recognize that the terms of participation in consumer culture are profoundly unequal, these terms are not simply reproduced in the culture itself.

The stuff of material culture

So how then are we to understand the specificities of consumer culture? One of the most important reasons for starting with the notion of material culture is that it allows an exploration of how things – whether they are gifts, commodities, or just 'stuff' – play a role in the making of culture. An influential example of this approach is provided by Mary Douglas and Baron Isherwood in *The World of*

Goods (1979). For Douglas and Isherwood, an anthropologist and an economist respectively, consumption as it occurs in all societies is 'beyond commerce', that is, it is not restricted to commerce, but is always a cultural as well as an economic phenomenon. Indeed, from their point of view, 'the essential function of consumption is its capacity to make sense' (1979: 612). Consumption is to do with meaning, value and communication as much as it is to do with exchange and economic relations. They suggest that the utility of goods is always framed by a cultural context, that even the use of the most mundane and ordinary of objects in daily life has cultural meaning. From this anthropological perspective, material goods are not only used to do things, but they also have a meaning, and act as meaningful markers of social relations. *It is in acquiring, using and exchanging things that individuals come to have social lives.*

Douglas and Isherwood suggest that it should be standard practice to assume that all material possessions carry meanings and to analyse their use as communicators; that we need to see goods as a communication system. This anthropological approach, they believe, should apply to both so-called traditional *and* modern societies. Indeed, Douglas and Isherwood suggest that the application of this approach reveals that there are similarities in the ways in which all societies – traditional and modern – make meaning through the use of material goods. One way they seek to demonstrate this is by showing the significance of goods in ritual.

Rituals, in the anthropological sense, give shape and substance to social relations; they fix or anchor social relationships, making sense of the flux of events, and containing the drift of meaning. They are a kind of ballast against cultural drift; as such, they are a fundamental component of all societies. While ritual can take a verbal form, as in greetings or prayers, it is more effective, Douglas and Isherwood argue, when it is tied to material things, for goods 'are the visible part of culture' (1979: 66). From this perspective, the use of material things – consumption – is a key aspect of ritual processes. Some examples of the use of material goods in ritual processes in contemporary American society are provided by McCracken (1988). He identifies a number of examples of such rituals, including: (1) possession; (2) gift; and (3) divestment rituals.

1 Possession rituals is the term used by McCracken to refer to rituals involving the collecting, cleaning, comparing, showing off and even photographing of possessions – in, for example, the creation and display of a collection of Elvis memorabilia, or the

decoration of a bedroom with posters. These rituals allow the owner to lay claim to a kind of personal possession of the meaning of an object that is beyond simple ownership. They are a way of personalizing the object, a way of transferring meaning from the individual's own world to the newly obtained good, and are the means by which an anonymous object – often the product of a distant, impersonal process of mass manufacture – is turned into a possession that belongs to someone and speaks to and for him or her. Possession, in this view, is not a static state, but an activity. Through possession rituals, individuals create a personal world of goods that reflects their experience, concepts of self and the world. Such rituals help establish an individual's *social identity*. And it is in rituals such as these that the performative capacity of goods is made visible; through performance, objects express certain aspects of a person's identity.

2   Gift rituals, especially those of birthday and Christmas, typically involve the choice and presentation of consumer goods by one person and their receipt by another. This movement of goods is also a movement of meanings. Often the gift-giver chooses a particular gift because it possesses the meaningful properties he or she wishes to see transferred to the gift-receiver. So, for instance, a woman who receives a dress is invited to define herself in terms of its style; the giver of flowers or chocolates may be asking the receiver to show properties of gentleness, or sweetness. In the same way, many of the gifts that are given by parents to children are motivated by a desire to transfer meanings as well as material possessions. From this point of view, the giving of objects on ritual occasions – birthdays, anniversaries, special occasions such as Valentine's Day – can be seen as a powerful means of *interpersonal communication or influence*.

3   Divestment rituals are employed to empty a good of meaning when it is transferred from one person to another. They are employed for two purposes. When an individual purchases a good that has been previously owned, such as a house or a car, the ritual is used to erase the meaning associated with the previous owner. The cleaning and redecorating of a newly purchased house, for example, may be seen as an attempt to remove the meanings associated with the previous owner. A second kind of divestment ritual takes place when an individual is about to dispense with a good, either by giving it away or selling it. An attempt will be made to erase the meaning that has been invested in the good by association. What such rituals suggest is a concern that the meaning of goods

can be transferred, obscured or confused, or even lost when goods change hands. McCracken suggests that the fear of dispossession of personal meaning resembles the fear of 'merging of identities' that sometimes occurs between transplant donors and recipients. In order to counteract this fear, the good is emptied of meaning in a divestment ritual before being passed along. What looks like superstition is an implicit acknowledgement of the *movable* quality of the meaning with which goods are invested, and of their significance in a system of symbolic exchange.

As a consequence of their use in ritual processes, goods come to be used for making visible and stable the basic categories of placing or classifying people in society. Goods act as sources of social identity and carry or communicate social meaning. They are capable of creating or enacting cultural assumptions and beliefs; they give such beliefs a reality, a facticity, what Douglas and Isherwood would call a concreteness, which they would not otherwise have. They have the effect of stabilizing human life.

What this discussion of the use of goods in rituals illustrates is that goods – things or stuff – can act as *markers or performers of social identity*, that they can act as *carriers of interpersonal influence*; and that their *meaning is movable*, that is, that it may be changed as goods circulate. For Douglas and Isherwood, the process of making goods meaningful in ritual is primarily *consensual*. It results from the active participation of everyone in a particular culture in a process of making meaning. They write:

> Goods are endowed with value by the meaning of fellow consumers . . . Each person is a source of judgements and a subject of judgements; each individual is in the classification scheme whose discriminations he [sic] is helping to establish . . . The kind of world they create together is constructed from commodities that are chosen for their fitness to mark the events, such as birthdays, weddings and funerals, in an appropriately graded scale. (1979: 75)

Douglas and Isherwood also suggest that individuals will strive to put themselves in a position from which they might gain not just access to but control of cultural meanings, and that individuals will adopt strategies to make sure that they are not marginalized by the system. However, they do not focus on the relationships between material culture, power and social inequality, and do not investigate the ways in which material culture may help create or consolidate inequality in any detail. In other words, at the same time as opening up a whole field of analysis – material culture – they put forward a rather static account of the operation of power and conflict. Yet, as the rest of the book will show, there are enormous differences in the way that the exchange of things is carried out in different societies and these differences are linked to issues of power and control.

Douglas and Isherwood do not really consider how modern systems of production, publicity and communication, such as the media and advertising, may affect individuals' participation in this process of making judgements and being judged. All goods are simply treated as 'a non-verbal medium for the human creative faculty' (1979: 62). Some would say that in adopting this approach, Douglas and Isherwood end up supporting the view that users or consumers make their own meanings, and that they fail to deal adequately with issues of symbolic power and control. As this book will go on to suggest, other writers believe that a distinctive feature of contemporary material culture is the extent to which the complex cultural dimensions of the contemporary economy have acquired a relative independence such that they can be distinguished as a discrete culture with its own norms, values and practices.

To sum up, Douglas and Isherwood suggest that it is possible to see continuities in the ways in which individuals make social meanings through their use of material goods in traditional and modern societies. Indeed, they suggest that there is nothing especially distinctive about the expressive use of material goods in modern societies. This argument is important insofar as it points to the symbolic role of objects and points to continuities between traditional and modern societies; in doing so, it challenges the sometimes exaggerated differences between them. It restores the 'cultural dimension to societies that are often represented simply as economies writ large, and restores the calculative dimension to societies that are too often simply portrayed as solidarity writ small' (Appadurai, 1986: 12). Such a perspective on material culture points to ways in which what Clifford calls 'some sort of "gathering" around the self and the group – the assemblage of the material world, the marking-off of a subjective domain that is not "other" is a pervasive feature of most, if not all societies' (1988: 218). However, in its emphasis on the often apparently timeless characteristic of ritual, it ignores contrasts between different worlds of things and the social lives they make possible.

Marshall Sahlins puts forward an alternative anthropological approach to material culture, focusing once again on the moment of use, relatively isolated from the cycle of production, distribution, use and reproduction. However, where Douglas and Isherwood draw on the concept of ritual, Sahlins (1976) draws on the anthropological concept of totemism to develop an analysis of consumption – especially food and clothing – in modern Western societies.

Totemism is the symbolic association of plants, animals or objects with individuals or groups of people, and is an important feature of many societies. In one of the most well-known analyses of totemism, Lévi-Strauss (1963) argues that it is a common process in which the natural world is divided into different groups of species and things in ways which reflect and create social differences. He argues that the term totemism covers relations, posed between two series, one *natural* the other *cultural*; that is, a natural object such as the sun, a plant or an animal comes to stand for, or be the symbolic representation of, a tribe or a social group. That tribe is recognized by its use of the object and its members' shared appreciation of what the object stands for. The object is thus simultaneously a natural and a cultural object; its meaning is closely tied to the ways in which it acts as a means of communicating the social hierarchies of the group for whom it has cultural significance.

Sahlins extends this argument, applying it to modern societies. He argues that modern societies have substituted manufactured objects for species or natural objects. In other words, manufactured objects such as a motorcycle, a drink, or an item of clothing act as totems in the modern world; and consumer groups are like tribes in traditional societies. Sahlins shows, for example, how items of clothing can act like totems, communicating distinct social identities and identifying different 'tribes'. He sees our clothing system not simply as a set of material objects to keep its wearers warm, but as a symbolic code by which its wearers communicate their membership of social groups. So, for example, the clothing that shows a distinction between men and women or between upper and lower classes also shows something of the nature of the difference that is supposed to exist between them. It communicates the supposed 'delicacy' of women and the supposed 'strength' of men, the supposed 'refinement' of the upper classes and the supposed 'vulgarity' of the lower classes. Clothing can thus be seen to communicate the properties that are supposed to inhere in cultural categories and that serve as the basis for their discrimination.

A classic example of this kind of anthropological analysis is to be found in Paul Willis's study of a motorbike club (1982). In the conclusion to this study, Willis suggests that the motorbike acted as a kind of totem for the group of young men who belonged to the club. Their dress, their appearance and their values were all linked to their

use and understanding of the motorbike, and in that way the motorbike marked them out from other groups. The motorbike was not
simply appreciated for its ability to get someone from A to B, that is,
for its utility as a means of transport, but as a totem of a certain kind
of working-class masculinity; it was part of a symbolic code.

> The motorcycle boys accepted the motorbike and allowed it to rever-
> berate right through into the world of human concourse . . . The lack of
> the helmet allowed long hair to flow freely back in the wind, and this,
> with the studded and ornamented jackets, and the aggressive style of
> riding, gave the motorbike boys a fearsome look which amplified the
> wildness, noise, surprise and intimidation of the motorbike . . . The
> motorbikes themselves were modified to accentuate these features. The
> high cattlehorn handlebars, the chromium-plated mudguards gave the
> bikes an exaggerated look of fierce power . . . The ensemble of bike,
> noise, rider, clothes, *on the move* gave formidable expression of identity
> to the culture and powerfully developed many of its central values.
> (1982: 297–9)

The bikers did not value clothing that protected the wearer from
the elements, or streamlined the body. Instead, they preferred loose
clothing that blew in the wind and allowed them to feel the excite-
ment of travelling, even though this reduced their speed. Similarly,
they customized their bikes by giving them high handlebars, which
meant that they were forced to sit upright. Once again, this restricted
the speed they were able to travel at, but gave them a frightening
appearance. In other words, the relation of these young men to the
motorbike was not a functional or instrumental one, but one which
allowed them to display a particular set of values, in this case, those
associated with a working-class masculinity.

At the same time, an individual member's relation to the use of the
motorbike provided the basis for hierarchies within the group. So,
for example, members who, while technically very skilled mechanics,
were very cautious riders were placed low on this internal hierarchy,
while members who risked life and limb were rated highly by other
members irrespective of their mechanical skills. Members who died
in accidents were ritually mourned, and were accorded the status of
heroes. In this way, members' relations to each other were mediated
through a particular understanding of the bike as a totem of working-
class masculinity.

This kind of analysis, once again, is drawing parallels between the
use of goods in traditional and modern societies. However, while
Sahlins, like Douglas and Isherwood, points to similarities in the use
of material goods as totems in traditional and modern societies, he
also identifies some differences. He writes:

> The object stands as a human concept outside itself, as man [*sic*]
> speaking to man through the medium of things. And the systematic
> variation in objective features [in manufactured objects] is capable of

serving, even better than the differences between natural species [as the medium of a vast and dynamic system of thought] because in manufactured objects many differences can be varied at once, and by a godlike manipulation. (1976: 43)

The question that arises here is how the object's manufacture or 'godlike manipulation' alters the functioning of ritual and the practices of totemism in modern societies.

More recently, the anthropologist Daniel Miller (1987) has elaborated a general list of ways in which objects contribute to the organization of social relations, the making of material culture.

1 *Function.* To put this simply, we do things with objects; they have functions for us. This is most obvious in relation to tools and machines but is also more generally true, although as Miller points out the register of use is privileged in some societies more than others. To put this another way, the idea that an object is useful or has useful properties depends on the existence of a particular way of life in which there are particular things to be done and particular ways of doing them. Modern Western societies are examples of those in which use – and the related values of effectivity, efficiency and so on – dominates object relations. The design ethos that form should follow function is an example of this philosophy. But even in such societies, Miller suggests, things have a capacity to separate themselves from the immediacy of utility.

2 *Self.* Miller points to the importance of objects in the creation of the subject's social identity – in other words, he suggests that not only is there a close relationship between objects and doing, but also between objects and being. Miller describes this in terms of the relationship of having and being.

3 *Space.* This is a two-way relationship – objects can make a space and space can make or define the meaning and value of objects. So, for example, one of the ways in which a house is made into a home is through the occupants' transformation of this space through the introduction and arrangement of objects. On the other hand, the value and meaning of an object is often tied to the space or place from which it originates. Miller gives the example here of the stone lapis lazuli, which he says has been valued not only for the brilliance of its colour, but also because it was derived from a single source, and thus signifies its origins in terms of distance, far-awayness or the exotic.

4 *Time.* Material objects are one of the principal means of objectifying

a sense of the past; so, for example, the signs of an object's age – from wear and tear to showing the patina of age – may contribute to a sense of the past, and the rapid turnover of objects in time is one of the things that can contribute to a sense of fashion or the new.

5 *Style.* Objects can be more or less stylized. Once again, this is not a fixed or universal property of objects for Miller, but instead is a consequence of the ways in which objects are related to each other within a particular society. Style emerges from the process of comparing things – whether and how they are similar to and different from other objects in the same domain. Understanding objects in terms of style means locating that object in relation to others, and then comparing it with others on the basis of selected dimensions. These comparisons create distinctions of style between objects.

In these five ways, Miller shows how objects have the capacity to integrate an individual into the normative order of the larger social group, where they serve as a medium for social relations or sociality, without presuming how they do so. Interestingly, Miller suggests that the last of these characteristics – style – is increasing in importance:

> style has achieved a certain autonomy in contemporary industrial society, going beyond its capacity for ordering to become itself the focus of concern . . . In this new world, all architecture, furnishing, clothing and behaviour are intended to relate to each other in a visibly coherent fashion. This works to break down all frames into a universal order of good design. (1987: 129)

The accessory is now to be understood not simply as a limited class of goods (of hats, gloves and bags), but in relation to a tendency in which more and more goods – including animals, as in the case of small dogs carried by celebrities – can be defined as accessories. And in the case of the dogs, the accessories have accessories – collars, jackets and so on. In the chain of shops called Accessorize goods are designed to demonstrate the verb, 'to accessorize'. An article in *Time* on the rise of design claims, 'Shopping for household items is no longer dutiful; it's part of a person's articulation of his or her personal style. Everything is an accessory' (Gibney and Luscombe, 2000: 54). An unrelated feature in the same issue has the heading, 'Wheelie good fun. Shiny, compact and cool, scooters have become Europe's ubiquitous accessory'

(Labi, 2000). An advertisement for a dinnerware company in the same issue asserts 'Accessories? A great way to forget your salad came in a bag. We know your life is often one big time crunch. So we do what we can to make things easier. Like offering you more matching accessories, in more patterns, than any other dinnerware company' (Lury, 2002: 217–18).

Miller's approach is especially interesting for the present study, however, because he is specifically concerned with material culture in the context of what he calls mass consumption (1987). He is at pains to address the sometimes derogatory implications of some uses of 'mass', acknowledging that modern material culture is often regarded as either trivial or degraded. He suggests that this 'anti-materialism' often stems from the belief that members of pre-industrial societies, free of the burden of artefacts, lived in more immediate, natural relationships with each other. He argues that this view is mistaken, and has prejudiced the analysis of the activities that comprise contemporary material culture. In his own studies of mass consumption as material culture, he attempts to adopt what he calls a non-dualistic model of the relations between people and things, studying neither people nor things in isolation from one another, without jumping to the conclusion that people are manipulated or subordinated in their use of things. For example, in an ethnographic study of shoppers in north London, Miller (2001) shows how the practice of shopping expresses and provides means of resolving contradictions in shoppers' lives; so, for example, clothes may be chosen because of their ability to express both a man's professional identity and his masculinity.

Miller argues that it is inappropriate to understand mass consumption in modern societies as a single thing, that is, in relation to the workings of a single, central hierarchical principle, whether this is the division of labour or the practice of emulation. He writes, 'As mass consumption, a particular array of objects may be found to represent and assist in the construction of perspectives relating to control over production or rivalry between consumers, but also to wider issues concerning morality and social ideals' (1987: 158). He argues for the necessity of analysing mass consumption in relation to 'a wide range of agents and relevant factors', including:

> forms of production and commerce and the demands of profit, the interests and constraints on manufacture, design, marketing and advertising, whose role it is to create the images of industrial goods in relation

to specified target populations, and the interests and constraints on the consumer population, who use and in their turn manipulate the meaning of these forms through differential selection, placement, use and association. (1987: 158–9)

He concludes that such an approach reveals the positive appropriation of goods by the pluralistic, small-scale communities that he believes make up the population of contemporary society. For Miller, then, mass consumption is the site at which a whole range of often self-contradictory and unbalanced desires, constraints and possibilities come together in a very incoherent process – what he describes as a kind of *practical kitsch*.

Despite this incoherence, Miller believes that mass consumption has the potential to produce what he calls an *inalienable culture*, that is, a culture invested by its users through a process of recontextualization of objects in specific sites with meanings that 'negate the abstraction of commodification'. He writes, 'Mass consumption may also be seen as . . . the creation of an inalienable world in which objects are so firmly integrated in the development of particular social relations and group identity as to be clearly generative of society' (1987: 204). Similarly, he argues that the sheer profusion of fashion, rather than overwhelming with its diversity, facilitates the building up of multiple social groups who define themselves through the assertion of a specific style. He also points out that:

> Small sections of the population become immersed to an extraordinary degree in the enormous profusion of hobbies, sports, clubs, fringe activities, and the nationwide organizations devoted to interests as diverse as medieval music, swimming, ballroom dancing, steel bands and fan clubs. The building of social networks and leisure activities around these highly particular pursuits is one of the strangest and most exotic features of contemporary industrial society, and one which is for ever increasing. There is no more eloquent confrontation with the abstraction of money, the state and modernity than a life devoted to racing pigeons, or medieval fantasies played out on a microcomputer. (1987: 209–10)

Material culture or consumer culture?

In a whole series of studies, Miller is at pains to illustrate the variety of contemporary forms of material culture, but other writers believe that it is possible – and necessary – to identify a coherence or consistency in the values and practices of contemporary consumption. Some of the most influential accounts describe this culture in terms of a consumer logic (Leiss, 1976) or consumer attitude (Bauman, 1990).

In relation to the first of these, Leiss (1976) argues that modern Euro-American societies are characterized by the growth of what he calls a high-intensity market setting in which individuals are trained to act as consumers. This growth is seen to have two key features: the number and complexity of available goods in the marketplace grows enormously and individuals tend to interpret feelings of well-being more and more exclusively in terms of their relative success in gaining access to high levels of consumption. However, he suggests that the intensification of commodity circulation has a number of negative effects as a result of the fact that the 'direct interaction between impulses and sources of satisfaction is broken; impulses are controlled and consciously directed towards an enlarged field of satisfaction' (1976: 61).

The negative effects include a fragmentation and destabilization of the categories of needing; the difficulty of matching the qualities of needs with the characteristics of goods; a growing indifference to the qualities of needs or wants; and an increasing environmental risk for individuals and for society as a whole. Together, these developments comprise what he calls a logic or ethic of consumption. Leiss does not think that there is anything 'inherently evil' in commodities and market exchange, but suggests that there is 'cause for concern' when commodity exchange becomes the exclusive mode for the satisfaction of human needs, displacing friendships and family relationships, engagement in political or community activities and so on.

Bauman (1990) shares similar concerns. He describes what he calls the consumer attitude as a way of life in which the market is the principal reference point:

> What does it mean to have and to display a consumer attitude? It means, first perceiving life as a series of problems, which can be specified, more or less clearly defined, singled out and dealt with. It means, secondly, believing that dealing with such problems, solving them, is one's duty, which one cannot neglect without incurring guilt or shame. It means, thirdly, trusting that for every problem, already known or as may still arise in the future, there is a solution – a special object or recipe, prepared by specialists, by people with superior know-how, and one's task is to find it. It means, fourthly, assuming that such objects or recipes are essentially available; they may be obtained in exchange for money, and shopping is the way of obtaining them. It means, fifthly, translating the task of learning the art of living as the effort to acquire

the skill of finding such objects and recipes, and gaining the power
to possess them once found: shopping skills and purchasing power.
(Bauman, 1990: 204)

For Bauman, the widespread adoption of the consumer attitude
means, on the one hand, that life is turned into an individual affair,
that public issues are individualized, and, on the other, that what it
is to be an individual is defined by consumer activity. This is seen
to have transformed the basis of modern politics, which is now concerned with the self-making of individuals (see chapter 8 for a more
detailed discussion of this politics).

Both the notion of a consumer logic or ethic and that of a consumer attitude offer powerful ways of thinking about consumer
culture. They suggest that it is possible to identify distinctive values
in contemporary material culture. Other writers have adopted a
similar approach. So, for example, Helga Dittmar (1992) argues
that modern Euro-American consumer culture is characterized by
the strongly rooted belief that *to have is to be*. In other words, people
are said to be coming to define themselves and others in terms of
what they possess. Indeed, Dittmar argues that most people describe
possessions as aspects of the self, and their loss is experienced as a
personal violation and a lessening of the self. In other words, material
possessions serve as key symbols for personal qualities, attachments
and interests. She sums up this view thus:

> in Western materialistic societies . . . an individual's identity is influ-
> enced by the symbolic meanings of his or her own material possessions,
> and the way in which s/he relates to those possessions. Material posses-
> sions also serve as expressions of group membership and as means of
> locating others in the social-material environment. Moreover, material
> possessions provide people with information about other people's iden-
> tities. (1992: 205)

In this perspective, consumer culture is tied to the development of
what is sometimes called the possessive individual (Macpherson,
1962; Abercrombie, Hill and Turner, 1986; Clifford, 1988; Pateman,
1988), that is, it has contributed to a conception of the ideal individual as the owner, not only of accumulated property and goods, but
also as owner of his or her self. From this point of view, consumer
culture is a source of the contemporary belief that self-identity is a
kind of *cultural resource, asset or possession*.

Another value that is widely associated with consumer culture is that
of choice. Indeed, the very understanding of choice as a positive value,

rather than as an act that may have positive or negative effects, is a sign of the dominance of consumer culture. Think here, for example, of the importance of choice as a value in contemporary politics – the value of having the ability to choose seems almost to have replaced the importance of the values of what we choose between. But what defines choice? Perhaps surprisingly, given how familiar the rhetoric of choice is today, this is not an easy question to answer. The dictionary definition of choosing is the selection from a number of possibilities, and choice is defined as the act or possibility of choosing. So, choice may be minimally understood as indicating a situation in which there are possibilities from which to select, and it may be the very availability of possibilities that is the source of the positive value sometimes attributed to choice. However, whether the differences between the possibilities to be selected from when choosing are meaningful is not something that is determined by choice or selection alone. As Henry Ford (the founder of the Ford car company) famously put it, the consumer can choose any colour as long as it is black. The relation between selecting and making selections available for choice is complex, subject to politics, the state and sometimes gross inequalities within and between producers and consumers.

Are you ready for personal branding?

Personal branding in this way involves defining who you really are, clarifying yourself. Many people don't like this; they prefer to hide. On the other hand, some have a natural talent for defining and communicating what they stand for. They are like talented musicians, playing the music by ear. Some find it more difficult: they need the music written down; they need a process of self-reflection, which for most people will be the introduction to self-development.

The benefit of this process is that you have to explore and express your own view of yourself and how you actually want to be perceived. This is something we seldom do for ourselves; instead we let others describe us.

We almost never think of ourselves in a structured way and very few of us deliberately try to manage and implement our own desired personality systematically.

So, are you really ready for personal branding? (Gad and Rosencrantz, 2002: xxii)

There are other questions too that can be asked of the elevation of choice as a positive value, including whether and how responsibility for the effects of the individual act of choosing one rather than another possible thing should be acknowledged. The positive evaluation of being able to make a choice sometimes seems to override this question. Does responsibility for the choices we make – to smoke or not to smoke? – lie with the producers and distributors who individually and collectively make available the possible choices, or with consumers, either as individuals or collectively? What role do objects and environments play in organizing our choices? How does the sweetness of sugar affect our tastes, for example? When we choose, are we responsible for ourselves as individuals, or for the effects of our choices on others, and if so, for which others? For our families, for those we do not know, for those who choose otherwise than we do (perhaps because they cannot afford the choices we make), for those not yet born, but who will live with the consequences of our choices? Think here about arguments for the importance of sustainable or green consumption, which highlight, in quite stark ways, the spatial and economic unevenness of relations between choices and (intended and unintended) effects of making some choices rather than others. If consumer culture has elevated choice as a way of being in the world, it also raises important ethical and political questions about the relation between the individual and the collective, and how we inhabit that relation.

> We can believe what we choose. We are answerable for what we choose to believe.
> (Cardinal Newman, letter to Mrs William Froude, 27 June 1846)

A further characteristic of consumer culture that has been identified by a number of writers is its contribution to a *reflexive* relation to identity (Beck, Giddens and Lash, 1994). The argument here is that through the provision of a knowledge-intensive environment – for example, in relation to lifestyle, taste, health, fashion and beauty – consumer culture provides the individual with resources to inform his or her choice and enhance his or her identity. This practice of reflexivity is often seen as contributing to the practices of self-fashioning. However, reflexivity is more than simply self-reflection, since it involves an ongoing, dynamic process in which individuals actively intervene in and respond to what is reflected back at them. This is not necessarily a straightforward process, but, rather, involves coming up against unintended effects, and confronting the limits of agency; the question of whether and how choice enables or frustrates this process of reflexivity is an important one for individuals and for society as a whole. The general suggestion being put forward in this book, however, is that consumer culture provides a very particular set of material circumstances in which individuals come to acquire a reflexive relation to identity.

Media, education and design agencies and political organizations are often in conflict with one another in the organization of this reflexivity in consumer culture, as different social groups work through or against them to define their interests. Indeed, some writers argue that the advice emanating from these different sources can itself be seen as part of a competitive game between these groups as to how aesthetics, ethics and politics are to be brought together in contemporary society. This is the view that consumer culture emerges in response to 'tournaments of value' (Appadurai, 1986) in which the politics of inequality, identity and experience are contested. Forms of expert knowledge available to individuals making choices have grown in importance as the distances from one another between producers, traders and consumers have increased, and are to be found in the invitations, prescriptions and advice of popular culture, the media, education and other agencies of the state as well as a variety of informal political and social movements and agencies. And knowledge is also, of course, embedded in objects themselves, including technological standards, infrastructures and networks. Indeed, the increasingly significant role of expert knowledge, information, aesthetics and design in the making and using of objects is sometimes what is meant by the term 'immaterial culture'. The point being made here is that even though objects still have a physical existence, the way in which we relate to them is increasingly organized in terms of knowledge and imagination.

This last point raises an issue about how this book itself and its illustrations and examples, variously drawn from the media, popular culture, academic and other research, are to be used or consumed. At times, the illustrations may seem to support the argument being developed in the text; at other times, they may contradict it; at others still, they may offer an ironic commentary on either the tone or the substance of the argument that the main text seeks to develop. One of the aims in including examples and illustrations from a wide range of sources is precisely to show the extent to which there is disagreement amongst 'experts' as to what the political or ethical implications of consumer culture may be. If the thesis the book develops is accurate, you, the reader, will be engaged in a reflexive process in which your relation to this expert knowledge – academic, journalistic, commercial – will both provide you with a way of evaluating objects and offer others a way of evaluating you. At the same time, though, the book is not intended as an advice manual, catalogue or a guide to etiquette; it is concerned with knowledge not as 'issue-bound instruction' but as 'illumination' (Bauman, 1992a: 22).

In the nineties, the conceptual artist Barbara Kruger made an artwork of the slogan 'I shop, therefore I am'. Off-Broadway theater pieces offered the audience a familiar 'supermarket of popular cultural references' and asked them to choose between alternative props and narratives. The economist Robert Frank wrote a book condemning the status-seeking consumption or 'luxury fever' that he saw replacing a concern for social equality. Another economist, Juliet Schor, described 'the overspent American', who maxes out credit cards after hearing coworkers talk about their own recent purchases. Rap musicians sang about Adidas shoes, gold jewelry, and the girl who 'look[s] as though [she] shops at Abercrombie and Fitch'. And a mixed-media installation by the artist Vera Frenkel juxtaposed photographs of a shopping mall with an ironic narration that began, 'This is your messiah speaking, instructing you to shop.' (Zukin, 2004: 17)

Conclusion

In this chapter, the value of considering consumer culture as a form of material culture has been outlined. The importance of things as carriers of meaning was emphasized, along with the fundamental point that it is in acquiring, using and exchanging things that individuals come to have social lives. However, it was also suggested that consumer culture is distinctive in a particular way, namely, that it is a culture in which the consumer emerges as an identifiable subject, a 'master category of collective and individual identity' (Trentmann, 2006a), and that this relates in important ways to the material characteristics of contemporary consumer culture.

This is not to argue that everyone is always or only a consumer in consumer culture. It is all too easy to take for granted the existence of 'consumers', as if participation in consumption immediately implicated everyone in the identity of the consumer. As many studies have shown, consumption involves extremely disparate types of practices that have been tied to a multitude of identities, not only that of the consumer but also, for example, the citizen, the mother, the teenager and so on. Trentmann himself quotes the sociologist Claus Offe who argued that consumers do not form a 'clearly delimitable and organizable complex of individuals'. Rather, 'the consumer' is an abstract category that defines certain aspects of the social actions of almost all individuals. Everyone and at the same time no one is a 'consumer': the identity of consumer is not taken up by everyone in the same way as is sometimes implied by accounts of a consumer logic or attitude.

This book will put forward the view that neither the capacity nor the desire to belong to the category of the consumer is equally available to all, and nor does participating in a consumer culture have uniform effects for people in terms of their identity. Rather, as a consequence of the unevenness of participation, consumer culture provides the conditions for a reflexive politics of value and identity. The understanding of consumer culture that is developed here, then, is that it is a form of material culture that produces the consumer as an identifiable subject in a process of reflexivity and plays a key role not only in the making of today's complex relations of inclusion and exclusion, equality and inequality, but also in how we make our experience of those relations meaningful.

2

Exchanging Things: The Economy and Culture

Introduction

This chapter will start by exploring the meaning of the term 'consumer culture', looking at a range of different theoretical perspectives on economy and culture. The aim here is to present these perspectives analytically, so that some of the insights about the relationship between economy and culture presented in the last chapter can be developed further. Beginning with an account of gift exchange – or the gift relation as it is sometimes called – this is followed by a look at commodity exchange. These two modes of exchange are often opposed, but this opposition is reviewed in the middle of the chapter in light of other approaches that point to the importance of cycles of exchange, and the interrelationship – indeed, interdependence – of these two systems in many societies. The final section of the chapter addresses those accounts of consumer culture that do not think it appropriate to understand consumer culture as derived from or as a response to production or systems of exchange, and instead give it a substantial degree of autonomy.

Getting and giving

The Gift: Form and Reason of Exchange in Archaic Societies, written by Marcel Mauss, a French anthropologist, was first published in 1925. What Mauss was trying to explain was how the gift – or rather the gift relationship – was central to the values and organization of what he calls archaic societies. He describes a process in which every gift produces a return or counter-gift in a chain of events that may accomplish

many things at once: goods (people and things) are exchanged and
(re-)distributed; war or peace may be established; competition or
collaboration result; marriages be made; alliances renewed or broken;
and status confirmed or lost. In short, in what he describes as a 'total'
gift economy, most social activities are structured by the exchange of
gifts between groups: markets, credits, contracts, marriage alliances,
appeals to the gods and more. In relationships of giving and receiving, the individuals and groups involved reproduce themselves and
the society in which they live. Yet, so Mauss says, giving and receiving are voluntary, disinterested and personal. How is this?

To address this paradox, Mauss asks himself several questions.
How does the gift relationship work? What is the nature of the obligation at issue here? Why is it that, in so many societies, at so many
periods and in such different contexts, individuals and groups feel
obliged not only to give or, when someone gives to them, to receive,
but also feel obliged, when they have received, to reciprocate what
has been given and to reciprocate either the same thing or its equivalent, or something more or better? Mauss here identifies three inter-
related moments in the gift relationship – the obligation to give, the
obligation to receive, and the obligation to reciprocate, and it is the
process of explaining this third moment in the gift relationship that
is central to his understanding of the gift. Two opposing forces are
contained in the gift relationship, he says, both of which compel reci-
procity or the obligation to reciprocate, and they are what combine to
explain the apparently paradoxical ways in which gift-giving is voluntary, disinterested and personal, *and* yet inexorably reproduces social
order. On the one hand, the gift decreases the social distance between
the protagonists because it is a form of sharing, and, on the other,
it increases the social distance between them because one is now
indebted to the other. This dynamic – contained in the act of giving
– produces the obligation to reciprocate and is also the reason why
it can be more or less antagonistic. So Mauss distinguishes between
non-antagonistic gifts or counter-gifts and antagonistic gifting, such
as, for example, potlatch – that is, ritual acts in which individuals and
groups compete in outgiving each other, in which the practices of
competition and rivalry prevail over sharing.

In trying to explain further what it is that obliges an individual or
group to reciprocate the gift received, Mauss suggests that gifts are
animated, that they have a spirit. As he describes it, the gift relationship makes possible a world where everything passes and re-passes
'as if there was a constant exchange of a spiritual matter, including
things and men, between clans and individuals, distributed between

social ranks, the sexes and the generations'. In the gift relationship, he says, 'things create bonds between souls, for the thing itself has a soul, is part of the soul'; or, again: 'What imposes obligation in the present received and exchanged, is the fact that the thing received is not inactive. Even when it has been abandoned by the giver, it still possesses something of him.' In a total gift economy, not only do people identify with things – totemism (discussed in chapter 1) – but things are an extension of persons, that is, they are animated. For Mauss, this acknowledgement of the importance of relationality between people and things in the making of persons and things is one of the most important aspects of a gift economy.

While *The Gift* is recognized as one of the founding texts of the discipline of anthropology, later anthropologists, including Claude Lévi-Strauss, have been troubled by Mauss's claim that gifts (things) are animated. Lévi-Strauss criticizes Mauss for taking the understandings of his informants as if they were an anthropological explanation of what he is trying to describe. Lévi-Strauss argues that it is the structure of the exchange relationship itself that must constitute the primary phenomenon for anthropologists, and not the individual operations into which social life breaks down, and he therefore proposes to focus on what he calls symbolic exchange. This emphasis on the system or structure of exchange has been a highly influential perspective, bringing together as it does an understanding of culture and economy in a single, unified account. As chapter 3 will outline, this notion of symbolic exchange has been taken up by some more recent theorists of consumer culture – notably Jean Baudrillard, who proposes that it is being destroyed in contemporary society.

While the criticism that Lévi-Strauss makes of Mauss is widely shared, it is also possible to argue that, by way of comparison with contemporary industrial societies, Mauss's idea of the animation of things can be illuminating. In the societies Mauss describes, it is accepted that the cosmos – the social world – is composed of human and non-human actors and of relations between both these kinds of actors. It is accepted that it is the relations between people and things that make people and things who and what they are. Once we see this in relation to so-called archaic societies, then we can, by way of contrast, recognize one of the distinctive characteristics of today's Euro-American societies, namely, that in such societies objects are believed to be dead and, once acquired by buying, have no relation to the person from whom they were bought. That is, we see, by means of the contrast with gift societies, what is normally taken for granted in Euro-American societies: in this case, that in such societies individuals and things are held to be not only different but also entirely separable and discrete, not defined in relationship to each other. This is a central part of a culture in which people experience exchange as the desire to appropriate goods, whereas in a gift-oriented economy people experience exchange as a desire to expand social relations (to be connected with more people).

What this comparison reveals, then, is that in contemporary consumer culture what it is to be a person is linked to the accumulation of discrete, separable or alienable things, owned by individuals as private property, while in a gift society what it is to be a person is not limited to the individual person and his or her possessions but is created in the circulation of things and other people. The contrast thus opens up a perspective on how it is that identity itself can come to be something – a possession – belonging to an individual self in Euro-American societies.

Like Lévi-Strauss, the contemporary theorist Maurice Godelier (1999) also takes issue with Mauss. He suggests that while the beliefs described by Mauss have an important role in some societies, they do not explain the true origin of the obligation to give in turn when one has received. Such beliefs may explain how the social actors – the indigenous people – think, experience and legitimate this obligation, but from Godelier's point of view, they are not only inadequate as anthropological explanations (as Lévi-Strauss argues), but they are false representations for the indigenous people themselves. Godelier is interested in what such beliefs mask, and to find this out he suggests that we need to see their effect. He argues that what is remarkable is that through the belief in animism, a metamorphosis occurs – instead of appearing to themselves as actors, humans appear to themselves as the target of actions (of spirits or gods, for example). In this way, the legitimacy of a social order is 'given' (it is god-given, what was meant to be, or a consequence of spirits). Godelier's perspective thus provides a way of explaining the *ideology* of a society in terms of relations of exchange.

Pierre Bourdieu is also interested in gift-giving for some of the same reasons. He suggests in *Outline of a Theory of Practice* (1977) that what makes gift-giving productive of a society's values and organization is its temporality. For Bourdieu, it is the interval between giving and getting that is important – in that interval is the possibility of strategy, of action – but this action, this strategy, is not to be taken as all there is. Instead, for Bourdieu, as also for Godelier, it is necessary to look at the significance of the interval between getting and giving in terms of how it allows what Bourdieu calls self-deception

– both individual and collective: 'the logic of time separating the gift from the counter-gift is what authorizes the deliberate oversight, the collectively maintained and approved self-deception without which symbolic exchange, a fake circulation of fake coin, could not operate' (1977: 6).

But what does this further discussion of gift-giving contribute to a discussion of consumer culture? Mauss himself originally associated the 'gift' and the 'commodity' with archaic and modern societies respectively. He describes how a distinction between persons and things has been slowly established in Western societies, where developments of Roman law gradually institutionalized a distinction between people and things. The institutionalization of this distinction is commonly held to be an important component of the making of what are called modern societies, and underpins legal restrictions on exchanging persons as if they were things (although its partial and unequal implementation is evident in the histories of the institutions of slavery, trafficking of people, and marriage) as well as underpinning legal conceptions of private property, and a belief in property in the person.

The drawing of a clear distinction between people and things is also sometimes described as part of a process of disenchantment (to be further discussed in relation to the notion of the post-social era, in chapter 3). This disenchantment is held to be evident in the ways in which, in a market economy, things are not only exchanged one for another through a universal currency – money – but in exchange are separated or alienated from those who made them. In expending labour for a wage you alienate yourself from what you have produced. In buying something you incur no debt, no obligation to the person from whom you buy, if you pay the set price. One of the questions a comparison with gift-giving raises is whether paying the price of something is really the same as paying the cost. Is the price we pay the full value of the thing? This takes us back to the questions of the morality of consumer culture raised in chapter 1, and the links between the economy, values and ethics. How does the vocabulary of choice as the market right of a consumer – as a way of relating to things – allow us to address these questions? Does it allow us to relate to things and people in the ways we wish or ways we can justify? And how can 'we' seek to answer this question? Can we do it on the basis of taking at face value what 'we' – the indigenous people – say about price or indeed about choice? Or is the rhetoric of choice – like a belief in the spirit of things – also a collective self-deception, a false representation, masking the effects of exchange and legitimizing the inequalities of our social order?

Buying and selling

Karl Marx's writings are the source of some of the most influential understandings of commodification, and of production and exchange for the market. Marx's analysis is not confined to capitalism alone; he is interested more generally in the importance of a mode of appropriation for a society: how humankind appropriates nature is central to his understanding of social organization. What is called material culture in this book is, for Marx, the objectification of social life. Under a capitalist mode of production, however, this objectification is turned against people in the processes of commodification. People are distanced from the production of objects and their full materiality, resulting in experiences of estrangement and alienation from the natural and material world as well as relations of inequality.

In developing this line of argument, Marx makes a distinction between producing something for one's own direct or immediate use and producing something within an alienating division of labour for exchange on the market. This latter process is the production of goods as *commodities*. It is important to note here that there is some debate within the Marxist perspective about the nature of the link, between the production of goods within a specific set of social relations and their production for exchange on the market, for the Marxist concept of the commodity (see, for example, Appadurai, 1986), and whether and how they are linked in contemporary forms of capitalism.

Marx himself argues that the cultural logic of commodity exchange is characterized by calculability, universality and abstraction, leading to the dominance of these values in capitalist societies. He identifies what he believes to be the unfortunate consequences of this – that is, the belief that things are not only separate from but also come to stand in for and replace relationships between people. In his terms, this is an important aspect of the ideology of capitalist societies: in a society dominated by commodity exchange we think everything – or more or less everything – can be bought and sold, and we fail to see that things are tied to people and people to things. Importantly for the claim developed in this book, that the consumer has emerged as a key category of identity, Marx argues that the 'product' of individual consumption – 'consumption that uses up products, as means of subsistence for the living individual' – is 'the consumer himself' (1967: 183). Marx thus locates the emergence of the category of the consumer as a key element of the ideology of capitalist societies.

Marx himself did not live to see modern consumer culture emerge, but he did describe the commodity's 'enigmatic' or 'mysterious' quality. This is said to arise from, on the one hand, the commodity's combination of material features that we can see, touch and smell, and, on the other, of the hidden social relations involved in its production. Leiss et al. describe this mysterious quality well; they write:

> Commodities are . . . a unity of what is revealed and what is concealed in the processes of production and consumption. Goods reveal or 'show' to our senses their capacities to be satisfiers or stimulators of particular wants and communicators of behavioural codes. At the same time, they draw a veil across their own origins: products appear and disappear before consumers' eyes as if by spontaneous generation, and it is an astute shopper indeed who has much idea about what most things are composed of and what kinds of people made them. (1986: 274)

Marx uses the term *fetishism of commodities* to describe the disguise or mask of commodities – a phantom objectivity – in which the appearance of goods hides the story of those who made them and how they were made.

But, you may ask, do consumers need to hear this story? In being deprived of it, are they experiencing a systematic distortion of communication within the world of goods itself? Marx suggests that they are. He argues that people's thinking about themselves and others is distorted by a *fetishism*, in which beliefs about the material products of labour – things – are a substitute for an understanding of the (unequal and alienating) social relations which made their production possible. As a result of commodity fetishism, Marx suggests, the social relations represented in an object come to appear absolutely fixed or given, beyond human control. It is in this way, in capitalist societies, that the legitimacy of the social order is sustained in consumer culture, and the reality of social inequality overlooked.

Marx further argues that the use of things is systematically distorted by the capitalist search for profit, which has led to the production of an ever-expanding range of products being sold due to increasing control over the market combined with manipulation of the consumer. This is hidden by *the mask* of the commodity, described earlier, and the many faces it presents in promotion and advertising. This is a view that understands consumer culture as a promotional culture (Wernick, 1991) and attributes the growth and values of consumer culture to changes in the organization of production, including not only the increasing production of objects for exchange on the market in pursuit of profit, but also a cultural condition of 'self-advantaging exchange' (Wernick, 1991: 181).

The argument here, then, is that the fetishism of the commodity in capitalist society is strategically manipulated in the practices of packaging, promotion and advertising. Adorno (1974), for example, speaks of how the dominance of exchange-value erases the memory of the original use-value of goods, leaving the commodity available to take up a secondary or ersatz use-value. From this point of view, commodities are manipulated so as to take on a wide range of cultural associations and illusions; this is the basis for what has been called *commodity aesthetics* (Haug, 1986). Advertising, it seems, is able to exploit this freedom to attach images of romance, exotica, fulfilment or the good life to mundane consumer goods such as soap, washing machines, cars and alcoholic drinks. These images or masks enable material objects to act as carriers of ideological meaning in social interaction. They encipher goods in symbolic codes that consumers cannot resist.

This is one perspective on the 'godlike manipulation' that Sahlins identifies, and it is seen as responsible for the rapid increase in consumer demand that characterizes modern Euro-American societies. Later chapters will discuss this view in more detail, but in the meantime it is important to note that other commentators on consumer culture – including many of those discussed in the rest of this chapter – have questioned the effectiveness of such masks to promote consumer demand. Indeed, it has been argued that, in relation to some goods at least, the so-called godlike manipulation of the producers is by no means infallible. It is also argued that people are neither passive nor gullible, and that their relations to goods are not exclusively defined by commodity-exchange or their positioning as consumers.

Cycles and circuits of exchange

In addition, however, even among the many writers who largely accept the importance of capitalism in the creation and organization of consumer culture, it is argued that consumer demand should not be understood in relation to the dominance of exchange-value alone, but simultaneously in relation to the activities of the state and other systems of production and exchange. In this regard, it is worth noting that in recent years the spheres of unpaid work such as housework, child and domestic care, non-monetized exchange, for example, voluntary or community work, and not-for-profit-monetized exchange such as that which takes place in the public or not-for-profit sectors have all grown in size relative to the commodified realm (Williams, 2005, cited in Moor, 2008). This points to the importance of looking at the relationship between different systems of exchange for an understanding of the characteristics of consumer culture.

One of the most influential writers to discuss the role of the state in the organization of consumption is Manuel Castells (1977), who has mapped the history of what he calls 'collective consumption'. This is the term he uses to describe the consumption of services and goods provided by the state for consumers as a public collective. This currently includes the provision of some housing, health care, transport and education in the UK, although the question of whether such services should continue to be provided by the state or the market is a long-standing subject of political debate. Central questions in this debate are: what conditions give consumers power, relative to producers, and under what conditions can consumers obtain what will give them well-being, satisfaction and pleasure? But there are also other questions. Do different groups have different (more or less, better or worse) access to services and goods, according to whether they are provided through the market or through the state? Does the medium of provision or distribution – the market or public service – contribute to social differentiation? Are differences in modes of access to goods not only the consequence but also the source of inequalities between different groups of people?

Zygmunt Bauman (1987) has argued that it is possible to identify two broad social groupings – the seduced and the repressed – on the basis of whether people's needs are satisfied by the market or the state. The seduced, he believes, are free to make decisions in the market arena and are incorporated into consumer culture; their lives are in large part devoted to the acquisition and display of commodities. The repressed are those who, lacking economic and cultural resources, are excluded from the market. They are not full members of the club of consumers; instead their lives are intricately entangled with the bureaucracy of the state.

We live, then, Bauman argues, in a society of two nations, not of exploiter or exploited, or even of the have and the have-nots, but of the seduced and the repressed, those free to follow their desires and those subject to surveillance and control through the bureaucratic regulations organizing state provision of services. (For a critique of this view, in which it is suggested that the category described by Bauman as 'repressed' is more adequately described as 'the poor', see Warde, 1994.) Some empirical evidence for this view is provided by Peter Saunders (1990) who identifies what he calls social cleavages based on differing patterns of consumption, and a major division between those who are dependent on the state and those who have personal property and private housing, pensions, education and health. (Bauman's analysis suggests that while not everyone participates in consumption on the same terms, society can be said to be dominated by a consumer culture or consumer attitude (Bauman, 1990; see chapter 1) insofar as it is the individual's relation to consumption – which he or she cannot control – that defines his or her social position).

It has also been pointed out that many of the goods and services provided, whether through the market or the state, are the subject of further work or transformation before they are finally used up, and thus that increasing consumer culture is likely to be linked to systems of exchange other than or as well as the market and the state. One of the most important of these relates to households, and what is sometimes called the domestic mode of production or housework. So, for example, food that is bought in a supermarket is normally prepared, cooked and presented before it is eaten, a set of activities typically but not always carried out by women for others in the household. While the preparation of meals, the washing and mending of clothes, the cleaning of the house and so on are readily recognized as housework, a number of writers have argued that housework includes not only practical, but also *emotional, sexual, reproductive and symbolic work done by women for men within family relationships* (Delphy and Leonard, 1992). It is not only work done on the house that is important here – the stylization and ordering of its furnishings – but also caring work in relationships, such as mothering, and work done by women on themselves for the pleasure or benefit of others, what has been called the work of femininity (Winship, 1987), that is, the work that women do on their appearance, manner and personal identity. In relation to all these kinds of work, labour does not only come *before* consumption, if by this is meant the purchase of goods on the market; it also comes after it. Additionally, this is a perspective that strongly challenges the view that consumer culture can be equated with leisure or free time.

Housework defined in this way does not fit the common preconception of work as paid employment, but it can be seen as work once it is situated in relation to the notion of a family economy (Oakley, 1976; Delphy, 1984). This economy exists alongside and is interlinked with industrial or capitalist economy. The family economy is typically structured by conditions of inequality, in which women tend to be in a position of economic dependence upon men, in part because of economic inequality in the workplace (Walby, 1997). This dependence is socially structured by relations of power within the household, the state and the labour market, and has meant that the amount of time a full-time housewife with children spends on housework stayed relatively constant throughout the twentieth century despite the introduction of so-called labour-saving devices (Anderson, Bechhofer and Gershuny, 1994). The amount of time that most men spend on housework has gone up slightly over this period of time; but it is still only between five and ten hours a week, even when the woman in the shared household is doing both the housework and paid work. In a heterosexual household, the man may offer to *help*, but housework is still typically assumed to be the woman's responsibility.

Delphy and Leonard (1992) argue that within the family there are three types of economic activity: production, consumption and the accumulation and circulation of property. They write that the inequalities generated by these activities will be missed if the family is assumed to be a natural unit, in which all members equally participate, and argue that:

> the fact that the family can be treated as a unit of production or consumption or of property-holding for certain purposes does not mean

that the family (in the sense of all its members) produce and consume and hold property together as a block, nor that all have the same economic status and identical interests. (Delphy and Leonard, 1992: 107)

As they go on to note, while it is often recognized that much production is carried out by members as separate individuals, this separation is not so clearly identified in relation to either property-holding or consumption. It is usually far from clear when authors speak of the family household as a 'unit of consumption' whether they are referring to the total consumption of all the members wherever it takes place, or just to that part of consumption which takes place within the home. Delphy and Leonard argue that even if 'family production' and 'family consumption' are used to refer to what is done or used by family members actually within the home, these processes are not the same for all the members of the family.

This last point, the existence of differences in the extent and quality of consumption of family members, is explained by contrasting the 'industrial economy' and the 'family economy'. Delphy and Leonard write:

> In the labour market, workers are paid a wage by their employer, but in the family-based household, members are maintained by its head. This means dependants have less choice as to what they get than if they were given money. What is provided for them is what is favoured (or at least agreed to) by the head. In addition, since much of what family members produce is consumed within the family, this in itself prevents goods and services consumed in the family being the same for all members. For example, when the husband and children consume meals served by the wife, she provides the services, so she cannot consume them in the same way as they do: as work done by someone else. She cannot both wait and be waited on. Hence, there are real problems in treating the family as a 'unit of consumption' in any analysis. (Delphy and Leonard, 1992: 108)

The point being made here is that the separate statuses of men and women are marked out by their different places in what only *appears* to be the same consumption space. While he is watching television, she is getting dinner. Even when everyone is seated at the dinner table, the woman is likely to be the one serving the food. She is the facilitator of other people's consumption as well as an active consumer in her own right.

In short, while it is often noted that it is women who make up the majority of consumers, in the sense that it is women who actually purchase goods on a routine basis, it is not so often recognized that they will generally go on to work on – transform, personalize, look after, keep clean and so on – the goods bought. Yet women typically work at transforming the goods and services of which men as husbands, children and other dependants are the final users. Indeed, given the relations of gender inequality within which much shopping and other housework is done, some feminists argue that it is inappropriate and misleading to consider shopping as an example of consumption, and suggest that it is more accurate to see it as part of family production – the work of selecting, transporting and transforming the raw materials or resources of housework. But it is also possible to suggest that both interpretations are correct. Shopping may be seen as an instance of consumption in relation to the cycle of commodity production (that is, production of goods for exchange on the market), but also as a moment of production in relation to household or domestic production (for exchange and use in the family). What this dual location of shopping illustrates is the importance of looking at *interlocking cycles* or circuits of production and consumption within society as a whole. It also shows that it is necessary to think of consumption not simply in relation to the market and commodification but also in relation to other economic systems, notably the family and the domestic economy.

In an alternative interpretation of the household and consumption, the anthropologist Daniel Miller argues that women's shopping can be seen as an example of a particular form of the gift-relationship described by Mauss – sacrifice. Miller suggests that women shop in order to be able to offer up goods (and their selves) to others. His argument here is that in contemporary Euro-American society the object of devotional sacrifice is no longer God, or even the domestic patriarch or husband, but the child or children. He further suggests that shopping is *not* an example of a relation to objects which substitutes for a relation to subjects (that is, it is not an activity dominated by commodity-exchange); it does not take the place of social relations but is a means of enhancing them: 'objects are the means for creating the relationships of love between subjects rather than some kind of materialistic dead end which takes devotion away from its proper subject – other persons' (Miller, 1998: 128). This example not only highlights the different frameworks of gift- and commodity-exchange but also shows very clearly how questions as to ideology and false consciousness arise (are women foolish to spend more hours a day working than men – and for less monetary reward – because of love for their husbands and children?), posing problems for how to understand the value and meaning of consumer culture.

However shopping is to be understood, though, the point being made here is the importance of looking at *cycles* of production and consumption, and the relations of exchange within these cycles. Alan Warde writes:

> frequently in the making of something that is 'finally consumed', several different cycles of production and consumption occur one after the other. This can be seen from considering the food chain as a whole. What we eat off our plates typically passes through a number of production processes (the growing, wholesaling, processing, retailing and domestic preparation) and several exchange transactions (some of which are often [misleadingly] called consumption) before final enjoyment as a meal . . . Analytically, it is worth recognizing the existence of sequential episodes of production and consumption, and to notice that episodes are not necessarily identical, and may involve specifically different kinds of social relationships. (1992: 18–19)

'Consumer demand' can thus be seen to be mediated by multiple circuits of exchange, only some of which are directly linked to the production of commodities for sale on the market, alongside those which are mediated by the state and/or the social relations of the household, while others are structured by the gift relationship.

Indeed a number of writers suggest that the opposition between commodity and gift has been over-stated. So, for example, Arjun Appadurai, while describing these forms as 'fundamentally contrastive and mutually exclusive' (1986: 11), also notes commodities may become decommodified and non-commodities may become commodified during the *biography* or *social life* of a thing. A number of studies of 'gift behaviour' describe situations where commodities are bought and then given as gifts outside the original consumption setting (Belk and Coon, 1993), or situations in which commodity and gift are conjoined, as in the case of some sales deals in chain stores and supermarkets, such as, for example, two-for-the-price-of-one offers.

Bird-David and Darr (2009) carried out one such study of deals in Israel, where, they say, such hybrid commodity-gifts are especially common, although examples are also to be found in other countries, including, for example, the gift of 'trial' products to buyers of cosmetics in the USA and Europe. By focusing their study on the 'action of buying', Bird-David and Darr are able to argue that what is involved in purchase is not simply the acquisition of a commodity but the opening up of what they call a relational space. An example of such a relational space is provided by the practice of one UK supermarket chain to give consumers spending above a certain sum a token which they can then, in turn, give to one of a number of charities selected by the supermarket. The consumer is then called on to make a choice of how to pass on this 'gift'. The supermarket promises to convert the tokens into money for the charities concerned.

Bird-David and Darr suggest that hybrid commodity-gifts are often infused with ambiguity and internal contradictions. For example, when two soap bars are packaged together and a small sign on the supermarket shelf informs the consumer that one of them is a gift, which is the gift and which is the commodity? Or, even more confusing, when an advertisement states that 30 per cent of the laundry detergent is actually 'free', is the same item imagined partly as a gift and partly as a commodity? Bird-David and Darr observe that shoppers have diverse ways of dealing with the ambiguities of hybrid commodity-gifts. These range from passive acceptance, through bargaining and negotiating over them, to outright refusal to accept them. They argue that the range of such responses reveals a continuum of hybrid gift-commodity types of conduct and ways of reasoning. In many cases, the shoppers hold to the separateness of gift and commodity categories – for example, by asserting 'There's no such thing as a free gift' – while simultaneously dealing with the hybrids.

The active consumer

Most of the approaches outlined so far understand consumer culture as emerging in response to changes in the organization of production and the exchange of goods, as well as state, family and household organization. In contrast to this, there are other approaches, which assert that consumption practices have an independent dynamic and are more than a passive response to production or other economic systems. These approaches are themselves diverse, but what they share is the view that consumption practices cannot be read off from production or exchange relations, but should be understood as having their own dynamic. It is a view summed up by Paul Willis who claims that he wants to 'rehabilitate consumption, creative consumption, to see creative potentials in it for itself, rather than see it as the dying fall of the usual triplet: production, reproduction, reception' (1990: 20).

An especially important view in this regard is what may be described as positional consumption. One of the most influential writers here is Thorstein Veblen (1925), who suggests that the use of goods in positional consumption came to have a special significance in modern Euro-American societies because it was linked to the emergence of a new social group in the early twentieth century, the *leisure class*. This class, Veblen claims, sought to publicly demonstrate its status through the use of consumer goods in leisure practices. The defining feature of the leisure practices of this class was a conspicuous abstention from all useful employment: abstention from anything productive was made visible or conspicuous by a spectacular display of consumption. Good taste became associated with the expression of distance from the world of work, the practical or the natural world, and was termed 'refined' or 'cultivated', and was dissociated from that which could be regarded as 'cheap' or 'vulgar'. In short, this class – the so-called *nouveaux riches* – made use of material goods to assert their social aspirations (or pretensions as others might describe them). Other writers suggest that it is not just this class grouping that has developed its own autonomous consumption practices, made visible through spectacular display, but many other groups as well, and this is only in part explained by a process of emulation by which lower groups in the hierarchy seek to imitate higher groups.

So, for example, another approach, proposed by Fred Hirsch (1977) among others, is that while historically only a small aristocratic elite engaged in positional consumption, more recently the people who make up the mass of the population have also come to do so. So one characteristic of modern consumption, according to Hirsch, is that it shows a *democratization* of positional or competitive consumption. However, he suggests that increasing consumption is a zero-sum game, insofar as what is bought is a position relative to others. Furthermore, he suggests that the expansion of the use of consumer goods as positional goods creates an overload of demands, which cannot be met, and, in turn, is leading to economic instability. The point being made here is that if goods function primarily as symbols, and all groups of individuals use them to establish distinctions between themselves and other groups of individuals, then there are, in principle, no limits to consumer demand. In other words, mass competitive consumption will have disorganizing effects on modern economies rather than, as is often claimed, being functional for the capitalist economy. However, other writers suggest that mass competitive consumption has its own rules (see the discussion of

Pierre Bourdieu in chapter 4), and is not necessarily disorganizing; rather, it is subject to cycles of *dis*organization and *re*organization.

Other writers identify other dynamics. So, for example, Carolyn Steedman writes movingly of a culture of longing and the envy experienced by working-class women in the UK:

> My mother's longing shaped my own childhood. From a Lancashire mill town and a working-class twenties childhood she came away wanting: fine clothes, glamour, money; to be what she wasn't. However that longing was produced in her distant childhood, what she actually wanted were real things, real entities, things she materially lacked, things that a culture and a social system withheld from her. The story she told was about this wanting, and it remained a resolutely social story. When the world didn't deliver the goods, she held the world to blame. In this way, the story she told was a form of political analysis that allows a political interpretation to be made of her life. (Steedman, 1998: 6)

Paul Gilroy (2010) describes other ambiguities. He observes the movement of African Americans between two poles: shoppers' rebellion and shoppers' resignation. In the first, 'the official value given to these prizes by a world of work and wages is supposedly altered, or at least ironically commented upon', while the second 'is defined most obviously by the mood of individuals who want to answer the sour impact of racism on their lives by buying in rather than dropping out' (2010: 26).

In a further twist on this perspective of positional consumption, it has been pointed out that the very qualities of certain goods may change as an effect of positional consumption. This is especially the case when the qualities realized in the consumption of a good depend not only on the provider but also on other people consuming the good at the same time. John Urry, for example, notes that part of a holiday experience is whether others are experiencing the beach or the wilderness with you, and is shaped by the cultural identities of these others. Michael Storper emphasizes the importance of what he calls *transactive positionality* in contemporary consumption practices:

> This is the case for some of the most important collective goods, such as schools or transportation. If everyone goes to public [state] schools, they have a certain range of qualities. If richer or better-prepared children go to private [fee-paying] schools, then not only do public schools change in relative status, but their absolute qualities may be changed as a result of the withdrawal of privileged students to private schools. (2001: 111)

As a consequence of this knock-on effect, he argues, the degree and shape of positionality in consumption becomes increasingly important for the life chances of all individuals, especially when one's position as a consumer is linked to organized distinctions between private or market and public or state consumption.

Positional consumption may also have implications for the generation of particular feelings, such as envy and resentment. Gilroy, for example, observes that shoppers' resignation can 'release violent envy and compound the petty hatreds of a steeply segregated world in which the interplay of material privilege and racial hierarchy is necessarily complex' (2010: 26). As Sianne Ngai notes, in contrast to an emotion such as fear, which only requires a single self to be pitted against a single other, competitiveness and envy emerge in relation to a 'numerated many'. She writes:

> Indeed, among our culture's current spectrum of negative affects, envy stands out as the only one articulated explicitly in response to a perceived inequality: a relative state of affairs that can be assessed only by comparison. [Competitiveness] . . . is likewise positioned: more specifically, the subject's position, relative and contingent upon the position of many others, in a larger hierarchical order . . . Both are responses to the positionally unequal distribution of a limited resource across this field: whether it be affect, capital, rights, or other symbolic goods. (Ngai, 2006: 111–12).

Storper himself suggests that the only way to slow down status competition and the negative affects of transactive positionality such as envy is to do so collectively, with 'mechanisms that simultaneously limit what our status competitors are doing' (2001: 112).

These examples certainly show the complex relations between individual and collective choices. However, many writers have argued that consumption is not (just) motivated by a desire for status, that the impulse to emulate is not the only engine of consumer demand and culture, but that it is also driven by the practices of hedonism, escapism, fantasy and the desire for novelty or 'identity-value' (Featherstone, 1991; but see Warde, 1992). All these accounts are also examples of a consumer-driven approach.

In his book *The Romantic Ethic and the Spirit of Modern Consumerism* (1989), Colin Campbell puts forward just such a view. He argues that consumption is not a direct response to production, but rather should be seen as springing from autonomous, independent sources. Central to this argument is Campbell's belief that people have independent desires to pursue pleasures; this is not a desire that has to be manipulated into being. However, he also suggests that there have been changes in the social organization and expression of the pursuit of this desire for pleasure or hedonism. He thus sees consumption as a voluntaristic, self-directed and creative process that involves shared cultural values and ideals, but one that has undergone a process of historical change.

Traditional hedonism, he suggests, was characterized by a concern with sensations, and pleasing the senses. Each pleasure was relatively finite or discrete and was associated with specific activities, such as eating. In this sense, it was standardized. There was a more or less direct connection between pleasure and satisfaction. However, a distinctively modern form of hedonism emerges from the late eighteenth century onwards in Western societies. This new form of hedonism is tied by Campbell to the emergence of the Romantic Ethic of the late eighteenth and early nineteenth centuries, which in turn is related to the Protestant Ethic of the seventeenth and eighteenth centuries. (The Protestant Ethic was argued to be an important contributing factor in the emergence of capitalism by Max Weber (1930).) Campbell notes that while the Protestant Ethic is commonly understood in terms of asceticism or puritanism (and thus might be seen to be hostile to the emergence of consumer culture), some strands within the ethic associated virtue with the charitable feelings of pity and sympathy. This, argues Campbell, was the basis of the growth of an emotionalist way of life in which the good man or woman could display his or her virtue through the display of emotions, especially those of pity and melancholy. In time, the expression of these and other emotions came to bring their own pleasure, rather than simply being a means of displaying virtue.

This way of life took on a wider cultural significance through the influence of the work of the Romanticists, a group of writers, poets and artists, including Keats, Wordsworth and Shelley, whose writings displayed a sometimes sentimental, nostalgic form of romanticism in which the individual longs to experience in reality those pleasures which can only be imagined. It is this Romantic Ethic, Campbell suggests, which provides the conditions for the emergence of a distinctively modern form of hedonism, in which pleasure is separated from satisfaction, but pursued in the art of daydreaming.

Pleasure is no longer given by specific activities, or associated with particular sensations; indeed, it is no longer localized or focused, but instead is a potential aspect or dimension of *all* experiences. This potential is to be found in the imagination; the individual learns to substitute imaginary for real stimuli, and by self-consciously creating and manipulating illusions or imaginary experiences or emotions in daydreams and fantasies, constructs his or her own pleasurable environment. Campbell argues that modern hedonism is characterized by a longing to experience in reality those pleasures created or enjoyed in imagination, a longing which results in the ceaseless consumption of novelty. Pleasure, once detached from specific activities, has the potential to be never-ending. Moreover, once the direct link between objects and sensations is broken, once it is mediated by daydreaming and fantasy, then images, as the vehicles of the imagination, become more and more important in modern forms of pleasure.

Consumption expresses the romantic longing to become an *other*; however, whatever one becomes is never what one wants to be. This is because the actual consumption or use of goods becomes a disillusioning experience. The actuality of consumption fails to live up to the dream or the fantasy. This persistent cycle of pleasurable expectation and disappointment explains the never-ending, insatiable character of modern consumption, why people continue to shop until they drop. Campbell thus explains what he sees as the inherent dynamism – the Walter Mitty principle – of modern consumption in terms of the ever-changing, never-satisfiable hedonistic desires of modern consumers.

Campbell's account of the emergence of modern consumption goes some way to explain a number of the characteristics of contemporary consumer culture that other commentators have noted. These include many of those that Mike Featherstone describes in terms of the aestheticization of everyday life (1991). He suggests that aestheticization is a consequence of 'the desire to be continuously learning and enriching oneself, to pursue ever new values and vocabularies, . . . [and an] unending curiosity in which the artist and the intellectual are heroes' (1991: 48). A key characteristic of the individual pursuing these heroes through the imitation of the lifestyles of artistic subcultures is what Featherstone calls a calculated hedonism, the calculated decontrol of emotions (1991: 71–2; see below, and for more discussion of this idea see chapters 4 and 8).

Featherstone suggests there are a number of historical precedents for this attitude or mode of consuming. One is to be found in certain artistic movements, including (as Campbell also suggests) Romanticism, but also the artistic avant-garde at the turn of the twentieth century. Amongst the latter (especially the Surrealist movement, whose members included writers (Jean Cocteau, Louis Aragon), playwrights (Eugene Ionesco and other so-called dramatists of the absurd), film-makers (Luis Buñuel), photographers (Man Ray and a host of others) and painters (René Magritte, Max Ernst, Marcel Duchamp, Joan Miro, and Salvador Dali)), there was an impetus to collapse the boundary between art and everyday life, to show that the most banal consumer objects and the kitsch and detritus of mass culture could be aestheticized and introduced as the subject of art.

Indeed, in his two *Manifestos of Surrealism* (1924 and 1929), André Breton described Surrealism in terms of 'the crisis of the object'. One of the ways in which this crisis was provoked was by pluralizing the contexts in which the object was perceived, specifically by removing it from the contexts where we conventionally perceive it and placing it in surprising ones. As it appeared simultaneously in multiple contexts, 'the object' was put in crisis because its solid identity could no longer be established. Another technique adopted by the Surrealists was to distort the scale of objects vis-à-vis one another. Both techniques had the effect of revealing the constructedness of objects, their dependence for meaning on context and conventional norms of perception. In the 1960s, postmodern art, reacting against what was seen as the institutionalization of modernism and the avant-garde in the museum and the academy, revived and built on these strategies. In some modern artistic practice, aesthetic value was to be found in the anti-work, in the 'happening', in 'performance art', in the creation of artworks that cannot be catalogued and preserved in the museum. Such art practices thus helped to bring art into everyday life.

Another precedent for modern consuming habits is found by Featherstone in the modernist notion of the artist as hero, as the advocate of radical values, challenging the consensus of public life and disturbing the complacency of domestic life. A complementary figure amongst elite groups was that of the dandy, the man (historically, dandyism was a role available more or less exclusively to (middle-class) men) who made his body, his behaviour, his feelings and passions, a work of art. This figure was the subject of much philosophical and literary writing in the nineteenth century, and was related to a particular understanding of pleasure, which 'was to be experience itself, and not the fruits of experience, sweet or bitter as they may be' (Oscar Wilde, quoted in Bowlby, 1993: 15). The dandy is *against* pleasure in the 'fruit' and *for* pleasure in the experience of tasting it, and celebrates an experiential-experimental openness to what is 'new' or 'exotic'. As Rachel Bowlby suggests, Oscar Wilde's *The Picture of Dorian Gray*, in which the hero Dorian Gray and his portrait swap places – the hero adopts as his own identity an artistic image, a portrait that does not age – can be seen as an investigation of the pleasures and costs of the lifestyle of a dandy:

[Dorian] exchanges a moral self for the unfettered freedom of the new hedonist, for whom 'insincerity' is 'merely a method by which we can multiply our personalities': 'Eternal youth, infinite passion, pleasures subtle and secret, wild joy and wilder sins – he was to have all these things.' There is no limit to what Dorian can have, to the number of 'personalities' he can adopt, to the experiences he can sample. All poses, all personalities, are equal, circumscribed by neither moral nor numerical boundaries, and referable to no state of authenticity from which they differ: 'Being natural', too, 'is simply a pose'. (Bowlby, 1993: 16, references omitted)

This is a description of the dandy as the ideal modern consumer: 'a receptacle and bearer of sensations, poser and posed, with no consistent identity, no moral self' (op cit: 23).

What Featherstone suggests is new today is that the practices of dandyism are no longer confined to artistic or elite enclaves, but are increasingly widespread. This is the project of turning one's life into a work of art. It is as if, Featherstone suggests, aesthetics has become the basis of decision-making in everyday life: put simply, the question is no longer, is this a good thing to do, but does it look good? (For a contrasting view on the relative importance of ethics and aesthetics in contemporary society, see the discussion of Lamont, 1992, in chapter 4.)

The term 'lifestyle' is a term that is sometimes used to refer to this new consumer sensibility (for example, Hebdige, 1988); through lifestyle, consumers are seen to bring a more stylized awareness or sensitivity to the processes of consumption. As a mode of consumption, or attitude to consuming, it refers to the ways in which people seek to display their individuality and their sense of style through the choice of a particular range of goods and their subsequent customizing or personalizing of these goods. This activity is seen by some to have become a central life project for individuals today. As a member of a particular lifestyle grouping, the individual actively uses consumer goods – clothes, the home, furnishings, interior decor, car, holidays, food and drink, as well as cultural goods such as music, film and art – in ways that indicate that grouping's taste or sense of style. In this use, lifestyle is an instance of the tendency for groups of individuals to use goods to make distinctions between themselves and other groups of individuals, and thus supports the view that consumption practices can be understood in terms of a struggle over social positioning. However, the notion of lifestyle emphasizes the symbolic or aesthetic dimension of this struggle.

A further condition for the development of consumer culture

identified by Featherstone is the rapid flow of signs and images that pervade everyday life in contemporary society. He suggests that the widespread availability of images, in conjunction with the heroization of the artist's way of life, has provided a context for the development of mass consumer-culture dreamworlds. Within these dreamworlds, the individual is said to be developing a capacity to de-control the emotions, to open him or herself up to an extended range of sensations, and gaining the ability to enjoy the swing between the pleasures of immersion in objects and detached distantiation from them. This can be seen in terms of the development of an aestheticized relation of the individual to his (and perhaps her) self-presentation. Featherstone writes that this controlled de-control of the emotions is brought about through 'techniques of the self which will permit the development of sensibilities which can allow us to enjoy the swing between the extremes of aesthetic involvement and detachment so that the pleasures of immersion and detached distantiation can both be enjoyed' (1991: 81). An important part of this calculating hedonism is an emotional and cognitive distancing on the part of the individual, since it is this distance that introduces the possibility of reflection on consumption and facilitates the adoption of playful and ironic ways of consuming. It can also be seen to have contributed to a *reflexive* attitude on the part of the individual to his or her identity, appearance and self-presentation.

Conclusion

As this chapter has progressed it should have become clear that it is not only not easy but also not appropriate to describe consumer culture in terms of a single theoretical perspective on economy and the culture. The theories outlined above are not necessarily exclusive; for example, the Marxist emphasis on the importance of commodity-exchange can be – and often is – linked to accounts that emphasize the importance of positional consumption. It seems likely that large-scale changes in consumer culture are associated with various sequences and conjunctures of economic and cultural processes. Nevertheless, it is also clear that it would be misleading to search for a single, overarching economic framework for understanding consumer culture. For one thing, there are significantly different national histories of consumption in various parts of the world, suggesting that there are multiple processes underpinning changes in consumption, each of which is likely to have its own periodicity, its own rhythms, and none of which is solely responsible for the complex patterns of contemporary consumer culture. It is perhaps for this reason that Jonathan Friedman claims:

> No theory of consumption is feasible because consumption is not a socially autonomous phenomenon. The best we can do is supply a framework of analysis. This framework must connect the macro processes of social reproduction with the formation of social projects of consumption as well as the interaction between them. (1994: 17)

3

Objects, Subjects and Signs

Introduction

If the last chapter focused on theoretical frameworks for thinking about the economy and culture in terms of the production, exchange and use of objects, this chapter will focus more directly on objects themselves. This chapter thus aims to foreground approaches that provide terms and methods of analysis that will address what is meant by the 'material' in material culture. Across all the approaches presented in this chapter there is the suggestion that what an object is – and the relations between matter, style and image it exemplifies – has changed historically. This focus on objects is part of a more general interest in science, technology and objects that has taken place in the social sciences and humanities over the last twenty or so years and includes a variety of approaches that combine analysis of 'the material' with that of meaning and communication. It often includes an emphasis on the agency of objects, that is, the capacity of objects to make things happen, without referring that agency back to the intentions of subjects or reducing what happens to unintended effects. What is at issue is whether and how it is possible to understand the attribution of agency or animation to objects as something more than naive, misplaced or ideological.

Importantly, the approaches outlined here do not simply want to add objects to subjects in the study of society, but instead draw our attention to the interrelationships between objects and subjects and show how the opposition between them is produced. The suggestion is that the everyday understanding of objects as discrete, inert or fixed entities, opposed to subjects, is a consequence or effect of particular relations between objects and subjects, that is, of networks of relations between entities. It also suggests that this everyday understanding of objects and subjects as opposed is changing as we become more and more entangled in networks with constantly changing objects that make relational demands on us. Such arguments provide an important framework for thinking about the conditions for reflexivity in consumer culture.

The approaches outlined here require thinking about the communicative and relational capacity of objects. This moves the analysis of communication and value beyond an exclusive concern with communication between subjects, an approach that has been widely criticized as inadequate for an understanding of consumer culture (Campbell, 1989, 1996). As Tim Dant notes:

> people communicate with objects in their culture directly, not simply via advertisements, instruction manuals or labels inscribed on their surfaces (such as 'Volume' printed beneath a control on sound equipment). Consumers communicate through sight, touch – and sometimes other senses – using their whole body to both make sense of and to make use of the things around them. This is not achieved through instinctual behaviour or even simple learnt behaviour but through the complex cultural acquisition of the meanings of objects that is characteristic of a particular formation of material civilization. (Dant, 2008: 15)

What is clear in all these accounts is the importance of understanding the 'articulation of the forms of relationality between persons and objects, images and materialities' (Cronin, 2004a: 108) for the study of consumer culture. They all insist upon considering the significance of objects, whether the focus is on object worlds, object–subject networks or object systems.

Commodity aesthetics

One of the most important accounts of the role of objects in culture derives from the Marxist perspective that links the expansion of markets and the growth of consumption to the expansion of capital and the intensification of commodity-exchange. As we have seen in chapter 2, one of the consequences of the production of goods as commodities for Marxism is that the basis for equivalence between goods is established in markets through the medium of money. There is thus a flattening of the qualities of goods as their values come to be measured in the quantitative terms of money, while at the same time other qualities and meanings are added through processes of advertising and promotion. Marx explains this paradoxical process – a simultaneous flattening and heightening of qualities – in terms of the enigmatic or mysterious aspect of the commodity, an analysis that has been extended in discussions of commodity aesthetics.

In the work of Stuart Ewen and Elizabeth Ewen (1976; 1982), for example, attention is paid to the role of '*the captains of consciousness*' – those working in marketing and advertising – in the shaping of American consumer culture in the first half of the twentieth century. In *Channels of Desire*, the Ewens report on an oral history study they carried out that shows how 'mass images', including those taken from cinema and advertising, played a role in the shaping of American consciousness in the early twentieth century. They point to the contributory role of the mass media and popular culture in providing a context within which promotional images could circulate. These images are seen to have created a vision of America that drew immigrants to 'the promised land', and Americanized immigrants on their arrival.

In one example, the Ewens tell how a firm's logo on a cotton bale evoked a utopian image of America in the mind of a young Czech working girl. They show that this logo produced an image for her of America as a land of abundance. The young woman came to see consumer products as magical objects, and the brand names and images of products became 'channels for her desires', emblems of wishes unfulfilled. Eventually, she emigrated to the USA, having already been introduced to the American way of life. Commodity aesthetics is thus deemed central by the Ewens to the creation of what they call the 'mass individual'. A more contemporary example of this process is the way in which consumer goods – whose existence was broadcast in the media – are said to have represented Western concepts of freedom, democracy and choice to those living in Eastern Europe before the collapse of communism.

However, the Ewens acknowledge that the development of modern consumer society is a contradictory and complex process. They argue that it is important to consider the historical context in which the manipulation of needs by producers and their agents occurs and is effective. They identify the disruptive nature of the experience of the processes of modernization as the context in which commodity aesthetics is able to take root. They suggest that the processes of urbanization and migration uprooted many people from familiar patterns of work, family and community, and from customary or traditional ways of understanding the world. They point out that people began to learn not only that 'others' were strangers, but also that they themselves were strangers to others. This experience, the Ewens argue, led to a sense of self as strange or alien. It was in this defamiliarizing context, then, that people became responsive to advertising and commodity aesthetics, since these discourses provided a common vocabulary and a shared way of relating to self and others.

The Ewens further argue that the use of a shared commercial vocabulary of image, appearance and style contributed to a shift away from a sense of self-identity understood in terms of internal or subjective moral and ethical values – that is, in terms of *character*, and attributes such as goodness or evil. It was replaced instead by a sense of self-identity defined in terms of external, presentational, often visual characteristics – that is, in terms of *personality*, judged by appearance, demeanour and style. The Ewens thus suggest that commercial promotion is effective because it enables people to respond to the often disorientating changes associated with modernization, and presents commodities as solutions to the problems of alienation, estrangement and disorientation raised by modern life, providing magical solutions, releasing unknown desires. As Sahlins puts it, goods allow Western society to turn 'the basic contradiction of its construction into a miracle of existence, a cohesive society of perfect strangers' (1976: 203, quoted in McCracken, 1988: 19).

Advertising has been identified by many other Marxist writers as

an important part of commodity aesthetics and processes of ideological mystification. So, for example, Sut Jhally writes:

> in non-market societies there is a unity between people and goods, but in capitalism there is a separation between object and producer. The world of goods in industrial society offers no meaning, its meaning having been 'emptied' out of them. The function of advertising is to refill the emptied commodity with meaning. Indeed the meaning of advertising would make no sense if objects already had an established meaning. The power of advertising *depends* upon the initial emptying out. Only then can advertising refill this empty void with its own meaning. Its power comes from the fact that it works its magic on a blank slate. (Jhally, 1989: 221)

The suggestion here is that advertising is a tool whereby consumers are controlled and manipulated, by the producers of goods who deliver things for which consumers have no real need, through the use of specialist types of aesthetic knowledge and the attachment of cultural values to goods in the production and distribution of products.

Commodity aesthetics is said to be a consequence of a capitalist mode of production, and is of profound importance in setting the conditions for a whole way of life. This restructuring of human needs is seen to have harmful effects. In a much-cited passage, Herbert Marcuse claims: 'People recognize themselves in their commodities; they find their soul in their automobile, hi-fi set, split-level home . . . social control is anchored in the new needs which [the consumer society] has produced' (1968: 24). Raymond Williams writes:

> If we are sensibly materialist, in that part of our living in which we use things, we should find most advertising to be of insane irrelevance. Beer would be enough for us, without the additional promise that in drinking it we would show ourselves to be manly, young at heart or neighbourly. A washing machine would be a useful machine to wash clothes, rather than an indication that we are forward looking or an object of envy to our neighbours. (1980: 172)

The imperative for the creation of these artificial needs is seen to come from the ever-increasing number of goods that capitalism must produce in order to survive. To avoid stagnation and the end of capitalism, manufacturers have to ensure that what is produced is also consumed, and they do so by the manipulation of the meaning of goods.

This line of argument is developed further in a study by Leiss, Kline and Jhally (1986) which looks at changes in advertising style and content alongside changes in the organization of production, thus enabling a focus on the aesthetic knowledge embedded in goods by producers and advertisers. This study identifies a number of different stages in American advertising during the course of the twentieth century, and suggests that these changes have implications for how commodities come to acquire meaning in social life. It suggests that the formerly artistic counter-cultural notion that life should be a work of art has been taken up and promoted in marketing and advertising as a way of selling the ever-increasing number of goods being produced.

This analysis suggests not only that advertising has become more important in contemporary economies, but also that changes in the style of advertising – and in particular a shift away from product features to the look of the product and its use in particular settings or lifestyles – have contributed to changes in our relations with objects as well as to how consumption is organized. The contemporary consumer is not invited to be rational or instrumental in their use of products, but instead to employ products in an expressive display of lifestyle. This change in relations with objects is attributed to the work of advertisers, marketers and publicists who seek to persuade the consumer to adopt a new role in the cycle of capitalist production and consumption. These captains of consciousness – to use the

I 1890–1925 The Product-oriented Approach
The central feature of ads during this period is the product itself – its function, features, price and the quality of its construction. The question for the consumer is assumed to be, what does this product do? That is, what is its functional or practical utility? Written text explains the 'reason-why' a particular product should be used.

II 1925–1945 Product Symbols
During this period, there was a shift in the focus of ads from the features of a product to its benefits for the consumer. The product was now presented in terms of its uses for the individual. The ads began to explore the non-practical aspects of use – there was an increasing emphasis on what the product could mean for consumers. The product itself became more abstract, representing a value achieved in use rather than a thing valued in its own right.

III 1945–1965 Personalization
Ads in this period were characterized not so much by representations of the product-in-use as by images of the consumer or user. Various motivations for consuming were represented, including the desire for social approval, pride in ownership, guilt and anxiety. Social interaction was shown to flow through the products people have, and the product itself might be personified, taking on human characteristics. So, for example, an ad from Chevrolet in this period claimed that the vehicle was 'More than a car – a member of the family'. Sometimes the product itself was represented as speaking, as if it were a person.

IV 1965–1985 Market Segmentation
This phase was characterized by the joint appearance of lifestyle ads and market segmentation. The focus of most ads shifted to the stylized identification of the consumer and the meaning of the act of consuming in a social situation. The product was displayed in a social context; the people who were displayed in the scene were not clearly defined by social role – instead they were situated within a particular consumption lifestyle. Consumption was represented in terms of the imaginary pleasures of certain settings and occasions – that is, in terms of a fantasy lifestyle – rather than in terms of satisfaction. These ads implied that by buying a particular product, the consumer would buy into a system of values, a way of life.

Ewens' phrase again – do this by highlighting the aesthetic or stylized dimension of the product, inviting the consumer to see and use the product in these terms.

However, other writers argue that multiple factors need to be taken into account to understand recent changes in commodity and commodities aesthetics: alongside changes in promotion and advertising must also be placed the intensification and reorganization of the labour process, through new flexible technologies, redesigned working practices, new methods of stock and inventory control and an increasing design intensity (Lash and Urry, 1994). Martyn Lee (1993), for example, suggests, 'Qualitative changes to the intensity and structure of labour and means of production tend to be reflected in changes to the commodity-form' (1993: 133). While this is a long-term process, Lee gives examples of a number of new or more marked characteristics of commodities that he suggests came to define the commodity form from the 1980s onwards. These include miniaturization – the reduction of the physical size of commodities in order to create new physical space, especially within the domestic environment, which may then make room for new commodities. Another development is the growth of what Lee calls 'compound commodities', that is, the compression or unification of previously discrete commodities, such as complete prepared meals, combined shampoos and conditioners, washing powders and fabric softeners, and alcoholic spirits and mixers. Mobile phones that are also cameras, videos, MP3 players, wireless Internet devices, GPS, notebook, address books, calendars, calculators and so on, yet fit into the palm of your hand, exemplify both trends.

Lee further argues that there has been an intensification of aesthetic obsolescence, that is, a more rapid turnover of styling changes. He argues that this is linked to small-batch commodity production that has been made possible by more flexible working practices, technologies, and improvements in the means of distribution. This process involves an increase in the use of aesthetic knowledge in production, requiring judgements of taste and aesthetic value in the design, development and production of such commodities. Importantly, he also suggests that one of the most significant developments in the commodity-form over recent years is the transition in production from *material* to *experiential* commodities. By this, he means that there has been a transition from production organized for the manufacture of durable and material commodities (washing machines, vacuum cleaners, cars, etc.) to the production of non-durable and experiential commodities (such as services, including, for example, tourism) which are either used up during the act of consumption or, alternatively, based upon the consumption of a given period of time, such as leisure or holiday activities. He concludes that there has been a 'de-materialization' of the commodity-form, with more commodities being 'time rather than substance based' (1993: 135). All these changes together, he argues, have resulted in the *fluidization* of consumption: the freeing up of the previously static and relatively fixed spatial and temporal dimensions of consumer culture.

In sum, this line of argument suggests that (post-)industrial societies have seen the intensification of commodity aesthetics – the manipulation of our relations to goods, in which promotion, advertising and imagery have a key role. These arguments about the effect of commodity aesthetics have been very influential in understandings of consumer culture, especially insofar as they point to the role of capital in the incitement of desire and challenge the naturalness of wants and needs. However, they have been criticized on a number of grounds. As noted in chapter 2, the centrality of capitalist production in the rise of consumer culture has been disputed. A further problem is that it is not always clear in such accounts how changes in the mode of producing goods have such a powerful or direct influence on consumption. It is also argued that the Marxist-inspired critique of advertising radically overstates the significance and effectiveness of advertising in contemporary culture, and implies that consumers are passive, suggestible and easily duped. What would Haug or Marcuse, for example, make of phenomena such as the genre of YouTube videos in which people record themselves unwrapping Apple products, or the involvement of consumers in creating ideas for new products?

Another problem with the Marxist account of commodity aesthetics is that although some attention is paid to the capacities of objects, the significance of the materiality of the objects themselves is often played down. There is a tendency for the objects themselves to disappear, and for image, style or emotional appeal to be seen as external to objects. However, as we shall see in chapters 5 and 6, recent neo-Marxist analyses have begun to explore the expansion of commodity-exchange in phenomena such as branding in ways that acknowledge more active relations between objects and images.

Style and things that matter

An alternative approach in the study of consumer culture is that provided by the early twentieth-century sociologist Georg Simmel. In his writings, Simmel emphasizes the interaction of subject with objects, and is concerned with how what he calls subjective and objective culture reciprocally shape each other. He argues that these cultures are not necessarily either symmetrical or analogous. Indeed, Simmel argues that in modern societies objective culture has become increasingly autonomous from subjective culture. He writes:

> Particularly in periods of social complexity and an extensive division of labour, the accomplishments of [objective] culture come to constitute an autonomous realm, so to speak. Things become more perfected, more intellectual, and to some degree more controlled by an internal, objective logic tied to their instrumentality; but the supreme cultivation, that of subjects, does not increase proportionately. (1971: 234)

Think here of a computer, a mobile phone or maybe even a washing machine. How much do you understand of how it works and how many of its capacities do you use?

For Simmel, the gap between objective and subjective culture is always mediated by the organization and practices of consumption. During the eighteenth century, he argues, objective culture was developed in relation to the ideal of the *individual*, by which he means an internal, personal value. By the nineteenth century, however, it is organized in terms of the concept of *education* in the sense of a body of objective knowledge and behavioural patterns that individuals must acquire by participating in the institutions of education, the scientific and technological professions and high culture. Simmel sees this in terms of the emergence of a partially independent objective culture, including the development of highly specialized objects whose use and meaning is often only understood by experts of some kind or other.

Simmel identifies a number of tendencies to explain how such a process might develop in modern industrial societies. The first of these is that the *sheer number of objects increases* to such an extent that any individual is incapable of comprehending the system of objects as an ensemble or totality. Second, with the *intensification of the division of labour*, exchange relations become increasingly complicated and mediated with the result that the economy necessarily establishes more and more relationships and obligations that are not directly reciprocal. The producer and the consumer lose sight of each other, with the consequence that no individual (neither producer nor consumer) is able to comprehend the technical and symbolic knowledge embodied by and as objects. As Simmel puts it:

Just as our everyday life is surrounded more and more by objects of which we cannot conceive how much intellectual effort is expended in their production, so our mental and social communication is filled with symbolic terms, in which a comprehensive intellectuality is accumulated, but of which the individual mind need make only minimal use. (1990: 449)

The third tendency identified by Simmel is that *the specialization of objects themselves* contributes to the process of their alienation from human subjects. This appears as an independence of the object, as the individual's inability to assimilate it and subject the object to his or her own rhythms. Simmel offers the example of furniture here, a case that he uses to demonstrate a growing estrangement between the subject and the products that ultimately invade even the more intimate aspects of daily life. He writes:

During the first decades of the nineteenth century, furniture and the objects that surrounded us for use and pleasure were of relative simplicity and durability and were in accord with the needs of the lower as well as of the upper strata. This resulted in attachment as they grew up to the objects of their surroundings . . . The differentiation of objects has broken down this situation. (1990: 459–60)

The number of highly specialized and increasingly frequently replaced objects makes an intimate and, as it were, personal relationship to each of them more difficult.

Here Simmel points not only to the rapidity of the consecutive differentiation of objects (a differentiation which he analyses in terms of fashion), but also to their concurrent differentiation. As a consequence of these tendencies, he suggests, objects increasingly present themselves in terms of an interconnected enclosed world that has fewer and fewer points at which the subjective individual can interpose his or her will and feelings. Together, he suggests, these tendencies help explain what he calls the stylization of life: on the one hand, style preserves the singular and specific while on the other hand it combines and equalizes things that are in reality different. He writes:

the more objective and impersonal an object is, the better it is suited to more people. Such consumable material, in order to be acceptable and enjoyable to a very large number of individuals, cannot be designed for subjective differentiation of taste, while on the other hand only the most extreme differentiation of production is able to produce the objects cheaply and abundantly enough in order to satisfy the demand for them. (1990: 455)

In some of his writings, Simmel seems to argue that the process of stylization is a counterbalance to the stresses and strains of modern life: 'What impels modern people so strongly towards style is the unburdening and masking of the personality that is the essence of style.' Take the case of fashion. For Simmel, it satisfies the individual's need for social adaptation and imitation, and, at the same time, it is a socially acceptable way of distinguishing yourself from others. However, although he sometimes suggests that the quest for style enables the individual to balance the pressures of modern social life, his later writings are more pessimistic. He speaks of what he sees as the increasing separation of subjective and objective culture not merely in terms of a crisis in culture or even a tragedy of culture but as a cultural pathology. In his terms, the unique subject or individual is subjected to enormous pressures by the extreme objectification of culture. Though modern culture made possible new developments of individuality, life in modern cities encourages a veneer of idiosyncrasy, a fascination with fashion, what he calls the blasé attitude and studied cosmopolitanism. All these are facets of what he terms 'exaggerated subjectivism'.

From production to signification: the logic of the code

The French philosopher Jean Baudrillard provides yet another account of the changing relations between objects, meanings and images. According to Baudrillard, we now live in a society in which the logic of production is no longer paramount; instead the logic of signification is all important. This latest stage in the development of capitalism is not just an extension of earlier stages, but a radical rupture, and thus requires new analytical concepts. We have moved, Baudrillard asserts, from a phase in the development of capitalism where the commodity-form was dominant to one where the sign-form prevails. Consumption is not be understood in relation to use-values, as material utility, but primarily in relation to *sign-values*, as *signification*. What makes his account so distinctive, then, is his focus not so much on either production or objective culture but on object-signs, and their organization as a system: although he makes reference to producers and consumers, the dynamic he identifies is largely internal to a system of object-signs.

This is clearly signalled in his early work – *The System of Objects* – and is developed throughout his writings. In this book, what interests Baudrillard is the relation between the rational technical system and the apparent 'irrationality' of needs of human beings and how this relation gives rise to ever-new needs. At this point in his thinking, Baudrillard is strongly influenced by Marxism and argues that it is what is happening in production that is important. His argument is that capitalism has in effect been able to act on need (including the need for pleasure), and has been able to produce human needs as an effect of its system of production. The potentially explosive lived contradiction between need and capitalist production has been displaced into the realm of object-signs in which objects are differentiated from each other through the working of an abstract code.

What Baudrillard is arguing at this stage in his writing is that there have been historical changes in the ways in which material goods acquire and convey meanings in modern societies. Objects are no longer related to in terms of their practical utility, but instead have become empty signifiers of an increasing number of constantly changing meanings. As more and more needs, wants and desires are brought into the realm of signification, individuals lose autonomous control and surrender to the code. A potentially infinite play of signs orders society while providing the individual with an illusory sense of freedom and self-determination (and here there are similarities with the ideas of repressive tolerance expressed by the analyst of Marxist cultural critic Herbert Marcuse). For Baudrillard, objects or things are not the focus of a lived relationship; this has become abstracted and annulled as object-signs proliferate. Revolution or even resistance is not possible. What is consumed is a de-negated human relationship, 'signified yet absent'; people live at distance not only from others but even themselves. In other words, while the new system of consumer capitalism appears to offer a new freedom or emancipation, this freedom is not what it seems. Rather, for Baudrillard, consumption assumes significance in modern societies as a new form of power that operates in terms of object-signs and their systemic articulation.

In his later work, Baudrillard extends this analysis, and moves away from a Marxist frame of reference to develop an analysis of signification as a system independent of production, but even in this early work he is attentive to the importance of semiotics. For example, the system of objects is understood in terms of the rise of a cybernetic imaginary mode 'whose central myth . . . [is] that of an absolute inter-relatedness of the world' (1996: 118). Within this cybernetic mode of information (not production), objects lose the substantiality and individual presence that was previously the source of their objective status; furnishing transmutes into interior decor in which what matters is not what an object is but whether it 'goes' with something else. Even the physical layout of rooms is significantly altered and connected in new ways. It is now space, and in particular the ability to communicate across the space of a distributed system, which has become the primary function of object relationships. Objects such as paintings and other art works lose their individual value and are repositioned within a new, interconnected, totality. An example of this is provided by the claim once made by Athena, a company that sold posters and cards, that the changing success of their prints could be linked to the changing popularity of the paint colours used in interior decor.

In the final chapter of *The System of Objects*, Baudrillard compares the traditional or primitive object-symbol with the modern object of consumption. The traditional object – and here he turns to the vocabulary of Mauss and Lévi-Strauss – is heavy with associations that are developed across a range of social practices and relationships; it is a symbol, and as such is interior to human society, and is never actually consumed in the sense of being used up. In the traditional system as he sees it, then, objects have the primordial function of being containers of a society's fundamental beliefs. This goes beyond their practical function and relates to their capacity to act as totems. They contain, embody or symbolize the natural or personal meaning of that society's world. So, for example, the house for him was symbolic of the human body; the object was anthropomorphized in poetic and metaphoric symbolism – windows, for instance, might be seen as the eyes of a house. The modern object, however, has become external to such symbolic relations and, in receiving its meaning in the context of a system of object-signs, has become part of a system dominated by marginal differences, or systems of pre-structured and impersonal differentiation. You choose a white or a pink or a black mobile phone, but the colours are relatively meaningless. In this way, he suggests, the code removes both objects and subjects from symbolic exchange.

> In the logic of signs . . . objects are no longer tied to a function or to a *defined* need. This is precisely because objects respond to something different, either to a social logic, or to a logic of desire, where they serve as a fluid and unconscious field of signification. (1988: 44)

Although in this extract Baudrillard appears to be suggesting that the logic of signification is tied to processes such as 'the social logic' or 'the logic of desire', in his later work he goes so far as to suggest that objects not only do not signify use-value but do not signify *anything* outside of themselves. Rather than people using objects to express differences between themselves, he proposes that people become merely the vehicles for expressing the differences between objects.

At the heart of a symbolic order, for Baudrillard, is the reversibility of the gift – the fact that it can and must be followed by a counter-gift; it is this reversibility that makes it different from the mode of contractual exchange dominating the contemporary consumer culture that is irreversible once completed. The logic of the new order is, he argues, *the implosion of the social*, its internal dissolution a consequence of its own contradictions. For example, according to a key commentator on Baudrillard, Mike Gane, the situation in contemporary society is that it appears as if the capitalist provides work to the worker: that is, it appears that the capitalist offers the worker a gift. In return the worker gives over or submits his life to the exploiter. But so, Baudrillard argues, the worker is put to a slow death.

To consider this initially rather surprising claim, consider the role of credit – or debt – in everyday lives. Baudrillard argues that until the end of the nineteenth century, for most people objects once acquired were owned in the full sense, for they were the material expression of work done. But, as Baudrillard puts it, today objects are with us before they are earned; they steal a march on the effort, the labour, that they embody, so that, in a sense, their consumption precedes their production. This inversion is, of course, one of the reasons for the traditional moral disapproval of the extension of credit, or, rather, debt.

However, Baudrillard believes that this disapproval has largely disappeared; we are instead actively encouraged to borrow money. Indeed, we believe it is our right as consumer-citizens to be extended credit, and companies compete for consumer debt with financial 'products' such as mortgages, life insurance policies and pensions alongside stocks and shares. However, Baudrillard argues that the economic duties of the consumer-citizen outweigh his or her rights. Thus, although he recognizes that people are learning how 'to make use of objects in complete freedom as if they were already theirs', his emphasis is on the obligations and costs incurred once the individual takes up the offer of credit. His concern is to challenge the purported freedom offered by the contemporary extension of credit. He notes that the length of time of repayment often coincides with the length of time over which an object will lose its value, thus ensuring that the consumer is never free of debt.

Indeed, he points out that the speed of 'using up' may sometimes outpace the speed of 'paying up' objects. As a consequence, he argues, credit cannot be integrated into everyday life without producing anxiety, the anxiety of meeting ongoing, periodic payments for something that is no longer of economic value. It is not clear who is giving or getting what.

The disruption to the order of everyday life caused by the intrusion of credit is further explored by Baudrillard in terms of its contribution to a shift in the terms of the economic valuation of the household. He points here to the different ways in which a sense of ownership may be legitimated, or not, in terms of possession as property. In the past, he suggests, the ownership of things was understood in Euro-American societies in terms of a set of property values linked to the social relationships of patrimony and secured by the apparent fixity of capital. The individual owned what he or she possessed and reward was seen to be linked to effort expended: objects 'were the material expression of work done'. In opposition to this, he argues, the individual's relation to possessions today is, as he puts it, 'conjugated in future perfect'. He further suggests that the ownership of goods no longer locates the individual in a relationship to either effort, that is, work done, or to the lineage of a family or customary group. Instead, the consumer system of objects now imposes its disjointed rhythms on the recurrences of everyday life.

The incitement to buy objects, including the offer of credit, means that rather than feeling a sense of security of ownership in the objects we earn through our labour or inherit from our family, we feel anxious in our possession of objects. Somehow, a sense of satisfaction eludes us. We are 'forever behindhand relative to our objects' since consumer goods now act as accelerators and multipliers of tasks, propelling us in a tendency to forward flight. As a consequence of the precariousness and disequilibrium credit introduces into our everyday lives, Baudrillard concludes, objects no longer represent payment from the past and security for the future; rather we are disconnected from our past and alienated from our future. So tight is our integration into the new system of production that 'private objects properly so called no longer exist'.

Baudrillard has been an influential critic insofar as he has opened up a way of exploring the organization of consumer culture, but many commentators are critical of what they see as the sweeping generalizations that he proposes. He is seen to have adopted an overly pessimistic interpretation of contemporary society, in which both producers and consumers are caught up in the endless reproduction of signs

with no escape possible, for he claims we live 'everywhere already in an "aesthetic" hallucination of reality' (1983, in Featherstone, 1991: 148). For some commentators this is a misleading claim, which over-states the significance of a system of signs.

The post-social and object worlds

Almost a century after Simmel, the contemporary sociologist Karin Knorr Cetina takes up the concern with the implications of the rise of objective culture or object worlds. She starts by noting that – in much sociology as well as in everyday life – the realm of the social has shrunk and become co-extensive with the human, noting that it was not always so. She thus acknowledges the historical impor-tance of animism and totemism referred to by the anthropologists in chapters 1 and 2. She explains the contemporary privileging of the human subject as a consequence of a long-term, ongoing, process of de-socialization or disenchantment in Euro-American societies. This process, she says, is continuing today: now even the social principles and structures of modernity – the nation, the family – are emptying out, losing some of the meaning and relevance they once had. But, she says, this is being offset by an enormous expansion of object worlds – of consumer goods, of technological devices and scientific objects. This is not only an expansion in the sheer volume of objects, but also in their value and significance. These two processes – the continuing contraction of the human social to the individual and the expansion of the world of objects – provide the conditions for what she calls a *post-social* world.

In its past, sociology has been concerned with the implications of the expansion of social policies, social thinking and social organization in the late nineteenth and early twentieth centuries, but Knorr Cetina argues that all three processes are now in decline. Indeed, she suggests there has been a retraction or withdrawal of social principles and structures, a slow erosion of belief in salvation by society and an increasing intensification of individualization. At the same time there is a second set of processes, running alongside the retraction of social principles – the rise of object worlds. One aspect of this is the increase in the volume of non-human things in the social world, but a second aspect is that many objects today can no longer be understood as fixed things of a material nature. Indeed, Knorr Cetina suggests that objects today can be defined almost as the obverse of this. She suggests that we no longer understand objects as material entities of a fixed nature; that objects now lack object-ivity.

Focusing on technological objects, consumer goods and exchange commodities, Knorr Cetina suggests that contemporary objects are characterized by a changing, unfolding character; things are now, she suggests, 'as much defined by what they are not as by what they are' (2000: 528). One illustration of this is provided by the many versions in which a product may appear: for example, Sony manufactured over 700 versions of the Walkman. She also points out that such objects make relational demands on us, at the very time when the increasingly isolated individual is facing a condition that Anthony Giddens describes in terms of ontological uncertainty. Knorr Cetina thus suggests that what makes contemporary forms of (post-)sociality distinctive is our solidarity with non-human or object worlds, and that these new forms of sociality pervade some of the most important sites of power in contemporary society – for example, the stock exchange and the government – and also mundane practices. She describes the relationality between subjects and objects in terms of an ongoing affinity between subjects conceived as structures of wanting and objects that are unfolding things, continually in the process of being defined. The implication is that solidarity with non-human

I don't worry much about having things. I worry plenty about relating to them. (Sterling, 2005: 79)

[B]y 'Artifacts' I mean simple artificial objects, made by hand, used by hand, and powered by muscle. Artifacts are created one at a time, locally, by rules of thumb and folklore . . .

By 'Machines' I mean complex, precisely proportioned artifacts with many integral moving parts that have tapped some non-human, non-animal power source. Machines require specialized support structures for engineering skills, distribution and finance . . .

By 'Products' I mean widely distributed, commercially available objects, anonymously and uniformly manufactured in massive quantities, using a planned division of labor, rapid, non-artisanal, assembly-line techniques, operating over continental economies of scale, and supported by highly reliable transportation, finance and information systems . . .

'Gizmos' are highly unstable, user-alterable, baroquely multi-featured objects, commonly programmable, with a brief life-span. 'Gizmos' offer functionality so plentiful that it is cheaper to import features into the object than it is to simplify it. 'Gizmos' are commonly linked to network service providers; they are not stand-alone objects but interfaces . . .

'Spimes' are manufactured objects whose informational support is so overwhelmingly extensive and rich that they are regarded as material instantiations of an immaterial system. SPIMES begin and end as data. They are designed on screens, fabricated by digital means, and precisely tracked through space and time throughout their earthly sojourn . . . (Sterling, 2005: 9–11)

worlds provides a kind of embedding in a shared life-world in object-dominated networks.

But how are we to understand these object worlds, and what are their implications for subjects? One approach is that developed by Tim Dant, whose work focuses on the ways in which meaning is communicated in material cultures. He makes a case for the importance of pragmatics rather than semiotics, by which he means – following Charles Morris – the study of the relation of signs to their interpreters. Following a study of people assembling flat-pack furniture and professionals working on cars, he identifies five aspects eBay is the product par excellence of the knowledge economy as content is continuously added by the users of the site themselves. This collective labour produces eBay as an 'epistemic object', characterized by two inter-related features. First, interaction, observation, use, examination and evaluation of epistemic consumption objects 'reveal themselves progressively', by increasing rather than reducing their complexity. Second, such objects demonstrate a propensity to change their 'face-in-action' vis-à-vis consumers through the continuous addition or subtraction of properties. The result is the possibility of a continuous knowledge project for consumers where uncertainty about 'what the object might offer next' motivates ongoing engagement. Because the epistemic object never stops signalling its unfolding possibilities . . . it sets up a cycle of revelation and discovery, always unclear and ill-defined; full of surprises, dangers, opportunities and promises allowing consumers to craft pleasurable daydreams. (Denegri-Knott and Molesworth, 2010: 59; references omitted)

of material interaction: intention, perception, orientation, manipulation and continuation. What is important about Dant's approach is the emphasis it places on a kind of communication with objects that is not mediated by language. He says, 'Human beings "read" what objects mean by engaging with them through their senses – this sort of reading does not involve a formal language that can be separated from the objects, but involves perceptual engagement with objects in their current state and relations with each other' (2008: 28).

An alternative framework, sometimes described as actor network theory (or ANT), also places emphasis on the conjoined agency of subjects and objects to convey meaning without language, but the focus is not on the subject's process of interpretation. This is an approach in which objects and subjects, things and people, are seen to jointly produce the social world in a network of non-humans and humans. Given the emphasis on the importance of relations between objects and subjects in this approach, and the deliberate decision not to privilege one of these over the other, the action that (jointly) emerges cannot be reduced to – or even analysed through terms derived from – a human or subjective point of view of meaning-making. An example of this approach is Mike Michael's (2000) exploration of the role of objects-in-everyday-life (the hyphens are important here!). He takes cases such as the driver-in-the-car, the person-on-the-couch-with-the-remote-control (or couch potato) and the human-dog-lead-dog (what he calls the Hudogledog) – and describes them as co(a)gents. He uses this term to draw attention not only to their interdependent agency but also to the cogency of that agency. It is a term that aims to capture the simultaneity and ambiguity of, on the one hand, distributed, exploded agency and, on the other, concentrated, imploded agency.

The characteristics of this co(a)gency cannot be reduced to either partner, subject or object, he says. Think, for example, of road rage as a description of activities of a driver-in-the-car; trolley rage – as the activities of a person-with-a-trolley said to be sparked by small children, slow packers, and change-fumblers; pavement rage – typified by aggressive comments and shoving; and phone rage – brought on by answering machines, voice mail and inefficient receptionists. In each case, Michael notes, the rage is a product of a person in relation to – or in a network with – an object: a trolley, the pavement or the telephone, and is a consequence of their relationship. There are interesting questions here, about how agency and responsibility – even emotion – may be distributed or delegated between objects and subjects. This kind of approach highlights the importance of relations between subjects and objects and provides a way of thinking about consumer culture in terms of changes in these relations, the becoming together of objects and subjects.

A further approach stresses the importance of information technology and the culture of computing for understanding how objects have changing effects in relation to subjects, transforming how subjects are produced in relation to objects. Some of this writing looks into the future, and considers how consumer culture may in the future be reorganized by developments in computing. So, for example, N. Katherine Hayles (2009) focuses on RFIDS, that is, radio frequency ID tags. These are small microchips no bigger than grains of rice, which have recently begun to be embedded in product labels, clothing, credit cards and the environment. Once activated, RFIDS can store information, including manufacturing date, delivery route, and the time and location when and where the product was purchased, or, in the case of a credit card, the name, address and credit history of the person possessing the card. But, more than this passive carrying of information, active RFIDs can be linked to embedded sensors to allow continuous monitoring of environmental conditions which can then be transmitted to a central, relational database and used to provide the consumer with further consumption choices. The development of objects with identities and the ability to communicate has the potential to transform advertising, since when they are coupled with mobile devices such as RFID-enabled mobile phones, tags can deliver location-specific information to individuals who may, for example, be able to receive a menu from three or four local restaurants or programmes from nearby cinemas. In addition, RFID tags, when coupled with backend databases, can lead to sophisticated 'behaviour inferences' that predict how particular people will act in a variety of situations and offer them individualized choices, and thus can be used by companies to attempt to manage markets and develop new products.

Hayles aims to think through the implications of this capacity to create animate environments with 'agential and communicative powers' (2009: 48). While recognizing the politically worrying issues of surveillance that are most obvious, she is also interested in how RFIDs, once combined with embedded sensors and relational databases, have the potential to de-stabilize traditional ideas about the relations of humans to products and the built world.

In this context, an 'Internet of Things' means 'a world-wide network of interconnected objects uniquely addressable, based on standard communication protocols', or, more widely: 'Things having identities and virtual personalities operating in smart spaces using intelligent interfaces to connect and communicate within social, environmental, and user contexts.' (<http://ec.europa.eu/information_society/policy/rfid/documents/iotprague2009.pdf>, accessed 4.8.09)

She conceptualizes this in terms of the movement of computation out of the box and into the environment – the emergence of a flexible, robust and pervasive 'internet of things' that 'senses the environment, creates a context for that information, communicates internally among components, draws inferences from the data, and comes to conclusions that in scope, if not in complexity, far exceed what an unaided human could achieve' (2009: 49). As she notes, many commentators believe RFID will revolutionize the ways in which products are manufactured, delivered, stored and inventoried, pointing out that both Walmart and the US Department of Defense, now require their vendors to attach RFID tags to their merchandise.

To think about the possible consequences of this revolution, Hayles draws on Bruce Sterling's notion of SPIME (the name he gives to a just emerging kind of object) worlds. For Sterling (a science-fiction writer and cultural critic), SPIME marks the transition from thinking of the object as the primary reality to perceiving it

After ten years of academic research and expert insight into the nuances of the Internet of Things, the latter is at last coming. Underwear that measures blood pressure, washing machines that start up only when electricity is cheap, smart meters that provide real-time, two-way communication between customer and electric power company – there are already many examples of real-world objects that eventually may become 'objects that blog'. (<http://ec.europa.eu/information_society/policy/rfid/documents/iotprague2009.pdf>, accessed 4.8.09)

as data in computational environments, through which it is designed, accessed, managed and recycled into other objects. As Sterling puts it, the SPIME is 'a set of relationships first and always, and an object now and then' (2005: 77); it is 'not about the material object, but where it comes from, where it is, how long it stays there, when it goes away, and what comes next' (2005: 109). Also likely to be transformed by RFID, Hayles suggests, will be ideas of private property, ownership and personal possession, since what we buy or consume will not necessarily have a fixed material existence.

George Orwell always had a fine ear for hypocrisy. Even so, quite what he would have made of last week's Kindle debacle, in which Amazon was accused of tactics reminiscent of Big Brother, is unclear. When it emerged that the company had secretly deleted copies of Orwell's novels from people's Kindle ebook readers because of a legal issue, the irony was too delicious to ignore: . . .

It turned out to be a copyright issue – MobileReference, the company that sold the copies, did not have the rights to use Orwell's work and Amazon was trying to erase its mistake.

The removal was enough to set off angry customers and, despite efforts to explain the mix-up, the outrage continued . . .

No wonder Amazon customers were so annoyed: it's as if they walked into a bookshop, only to discover that the shop was a library and they had to give it back . . . (Johnson, 2009: 2).

Conclusion

This chapter has introduced a range of perspectives that describe the characteristics of objects and object-relations in contemporary societies. There is a claim – in some of the approaches outlined here – that the role of objects in the social world is changing in important ways, and that there is a need to develop new concepts and ways of understanding object–object relations as well as subject–object relations. The different approaches outlined here propose (sometimes contrasting) views of what might be described as the material-semiotic or material-pragmatic effects of subject–object networks and systems of objects. Very importantly, this opens up the issue of how to think about consumer culture in ways that are not limited to symbolic exchange or even conscious or purposive communication between people. They suggest that material culture provides an increasingly reflexive environment for the making of identities at the same time that the nature of that reflexivity may be changing.

4

Capital, Class and Consumer Culture

Introduction

In what follows, a brief discussion of the historical development of modern consumer culture in the UK will be presented, but it is not a comprehensive account or even an overview. Instead, the main concern of the chapter is a presentation of an interrelated set of accounts of the relations between capital, class and contemporary consumer culture in the UK in the second half of the twentieth century. These accounts describe a shift from Fordism to post-Fordism or, as it is sometimes described, from organized to disorganized capitalism. This leads into an analysis of class, cultural capital and consumer culture developed by the French sociologist Pierre Bourdieu that has been taken up in the UK and the USA. There is then a brief discussion of the implications of the increasing importance of what is called immaterial labour for the economy. This begins to show the complexity of current interrelationships between the contemporary economy and consumer culture, and the notion of prosumption is briefly introduced. The following chapters will complicate the story still further.

Histories of consumer culture

How are we to explain the emergence of modern Euro-American consumer culture? This is a very big question, impossible to answer with a single thesis. Let me take the case of the emergence of fashion in England as an example of how problematic it is to try to develop a single explanation.

It is sometimes assumed that the development of modern consumer culture is a direct consequence of the Industrial Revolution. But a radically different view is developed by McKendrick, Brewer and Plumb (1982) who look at the rise of fashion across the domains of clothing, pottery and newspapers and print prior to and parallel with the Industrial Revolution, which, so they propose, together amounted to a revolution in consumption. In relation to clothing, they acknowledge the importance of developments in production and distribution of goods, including the increasingly rapid obsolescence of style, a speeding up of the diffusion of fashion knowledge, the use of marketing techniques such as the fashion doll and the fashion plate, the participation of previously excluded social groups, and new ideas about consumption and its contribution to the public good. But, importantly, they also propose that the spread of fashion was dependent upon a new consumer sensibility, a kind of progressive emulation among the lower middle classes and a new fondness for novelty. For McKendrick et al., a 'revolution' in consumption was a 'necessary analogue [not an effect] of the industrial revolution' (1982: 9).

They locate this revolution in consumption in the second half of the eighteenth century in England, in the context of a society that was becoming less hierarchical as a result of the status aspirations of the new bourgeois classes. The possibility of social advancement was to be found in the conspicuous emulation of the consumption of the nobility. According to McKendrick et al., once the pursuit of luxury became possible for an ever-widening proportion of the population, its potential was released and it was this revolution in sensibility that was the engine for growth, and was itself 'a motive power for mass production' (1982: 66).

Yet while this identification of independent origins for a consumer revolution has been very influential – it helped establish the field of consumption studies – there is, in fact, little agreement as to the time and location of the origins of consumer culture even in the context of the UK, let alone elsewhere. Instead, the general consensus is that not only is there not a single explanation for the consumer revolution, but that there was not a single consumer revolution. Rather, the view emerging across a range of disciplines is that consumer cultures are best viewed as long-term phenomena with multiple geographies (some smaller, some larger than the nation) and a variety of histories. There is an increasing body of literature that is beginning to explore this complex set of processes without trying to find a single cause, especially as the importance of relations of exchange between countries and regions is acknowledged more fully (see, for example, Mandel and Humphrey, 2002; Garon and Maclachlan, 2006; Trentmann, 2009; and chapter 5).

So, for example, one of the most important claims made in histories of European consumer culture is that its emergence is linked to a significant growth in the scale and complexity of material culture *prior* to the Industrial Revolution. These changes are linked to the trade with and exploitation of colonies by some European countries, which involved not only the geographical expansion of trade routes and increasing numbers and kinds of transaction but also the import of luxury goods, including perfumes, silks and linens, and then sugar, coffee, tea and cocoa. As Trentmann puts it, 'Cotton textiles were as successful, fashionable and desirable in the late 17th and 18th centuries as jeans have been since the 1950s' (2009: 192).

The availability of these luxury goods contributed to the spread of a hedonistic-aesthetic attitude towards material culture, which, so some commentators suggest, was also linked to a slow process of secularization of love. This is a view put forward by, for example, Sombart (1967) who argues that a secularization of love came about as the result of a slow but progressive emancipation from religious institutions and rules. This, he argues, contributed to the emergence of cultures of earthly enjoyment of beauty and is associated with a new 'hedonistic-aesthetic conception of the woman and of love for a woman'. In other words, long-term transformations in gender relations are seen to be one element in the development of consumer culture, involving not only relations between men and women but also a self-reflexive relation by women in relation to themselves, including, for example, changes in conceptions of beauty and femininity.

Other commentators, including notably Mukerji (1983), propose that the emerging modern attitude towards consumption was part of the rise of 'materialist values', meaning an interest in the properties and qualities of material things. The suggestion here is that the availability of new and unknown products in Western European markets in the sixteenth and seventeenth centuries provoked people into cultivating a capacity for cultural classification, displayed for example in pictorial prints and maps, pushing them to develop increasingly sophisticated materialist cultural attitudes as well as contributing to the advancement of scientific and technological thought. This materialist culture 'shaped the environment in which capitalism could develop' (Mukerji, 1983: 15).

The emergence and development of consumer culture is understood in both these accounts as neither an effect of, nor unrelated to, changes in the organization of production in Europe alone, but as part of a set of complex, dynamic and transnational relations between the economy and culture. They recognize the importance of the interplay between specific cultures, national policies and movements of objects, ideas, money and people between countries. Instead of a localized Western birth of consumer culture, these and other studies demonstrate the importance of contact zones, the exchange of goods and knowledge, and processes of incorporation, emulation and assimilation in a transnational space for the emergence of consumer cultures everywhere.

To suggest that consumer culture is not to be understood as the direct effect of changes in production in a single local or even regional context (for example, industrialization in Europe) is not an argument that production is unimportant or that an historical understanding of capitalism has nothing to contribute to an understanding of consumer culture. Rather it is an argument that our understanding of the economy and capitalism is improved if consumer culture is not seen as entirely determined by production, or by developments in a single country alone. It is to show the value of looking at complex, iterative and multidimensional relations between 'production' and 'consumption' – some of which may be understood in terms of the growth of markets and relations of exchange and distribution – *and* considering the importance of cultural, scientific and technological processes for understanding changes in the economy. Having made this point at a general level, let us now turn to some recent influential accounts of the relationship between capital, class and consumer culture in the shift from Fordism to post-Fordism, that is said to have occurred in the second half of the twentieth century in the USA and various European countries (to different degrees and in different ways).

From Fordism to post-Fordism

In many accounts of the development of consumer culture, great importance is placed upon the growth of mass production and market relations. From this perspective, it is capitalist relations of production that 'produces' mass consumption as the purchase of commodities, and the identity of the consumer as the user of commodities. Additionally, an individual's access to consumption is held to be largely structured by the distribution of economic and cultural resources, which themselves are determined in crucial ways by the wage relation and social class. In this perspective, then, it is the inter-relationship of capitalist relations of production and consumption that is important to the understanding of consumer culture. The point here is that very few accounts of the rise of consumer culture are simply production-led: even in Marxist-inspired accounts, along-side an emphasis on the social relations of production, attention is also paid to the organization of commodity-exchange, the develop-ment of commodity-fetishism, the increasing significance of forms of knowledge and expertise, positional consumption, the role of cultural intermediaries and the growth of a calculating mentality. The need of producers to incite demand is recognized, but so too are the ways in which consumer practices and desires are linked to class position and class antagonisms, as well as, more recently, the rise of the politi-cal discourse of neo-liberalism (Harvey, 2005). In short, a whole complex of cultural, social and political as well as economic relations is involved.

To explore the one case example of these complex interrelation-ships, we will turn to a brief description of the shift from Fordism to post-Fordism. Put simply, Fordism refers to the system of mass production and consumption characteristic of developed industrial economies during the 1940–1960s. It includes an emphasis on manufacturing, the organization of labour according to principles of scientific management, sometimes known as 'Taylorism', assembly-line production, and the standardization of products. Economies of scale are achieved by spreading capital expenses, such as the build-ing and maintenance of factories, and investments in machinery and equipment, over large volumes of output, leading to a reduction of unit costs. Economies of scope are put into place by organizing the division of labour in such a way as to make labour more cost-effective (if usually less skilled), typically through, for example, assembly-line production. At the same time, the Fordist workforce, which consisted of primarily (male) semi-skilled manual workers, increasingly came to develop a strong sense of collective solidarity and class identity, expressed in labour movement organization and politics.

The reason this system of production came to be called Fordism is that it was exemplified by Henry Ford's system of mass auto-mobile production. A defining characteristic was standardization – standardized parts, standardized manufacturing processes, and a relatively easy to manufacture standard product. For this reason, it is sometimes argued that the car is the quintessential commodity form of the twentieth century (Dennis and Urry, 2009). But Fordism does not only describe a particular organization of production: the high levels of production typical of Fordism were combined with persuasion to spend and included policies to stimulate demand through a combination of low prices, high wages, advertising and the lifting of regulations to make consumer credit more easily available. In other words, Fordism was a combination of industry and state policies affecting both production *and* consumption in interrelated ways.

Initially, Fordism was a largely North American regime: neither Fordist principles of production nor the associated political strategies to develop consumption and the identity of the consumer were taken up outside the USA. As Frank Trentmann says, 'The universal, mobile persona of the consumer was not easily grafted on to nation-states, with their respective legal traditions and territorially bounded notions of citizenship' (Trentmann, 2006b: 13). He argues that it was in fact the Second World War that meant that the consumer became a social actor and object of state policy in Europe. 'More than choice, affluence and shopping arcades, it was the need to rationalize scarce resources in war-time or to boost demand to overcome economic depression that made states identify consumers as a core target of public policy' (2006b: 12).

However, even as Fordism began to be taken up outside the USA, more global and more flexible techniques of production were being introduced by companies, including IBM, who introduced systems such as total quality management (TQM), 'lean' manufacturing, just-in-time (JIT) delivery, and price-based costing, as well as, a bit later, the Toyota Production System. The introduction of these systems of flexible production was supported by developments in communications, logistics and information processing. Instead of producing mass or standard goods, firms found it more profitable to produce differentiated product lines targeted at mini-mass or niche groups of consumers. This was because, rather than investing large amounts of money on the mass production of a single, standardized product, firms could now bring together flexible combinations of workers and machines in response to changes in consumer demand.

At the same time companies employed labour wherever in the world it was cheapest, leading to a new international division of labour. Advertising, design and marketing became more important in the organization of production as they were used to identify and differentiate these dynamic markets, thus enabling an increasingly intricate calibration of supply and demand. These changes went along with a series of developments in distribution and retail. One notable innovation here was the barcode that enabled retailers to produce more accurate inventories, to automate reordering, and improve market research and analysis, feeding back into the production process. Stuart Hall sums up the consequences of this shift as follows:

> more flexible, decentralized forms of labor process and work organization; decline of the old manufacturing base and the growth of the 'sunrise', computer-based industries; the hiving off or contracting out of functions and services; a greater emphasis on choice and product differentiation, on marketing, packaging, and design, on the 'targeting' of consumers by lifestyle, taste and culture rather than by categories of social class; a decline in the proportion of the skilled, male, manual working class, the rise of the service and white-collar classes and the 'feminization' of the work force; an economy dominated by the multinationals, with their new international division of labor and their greater autonomy from nation-state control; and the 'globalization' of the new financial markets, linked by the communications revolution. (1992: 58)

This new system of flexible production and consumption – what has come to be called post-Fordism or flexible accumulation – reduced the demand for unskilled labour in Europe and North America, and with this reduction came a decline in the political influence of unions. At the same time there was a growth in services, including, for example, tourism (Urry, 1990), and an increase in the participation of women in the labour market (Walby, 1990, 1997). These new forms of labour were organized as a core of multi-skilled workers and a periphery of semi- and un-skilled workers in ways that were highly gendered and racialized. At the same time, consumption practices became an increasingly significant source of identity for people as a greater range of products was directed at specific target markets.

As noted in chapter 3, Martyn Lee argues that these changes contributed to a change in the commodity form and a *fluidization* of consumption, with a diversification of individual consumption times and spaces and the freeing up of the previously static and relatively fixed spatial and temporal dimensions of social life. Others, for example, Rifkin (2001), have described some of the same changes in terms of the rise of an 'experience economy', and have pointed to the increasing importance of access to (a continually changing) product rather than outright ownership. If we return to the case of the car company Ford, we can observe how, in recent years, the company have come to make more money from the financial deals in which people purchase their cars than from the sale of the cars themselves. From this point of view, the Ford company is a financial services provider rather than a manufacturer of cars: the majority of its profit derives not from the one-off profit it makes when a single car is sold to many individual consumers, but from the financial arrangements in which many individuals purchase not a single car, but enter into an ongoing financial relationship with the company.

A contrasting but related perspective is provided by Luc Boltanski and Eve Chiapello (2007) who argue that in response to the economic and political crises of the 1960s and 1970s capitalism came to acquire a new 'spirit', in the form of networked organization, flexible production, subcontracting, casualization of labour, segmentation of markets, the intensification of work and increased job competition or precariousness. In such networks, they argue, activity becomes the standard of value for personal success: what becomes important – and economically valuable – is to be always pursuing some sort of activity, always to have a project, ideas, to be looking forward to, and preparing for, something to do.

What these changes add up to has been a matter of some debate, and there is considerable dispute about the extent and economic and political implications of the shift from Fordism to post-Fordism (Piore and Sabel, 1984; Lash and Urry, 1987, 1994; Harvey, 1989, 2005). However, what will be focused on is the claim that the distinctive uses of consumer goods by a particular social group – the developing middle classes – also came to play a part in the shift from Fordism to post-Fordism. From this point of view, there is a complex interplay at work, which can be represented in terms of a *cycle* of processes, feeding into and reinforcing each other, with no single moment in the cycle – production or consumption – able to be identified as more important than any other.

Class and taste

In the analysis outlined here, post-Fordism is understood not simply in terms of changes in production, but in terms of interactions between production and consumption, in which the activities of the so-called 'new' middle classes, who are to be found in the rapidly expanding service and white-collar occupations, are especially important. The kinds of labour performed in these occupations is important here: it typically involves work that combines adherence to bureaucratized rules with notions of professional autonomy and an engaged responsiveness to the environment. This mode of working is said to encourage innovation within a quasi-professional ethos, thus providing a distinctive space within which a shared culture, or way of life, can be sustained. At the same time, the groups employed in this rapidly growing sector of the economy are highly visible and given perhaps a disproportionately loud voice by what have come to be called cultural intermediaries.

The general argument being developed here then is that, through the development of a shared culture, the new middle classes came to assert a distinctive identity vis-à-vis other class fragments. This was, in part, achieved in their work-lives, a self-promotion that is most clearly visible amongst the members of occupations in the media, design and fashion worlds themselves. Consider, for example, a feature in the upmarket women's magazine *Elle* which features an article about a new shop opened by three women 'behind the latest counter culture', one of whom is quoted as saying '"We know what we like. We're not interested in producing anything we wouldn't wear ourselves"' (Scott, 1995: 27). Indeed, Pierre Bourdieu suggests that the emerging lifestyle of the new middle classes embodied a new social consciousness, in which the very distinction between work and leisure is problematized. A contemporary example of an object used to elaborate this lifestyle is the BlackBerry – an electronic personal organizer.

'It completely allows me to mix business with pleasure.'
    Prateek S., NY
This year, I visited Asia, the Middle East and Europe for work and my BlackBerry Pearl allowed me to work there as though I had never left the office. I took pictures with my new Pearl and then viewed my spreadsheets. I got instant flight delay alerts and stock quotes, all on the way to the airport. It completely allows me to mix business with pleasure.

'For a girl, it's like having all your make-up in one compact case!'
    Cindy P., ON
I love my BlackBerry Pearl because it is so easy to use, whether it's text messaging friends or receiving an email. It is so much better than having to carry a separate agenda around, when everything you need to be organized is included in this little device. For a girl I guess it's like having all your make-up available in one compact case.

'Because my clients don't know where I am.'
   Rick S., WI
Why do I love my BlackBerry? Simple. It's because my clients
don't know where I am.

'I can glance at my BlackBerry and feel connected to my family.'
   Wynne B., CA
My BlackBerry is an essential tool for business – especially since
I am in sales and on the road often. But that is the common
reason for loving your BlackBerry. Why do I REALLY love my
BlackBerry? Because I was able to scan in my first ultrasound
picture of my first child (due February, 2007), email it to myself
and load it as my wallpaper on my BlackBerry. So while I am
traveling and running around the country closing deals, I can
glance at my BlackBerry and feel connected to my family and my
priorities – and always remember why succeeding in my career is
so important.
   (BlackBerry website: <http://uk.blackberry.com>; accessed 9
April 2009)

In general terms, Bourdieu argues that the new bourgeoisie is:

the initiator of the ethical retooling required by the new economy from
which it draws its power and profits, whose functioning depends as
much on the production of needs and consumers as on the production of goods. The new logic of the economy rejects the ascetic ethic of
production and accumulation, based upon abstinence, sobriety, saving
and calculation, in favour of a hedonistic morality of consumption,
based on credit, spending and enjoyment. This economy demands a
social world which judges people by their capacity for consumption,
their 'standard of living', their lifestyle, as much as by their capacity for
production. (Bourdieu, 1984: 310)

The increasing importance of hedonistic consumption is seen to
provoke changes in production, enforcing a greater flexibility in types
and speed of production processes. The lifestyle and tastes of this
new class fraction is thus held both to have been created by, and contribute to, the development of the capitalist economy and consumer
culture in the post-Fordist era.

Habitus and habitat

In order to consider this view in more depth, let me outline Bourdieu's conceptual framework, especially the highly influential analysis of consumption and the dynamics of taste informed by a large-scale empirical study of French society in the late 1960s, *Distinction* (not published in English until 1984). In this weighty book, Bourdieu provides a critique of, and an alternative to, traditional or common-sense understandings of taste as something so intangible, fluid, and subjective that it cannot be analysed. He argues, instead, for a view of taste as a social phenomenon; he suggests that taste is not the result of individualistic choices, but is socially patterned in particular ways.

Generally, Bourdieu is concerned with social reproduction, that is, with how societies reproduce or maintain themselves over time, not simply as a set of individuals, but as individuals in certain groupings in certain relations of power to each other. As part of this general project, he argues that the resources or assets of different social classes are as much *symbolic* as economic, political or organizational (remember here the links drawn between the symbolic and the economic in the work of the anthropologists discussed in chapters 1 and 2). For Bourdieu, taste is a key mechanism for organizing the distribution of symbolic resources; as such it is an important part of social reproduction. He describes how individuals struggle to improve their social position by manipulating the cultural representation of their situation in the social field. They accomplish this, in part, by affirming the superiority of their taste and lifestyle with the view to legitimizing their own identity as 'what it is right to be'. Disputes about taste are not trivial from Bourdieu's point of view, but are tied to the reproduction of class relations: the reproduction of a shared cultural style contributes to class reproduction.

In exploring the significance of taste for social reproduction in contemporary society, Bourdieu looks at the interplay between cultural and economic capital; he believes that people actively invest cultural capital to realize economic capital. More particularly, he argues that cultural capital has become increasingly important in recent years, as, in many Euro-American societies, the economic differences by which class distinctions have traditionally been signalled have become less clear-cut although, as noted in chapter 1, there still remain deep and enduring economic inequalities. On the basis of his large-scale study of French society he argues that the increasingly important relationship between economic and cultural capital gives rise to a number of competing groups within the middle classes in particular. He identifies three principal groups in French society. A dominant group is comprised of senior industrial managers who have a great deal of economic capital but relatively little cultural capital. A second group is clustered in a rapidly growing set of occupations, including the media, the so-called caring professions and marketing. These have less economic and more cultural capital. A final group is low in economic but high in cultural capital; they include teachers, artists and the like. For Bourdieu, these groups, and others in other class formations, are engaged in a constant struggle with one another to improve their social position, by using and enhancing their possession of the different types of cultural and economic capital. For Bourdieu, these struggles over taste that continue today are highly significant for social reproduction. Indeed, and this is the point at which we return to the argument outlined above, the struggles over taste are said to have contributed to the transition from a Fordist to a post-Fordist society.

One of the most important terms in Bourdieu's analysis is that of *habitus,* a term that derives from the idea of 'habit, custom and the state of things' (Slater, 1997: 62). It is defined by Bourdieu as a system of dispositions, a system that organizes the individual's capacity to act. He writes that habitus is:

> a system of lasting, transposable dispositions, which, integrating past experiences, functions at every moment as a matrix of perceptions, appreciations and actions and makes possible the achievement of infinitely diversified tasks, thanks to analogical transformations of schemes permitting the solution of similarly shaped problems. (1977: 83)

Habitus is evident in the individual's taken-for-granted preferences about the appropriateness and validity of his or her taste in art, food, holidays and hobbies. It does not simply refer to knowledge, or even competence or sense of style, but is also embodied, literally. That is, it is inscribed in the individual's body, in body size, shape, posture, way of walking, sitting, gestures, facial expression, sense of ease with one's body, ways of eating, drinking, amount of social space and time that an individual feels entitled to occupy; even the pitch and tone of voice, accent, and complexity of speech patterns are part of an individual's habitus. All these things, according to Bourdieu, are bodily manifestations of your habitus. It is shaped primarily in childhood within the family and schooling by the internalization of a given set of material conditions. In this way, an individual's habitus is linked to his or her family, group, and, perhaps most importantly for Bourdieu, the individual's class position.

The habitus is not just a random series of dispositions, but operates according to a relatively coherent logic, what Bourdieu calls the *logic of practice*, and this is organized by a system of classification. The habitus, which operates below the level of individual consciousness, is what will shape an individual's apparently personal taste through the way in which the individual applies the system of classification. The system of classification operates with dichotomous distinctions like high/low, masculine/feminine, white/black, distinguished/vulgar and good/bad. These principles of categorization are initially developed in specific situations, but come to be applied across a wide range of situations as non-conscious regulating principles.

It is the application of these principles as a distinctive mode of cultural consumption that is recognized as taste, or lack of it. It is in operation, for example, in the particular way in which domestic goods are assembled together for display in an interior decor magazine – a book of poems casually laid on a coffee table, or the selection of a large leaf and a single stem of flowers rather than a bunch of flowers to show off a jug, for example. According to Bourdieu, what seems like an individual practice – taste – is regulated by the logic of practice and is always a variant of class practice.

Indeed, the source of divisions in taste in contemporary society is attributed by Bourdieu to the workings of class in modern society. The immediacy of working people's tastes derives from the immediacy of their work experience, and the pressure imposed by their needs. A person who carries out manual labour, and whose access to the basics of sustenance and comfort is not guaranteed, has a respect and a desire for the sensual, physical and immediate. An individual who has been brought up in the abstractions of education and mental labour, and who is certain of obtaining daily necessities, cultivates a distance from these needs, and affects a taste based in respect and desire for the abstract, distanced and formal. These objective conditions are interiorized through habitus as desire expressed in taste.

This notion of habitus is an attempt by Bourdieu to develop a *social* analysis of taste; it acknowledges the social conditions for the acquisition of taste, but also allows some space for human agency. Bourdieu suggests that although the logic of practice which structures the habitus and thus an individual's taste is determined by a particular material set of conditions, the individual's practice is always also a strategy in situations of which the outcome is uncertain, not least because these strategies are opposed by the strategies of other individuals. So, although the habitus provides a framework for action, it is not static, and can be shaped by the outcome of the interaction of the strategies adopted by different social groups.

Moreover, according to Bourdieu, as part of the process of social reproduction, classes in competition with each other attempt to impose their own habitus or system of classification on other classes, as part of their more general struggle to become dominant. What he calls the cultural field is central to this competition, and its organization can itself be seen to be the cumulative result of these struggles. Education has been a central institution in the development of this system insofar as it provides a key route to the appreciation of high culture that historically has been defined by its spatial and temporal apartness and abstraction from the immediacies of everyday life. It produces specialized groups of users or consumers of art, who then may form the basis of new cultural markets.

Bourdieu conceptualizes the cultural field as if it were an economy. He argues that it is characterized by markets, competition, inflation and attempts at monopolization. As part of this understanding of the operation of the cultural field as an economy, a key concept for Bourdieu is 'cultural capital', the sedimented knowledge and competence required to make distinctions or value judgements, such as being able to make judgements about works of 'art' and 'non-art'. Bourdieu suggests that different classes and different class fractions are engaged in a series of struggles with each other to increase the volume of cultural capital they possess, and to increase the valuation placed on the particular forms of capital they possess. He argues that in the second half of the twentieth century new class fragments found 'ardent spokesmen in . . . the directors and executives of firms in tourism and journalism, publishing and the cinema, fashion and advertising, decoration and property development' (1984: 310–11). He uses the term 'cultural intermediary' to describe these spokespeople.

An earlier example of these struggles in British society was the attempt by literary critics such as F. R. Leavis and Denys Thompson in the early and mid-twentieth century to build up English literature as a discipline in British universities (Mulhern, 1974). This was achieved through the elevation of particular principles of reading as the preferred techniques of literary criticism, and by establishing what has come to be called the literary canon, that is, a selection of writings that are held to be the best of English literature. These critical and pedagogic strategies contributed to the formation of an educated public for certain kinds of fiction – particularly novels. They helped consolidate the development of two levels of literacy – being able to read and being well-read – and also trained certain groups in a literary mode of appropriation, including the skills of: intense contemplation of a text; following its narrative from beginning to end; and interpreting the text in relation to an individual author's *oeuvre* of work. It can thus be seen to have contributed to the creation of the distinction between high and popular culture in the cultural field by institutionalizing particular techniques for the appreciation of literary value in terms of originality and uniqueness. This skill is not a neutral set of techniques for identifying the inherent value of literature, but, rather, is a set of techniques for legitimating the values of an emerging fraction of the middle classes and their mode of critical consumption. Through the production of this culture, this new class fraction not only shaped tastes and challenged the authority of established taste-makers but also pursued their own legitimacy and power (Lash, 1990).

In Bourdieu's terms, differential access to literary consumption is thus a crucial aspect of the reproduction of class and class conflict – being able to show that you are well-read is an important aspect of class domination, and the success of Leavis and his colleagues was to set the terms of judgement according to the values of an emerging professional fraction of the middle classes. It might be argued that the value of this way of reading has come to be extended to other texts, such as, for example, film. For some people, it is more important to know the name of a film's director rather than those of its stars. But in Bourdieu's own analysis of the cultural classifications emerging in France towards the end of the twentieth century, it is their control over many aspects of the mass media as well as high culture that has allowed the new cultural intermediaries to invent 'a whole series of genres half-way between legitimate culture and mass production' (1984: 325–6). And while Bourdieu may have had more conventional types of cultural producers in mind, others have included 'practitioners in design, packaging, sales promotion, PR, marketing and advertising' within this category (Nixon and du Gay, 2002; Julier and Moor, 2009).

While Bourdieu's approach has been highly influential, a number of problems have been identified. As Michele Lamont notes (1992: 182–3), Bourdieu assumes that *differentiation*, the marking of difference, leads directly to *hierarchalization* – the ranking of difference. This is a view of the expression of taste as a form of one-upmanship, but, Lamont argues, it is not necessarily so. Bourdieu's assumption is a consequence of his view that meanings and values are defined relationally or structurally in relation to each other within a closed or stable power field. A field is defined here as a competitive system of social relations, which functions according to its own specific logic or rules: 'A field is a space in which a game takes place, a field of objective relations between individuals and institutions who are competing for the same stake' (Bourdieu, quoted in Moi, 1991: 1021).

Lamont stresses that contemporary societies are dynamic, that is, that fields are not necessarily either stable or closed; rather, they may be open, fluid and subject to rapid movements. Lamont also argues that contemporary societies are made up of a *number* of partly overlapping spheres of competition and comparison, with different logics and different criteria of evaluation. Even more challenging to such accounts is the opinion that Bourdieu adopts a view of culture that is too calculating or instrumental because he has a limited conception of the economy as a matter of self-interested calculation. As one commentator notes:

> On some level, what Bourdieu is saying is undeniably true. There is no area of human life, anywhere, where one cannot find self-interested calculation. But neither is there anywhere one cannot find kindness or adherence to idealistic principles: the point is why one, and not the other, is posed as 'objective' reality. (Graeber, 2001: 29)

Lifestyle

An important development of Bourdieu's argument is provided by Mike Featherstone (1991), who argues that the new middle classes are distinguished by their pursuit of expressive and liberated lifestyles. He claims:

> Rather than unreflexively adopting a lifestyle, through tradition or habit, the new heroes of consumer culture make lifestyle a life project and display their individuality and sense of style in the particularity of the assemblage of goods, clothes, practices, experiences, appearance and bodily dispositions they design together into a lifestyle. (1991: 86)

They have a very strong commitment to fashion, that is, to the rapid and playful transformations of style. So much so, Featherstone suggests, that the alertness of the new middle classes to new popular styles and the marketability of the new creates conditions in which styles travel faster, from the popular to the avant-garde and vice versa. This is seen to have contributed towards the breakdown of previous distinctions between high culture and popular culture, the old and the new, of the nostalgic and the futuristic, of the natural and the artificial, a set of breakdowns which is said to characterize postmodern culture.

As was noted earlier, Bourdieu also suggests that these groups have a novel approach to pleasure. The old bourgeoisie is argued to have based its life on a morality of duty, with a fear of pleasure, a relation to the body made up of reserve, modesty and restraint, and associated every satisfaction of forbidden impulses with guilt. In contrast, the new middle-class groups urge a morality of pleasure as a duty. This doctrine makes it a failure, a threat to self-esteem *not* to 'have fun'. Pleasure is not simply permitted but demanded, so that the individual is encouraged to work at pleasure. This has contributed to what Featherstone calls a *calculating hedonism*, a hedonism in which the individual strategically moves into and out of control, enjoying the thrill of the controlled suspension of constraints. This hedonism is sometimes understood by Featherstone in relation to a process of *heroization* of the consumer, who is prepared to experiment with his or her self-identity, strategically to calculate the risks involved in the temporary abandonment of restraint involved in excessive consumption.

The growth of the so-called new middle classes has, however, seen its own internal struggles. Featherstone believes the growth of new media-related professions and marginal service industries such as restaurants, craft shops and therapy clinics is related to the need, because of the relative democratization of education, to create jobs and provide services for members of the old bourgeoisie. These are occupations where inherited as opposed to acquired cultural capital can be put to most profitable use. At the same time, however, members of this old bourgeoisie are likely to display an aesthetic asceticism in contrast to a traditional or commercial bourgeois preference for sumptuousness. Featherstone describes the symbolic subversion of the rituals of bourgeois order demonstrated by, for example, intellectuals in the display of so-called ostentatious poverty. This is evident in the tendency to dress casually even when at work, to favour bare wood interiors and the preference for outdoor solitary activities like mountaineering, rambling and fell-walking.

In contrast, the new petits bourgeois – who make up the lower echelons of the service class – are seen to be developing a lifestyle in which they actively struggle for self-improvement and self-expression. Featherstone offers particular examples of this; so, for example, he holds that members of the petit-bourgeois class fraction are uneasy in their own bodies, 'constantly self-consciously checking, watching and correcting [themselves]' (Featherstone, 1991: 90). This, he suggests, explains the current popularity of body maintenance techniques,

sports and forms of exercise such as aerobics, and health products –
vitamins, ginseng and royal jelly – for this group of consumers. This
anxiety is related by Featherstone to the relatively insecure position
of the new petit bourgeois.

As Martyn Lee notes, this group is the class fraction that 'was the
chief recipient and beneficiary of the expansion in the higher educational sector that took place within most Euro-American societies
following the Second World War' (1993: 167). He argues that the
expansion was directed towards education focused on occupational
vocation, with an emphasis on training and specialized occupational
skills that contrasted with the previous emphasis on the cultivation
of the individual and abstract learning. In Featherstone's terms, this
expansion provides an uncertain basis for the realization of cultural
capital, and it is the emerging, incomplete or not fully formed relationship to the educational field which is said to explain the anxious
lifestyle of the new petit bourgeois. Featherstone writes:

> The new petit bourgeois is a pretender, aspiring to more than he is, who
> adopts an investment orientation to life; he possesses little economic or
> cultural capital and therefore must acquire it. The acquisition of the
> latter makes him open to being perceived as an autodidact, the product
> of the education system, who betrays an anxiety about using the right
> classification, who is always in danger of knowing too much or too little
> . . . The new petit bourgeois therefore adopts a learning mode to life; he
> is consciously educating himself in the field of taste, style and lifestyle.
> (Featherstone, 1991: 90–1)

This generation of the middle classes is the first to have experienced the full force of what Raymond Williams (1974) calls *mobile
privatization* – the reorganization of domestic life so that, via the
television and other forms of consumption, it offers a safe space of
almost unlimited access to other places and times, 'elswheres' and
'elsewhens'. Television can thus be seen as an alternative or complementary medium of education for this generation. And, since the
post-war generation has witnessed the evolution of television from a
period in which it was highly dependent on the radio for its mode of
address and programming style towards self-referential forms that
exploit and play upon the evolved forms of television itself, it is familiar with strategies for discovering new significance in the already well
known, and establishing a playful distance from established styles
(King, 1989). Thus, according to Featherstone, the media, together
with the (relatively) democratized institutions of higher education,
have trained the new middle classes in ways of making meaning that

encourage the development of lifestyle as a self-conscious project, in which the display of taste plays a key role, so accelerating the shift towards a post-Fordist society.

Featherstone's account has been influential but it is hard to compare directly with that of Bourdieu since it is not based on a large-scale study, and draws largely on British sources. From a different national perspective, an earlier study by Michele Lamont (1992), comparing how members of the French and the American upper-middle class define what it means to be a 'worthy person', points to a number of problems with the Bourdieu framework. Her data suggests that Bourdieu greatly underestimates the importance of moral preferences while he exaggerates the importance of cultural and socio-economic resources. Lamont also suggests that Bourdieu neglects the importance of distinctive national cultures in providing and organizing a cultural repertoire which provides a backdrop for struggles over taste. She writes, 'individuals do not exclusively draw boundaries out of their own experience: they borrow from the general cultural repertoires supplied to them by the society in which they live, relying on general definitions of valued traits that take on a rule-like status' (Lamont, 1992: 7).

Comparing the French and American cases, Lamont shows that cultural boundaries, that is, boundaries between groups drawn on the basis of education, refinement and cosmopolitanism, are much weaker and more loosely defined in the United States than in France. This is ascribed to the relatively greater importance of high culture and materialism in France and in America respectively. She suggests that while cultural egalitarianism reinforces anti-intellectualism in the United States and generates a more open culture, materialism in France is weakened by the low level of geographical mobility characteristic of this society. One consequence of the relative looseness in drawing cultural boundaries in the United States is that cultural boundaries are less likely to lead to socio-economic boundaries being drawn, and thus less likely to contribute to socio-economic inequality, than in France.

There is, however, a certain amount of empirical evidence to support the interpretation of the importance of lifestyle in contributing to economic change in the UK at least, including a study of the British middle classes by Savage et al., *Property, Bureaucracy and Culture* (1992). In this study, Savage et al. explore the changing structure of the middle classes in relation to their ability to mobilize three kinds of assets – organization, property and cultural assets. They argue that, historically, the three types of asset have given rise to three distinct groupings within the middle classes, with the distinction between the professions on the one hand and the managerial and propertied sectors on the other being particularly strong. However, they also point to the need to recognize the importance of 'organization man', that is, those employed in organizations – including managers – who are dependent on organizational assets, a group which Bourdieu neglects in his own study.

Using data from the British Market Research Bureau's 'Target Group Index' (TGI is an annual survey of 24,000 adults, with respondents asked to give details of a wide range of consumption habits) Savage et al. suggest that there is a strong association between high incomes, educational attainment and a new culture of health and body maintenance. More particularly, they believe that all three of the groupings mentioned earlier can be identified with a specific set of tastes. The first group, primarily located in the public sector professions, display an ascetic style, using their leisure time to exercise and take part in sporting activities as well as having high culture pursuits. Managers and public-sector bureaucrats, on the other hand, have an unremarkable culture; there are no pastimes or pursuits that particularly single them out. In contrast, private-sector professionals and specialists adopt a so-called postmodern lifestyle. This lifestyle is paradoxical in that it brings together apparently contrasting activities and interests; its advocates show an interest in health, exercise, sport and fitness, but they are also fond of the good life, as manifested in champagne drinking and gourmet food. Savage et al. write 'high extravagance goes along with a culture of the body: appreciation of high cultural forms of art such as opera and classical music exists cheek by jowl with an interest in disco dancing or stock car racing' (1992: 108).

They make a number of further claims on the basis of this study. First, they found that organizational assets are of declining importance as companies are becoming less reliant on organizational hierarchies in which managers have clear positions of authority. At the same time, companies have increasingly come to need the skills and knowledge of professionally trained people who can move between companies. In response to this, managers try to convert organizational assets into other forms; for example, they may seek property assets by becoming entrepreneurs, or cultural assets by acquiring professional qualifications. At the same time, Savage et al. suggest that what were once the practices of an 'alternative' middle-class minority, who opposed the values of materialism, have now been adopted on a large scale by those with much greater economic resources. However, in the process, this set of values has been positioned as one of a number

of lifestyles from which this group can 'sample' and, as a consequence, 'A 1960s-style counter-culture has been transformed into a
1990s-style post-modern cultural conformity' (Savage et al., 1992:
113). Putting these processes together, Savage et al. believe, shows
how cultural assets, as mobilized by some fragments of the service
class, are becoming increasingly influential in determining not only
class formation, but also, indirectly, the organization of production as
the economy responds to the shifting patterns of consumer demand.

This view is further supported by more recent studies looking at
class and cultural capital in the UK (such as a later study conducted
by Savage in 2007 with a new team of researchers – Le Roux, Rouanet
and Warde), which reveal clear and marked patterns of differentiation in tastes in the UK. The findings of this study support those of
the earlier one that there is indeed no simple opposition between
high and popular culture, but indicate that there is a tension between
those who are multiply culturally engaged or are culturally omnivo-
rous (that is, people who participate in multiple cultural pursuits)
and those who are largely culturally disengaged or disinterested. This
axis is strongly associated with class but, significantly, is also linked to
age. In particular, there is a tension within the middle class that sets
the young against the old.

In exploring how cultural participation is linked to class boundaries, this later study outlines a (different) three-class model, with key
boundaries between a service or professional class (24 per cent), an
intermediate class (32 per cent, including lower managerial workers,
supervisors, the self-employed, senior technicians and white-collar
workers) and a large working class (44 per cent, including lower
supervisors and technicians). Their findings suggest that class
boundaries in the UK are being redrawn through an increasing interplay between economic and cultural capital, especially that form of
cultural capital linked to education. So, for example, those members
of the service class who do not possess graduate-level qualifications,
especially those in lower managerial positions, are more similar to the
intermediate classes than they are to other sections of the professional
middle class. There is also a process of boundary-redrawing at work
with respect to the working class, where lower supervisory and technical occupations have been downgraded so that they have become
similar to those in semi-routine and routine positions.

A common concern in these many explorations and developments of Bourdieu's approach in different national contexts is that
the processes by which cultural capital is transformed into economic
capital are not always clearly or accurately identified. One of the

most obvious ways in which this is done is through the acquisition of educational qualifications, legitimated by the state and professional associations, which may then provide an entrée into occupations, thus providing a route for the transformation of an individual's cultural capital into economic capital. However, other techniques of transformation are not always clearly identified and, in particular, it is not clear how taste, in the sense of a set of cultural preferences or a lifestyle (rather than educational attainment), may be converted into economic capital. Roberta Sassatelli also makes the important argument that 'not all styles of consumption are easily reducible, even with the mediation of habitus, to the economic, cultural or social capital of those who adopt them', and notes the importance of other factors, including 'very rapid style changes and quest for novelty in contemporary markets', the role of mediating agencies and organizations, and social movements such as environmentalism (2007: 95–7).

Bourdieu himself suggests that the distinctive tastes of members of the dominant class act as status markers and facilitate integration into this group, and that outsiders who have not been socialized into these aesthetic dispositions at an early stage cannot easily become integrated into high-status groups, but this is a difficult claim to substantiate. As noted above, however, he also proposed an increasingly important role for cultural intermediaries. As mentioned earlier, for Bourdieu, the growth of these occupations is closely linked to the emergence of a class fraction whose tastes, classificatory schemes, dispositions, lifestyles and working practices often clashed with those of the established middle class (Featherstone, 1991; Lash, 1990). The positions of power and control in the mass media occupied by members of this group allowed the assembly and circulation of cultural products (advertising, television, film) that embodied new tastes and values, leading to the creation of a whole range of 'half-way genres' (Bourdieu, 1984: 326). This is more than simply a democratization of access to high culture, but a transformation of the cultural field. One of the interesting issues here is how both the cultural and economic fields are being transformed by not only mass media but what were once, not so long ago, called new media, that is, mobile, digital media.

It is now being argued, for example, that social media and participation in communicative modes of consumption enabled by such media are becoming increasingly important in the emergence of 'consumption as production' in post-Fordism, or what is sometimes called 'cognitive capitalism' (Arvidsson, 2006, see chapter 6) or 'prosumer capitalism' (Ritzer and Jurgenson, 2010). In the argument put forward by Ritzer and Jurgenson (2010), for example, it is proposed that the capitalist economy – and even the pre-capitalist and non-capitalist economies – has always involved what they call 'prosumption'. In this perspective, prosumption involves both production and consumption rather than referring to activities typically positioned as one or the other. The term itself is generally attributed to Alvin Toffler and his discussion of *The Third Wave* (1980); this, he proposed, was replacing a second wave of economic development that had separated production and consumption. Ritzer and Jurgenson adopt and develop this idea. They argue that while prosumption has always been important, it has recently acquired even greater significance as a result of the rise of the Internet and Web 2.0 (that is, the user-generated Web, including Facebook, YouTube, Twitter). In what is an emerging prosumer capitalism, they argue, control and exploitation are acquiring different forms from those in other types of capitalism. There is a trend towards unpaid rather than paid labour, and the system is characterized by abundance where scarcity once predominated. This perspective clearly originates in a North American context, and it is debatable how widespread abundance or prosumption really is. Nevertheless, it is important to recognize this approach here insofar as it proposes that the opposition between producers and consumers was never absolute and that prosumption – a form of activity involving both production and consumption – may have an important role in contemporary capitalism.

Life, labour and love

Some more recent discussion of the economy – such as, for example, those of Virno (2004), Hardt and Negri (2001), Terranova (2004) and Lazzarato (2004) – develop this line of argument from a different political perspective. They propose that contemporary forms of production are coming to involve all aspects of social life, including communication, knowledge and affect. So, for example, Lazzarato provocatively proposes that firms do not produce goods as such, but instead produce worlds in which goods exist. The production of these worlds extends outside what is traditionally defined as the economy, outside the factories of Fordism, entering everyday life. They can be both real and virtual spaces, domestic and commercial themed environments, including Second Life, Disney World and other leisure, sport and holiday resorts. In such worlds, marketing efforts are not designed to control consumption directly but are attempts to 'grow' the life-worlds of consumers by fostering the conditions in which

consuming subjectivities and activities emerge. As he says, 'consumption consists not in buying or destroying a service or product as political economy and its critique teaches us, but means first and foremost belonging to a world' (2004: 96).

Similarly, Tiziana Terranova argues that in the shift towards post-Fordism, 'work processes have shifted from the factory to society, thereby setting in motion a truly complex machine' (2004, 74). In the move from mass production to flexible specialization, she says, a clear demarcation between labour and (the rest of) life becomes hard to sustain. As the discussion of branding in chapter 6 will outline, some companies not only draw on the labour power of their workers but also engage consumers in production processes. From a business point of view, this can be seen in terms of 'value co-creation' (Prahalad and Ramaswamy 2004; Wilmott, 2010), or a new 'wikinomic' model in which companies put consumers to work (Tapscott and Williams 2007). From the perspective of the writers outlined here, however, this is not collaboration since the value of the 'activity' or labour of consumers is not adequately recognized, and is produced in unequal and asymmetrical relations.

Lazzarato uses the concept of immaterial labour to explore these changes. The term is not meant to imply that labour is disembodied or incorporeal since labour processes always involve mind and body. The immateriality of immaterial labour refers instead to the salience of certain characteristics of the product: according to Lazzarato, immaterial labour produces the informational and cultural content of commodities. This content is informed by social relations and brings (new) social relations into being. Production and consumption can no longer be separated from each other in a neat way; commodities deeply affect the consumers who use them and the consumers themselves transform the commodity in use. Hence, the consumer has a continuous productive role. This kind of consumer productivity, Lazzarato stresses, is not a matter of individual creativity and authorship but is collective and distributed in uneven and unpredictable ways in the social relations of use.

In a related discussion, Terranova's use of the term 'free labour' is illuminating, especially insofar as the focus in her work on networked economies reveals the importance attached in these approaches not only to the Internet, but also to other kinds of networks and social relations in the contemporary economy. So, for example, Terranova observes that many online services are based on the continuous contributions of users or consumers: peer-to-peer networks, social media channels, blogs, micro-blogs or community websites provide a world or platform for action which remains valueless unless it is filled with 'life'. According to Terranova, this 'life' should be considered as what she terms 'free labour', 'free' both in the sense of 'not financially rewarded' and 'willingly given' (Terranova 2004, 93–4). Whether users give feedback to improve goods and services, modify software, add new cultural meaning to products, participate in online discussions and mailing lists, or simply recommend companies or products to their friends, 'free' participation is a crucial part of contemporary value production. American Apparel and Zara are examples of companies whose use of such economic strategies has led to them being described as 'hip neo-Fordism' (Moor and Littler, 2008).

Terranova's emphasis on digital media and the Internet is revealing, however. By supporting her argument through reference to the Internet she raises problems – at least by implication – for the other accounts discussed here. These problems are to do with whether and how the changes Terranova identifies in digital and other network economies apply as widely as is implied in some of the other accounts. In other words, is this approach generalizing from the networks of the digital economy to the economy as a whole without sufficient evidence? This is a question that can only be answered empirically, in an investigation of whether what these writers describe is a trend that will come to dominate the economy as a whole or only the logic of a sector (Castells, 1996). What is important about this perspective from the point of view of consumer culture, however, is the way in which it opens up how we might think about consumption and its relation to production. It also raises important questions about how to think about culture itself in this new economy. Is this a culture that is dominated by the meanings of symbolic exchange, or are other less meaningful but still powerful forms of signification, especially those to do with information such as transactional data, relational databases and profiles, increasingly important? What new forms of culture are at play in contemporary forms of cultural capital? And what forms of (intellectual) property are important? These are questions we will return to in chapters 6 and 8.

[The] trend towards putting consumers to work – turning them into prosumers – accelerated after the birth of the fast-food restaurant in the mid-1950s. Among the examples are:

- pumping one's own gasoline at the filling station;
- serving as a bank teller at the ATM machine;
- working at the check-out counter at the supermarket by scanning one's own food, bagging it, and paying for it by credit card;
- using electronic kiosks to check into a hotel and at the airport, to purchase movie tickets, etc.;
- co-creating a variety of experiences such as moving oneself through Disney World and its many attractions or serving as an 'actor' in the 'theatre' staged by Starbucks to create the image of an old-fashioned coffee house;
- using do-it-yourself medical technologies (e.g. blood pressure monitors, blood glucose monitors, pregnancy tests) that allow patients to perform, without recompense, tasks formerly performed by paid medical professionals;
- being a caller on a call-in radio show;
- being part of Reality TV;
- being involved in amateur pornography. (Ritzer and Jurgenson, 2010: 18–19, references omitted)

Certainly this more recent approach to the economy demonstrates how the sphere of production has been broadened within contemporary economic practices. It is not limited to the manufacture of products as fixed things or closed objects as it also includes the production of sociality, affects, relationships or immaterial assets, as well as objects that compel participation, and are themselves constantly changing as they are transformed in real-time use. It is not limited to physical or mechanical labour but extends to life itself, as everyday activity is recognized as productive in this perspective. Finally, the relation between production and consumption is not understood in terms of a simple mechanistic logic but follows more complex causalities of iteration and entanglement. Most writers would suggest that production and consumption still can and should be distinguished, but these perspectives point out that it is important to recognize where, how and by whom this distinction is drawn, and with what implications for the recognition of value.

Conclusion

This chapter has outlined a number of accounts of the interrelationship between class, the market and consumer culture in the shift from Fordism to post-Fordism. It began with the work of Bourdieu and Featherstone, who argue that taste is a social phenomenon and is the result of struggles between different class groups. As part of this struggle, they suggest that the new middle classes, whose size and significance in society is said to have increased as a result of a shift from a Fordist to a post-Fordist economy, have developed highly visible forms of lifestyle. The new and distinctive use of consumer goods these lifestyles involve has, in turn, accelerated the shift from Fordism to post-Fordism as a consequence of the increasing importance attached by those members of new middle classes who act as cultural intermediaries to specialized and increasingly stylized forms of consumption. The determining or causal links between changes in production and changes in consumption can thus be seen to operate in both directions.

It was pointed out, however, that this kind of explanation tends to focus on the impact of a small number of circuits of exchange, especially those routed through education, high culture and the state, and has tended to ignore circuits of exchange that are mediated by the media, popular culture and the market. It also tends to work within a national frame, and play down the importance of transnational exchanges. The final section of the chapter thus introduced a number of accounts that emphasize the fluid, open and dynamic nature of relations between production and consumption in the contemporary economy, especially insofar as they are developing in digital and interactive media. These developments raise important questions about what counts as cultural capital today, as well as focusing attention on the multiple forms of signification at work in consumer culture. The following two chapters explore these issues further.

5

Circuits of Culture and Economy: Gender, Race and Reflexivity

Introduction

This chapter takes up the theme of reflexivity outlined in the previous chapter, and explores its relevance for explaining the emergence of the consumer as a master category of identity. It does so by looking at the participation of social groups characterized by race and gender in practices of consumption and consumer culture and adds them to the class-based analysis outlined in the preceding chapter. Although, as discussed in chapter 3, it is widely accepted that no single explanation can account for the diverse histories of consumer culture in different societies, there is also a general acceptance of the importance of what Roberta Sassatelli calls 'cross-fertilization between different social groups, other than mere economic exchange' (2007: 10). This chapter can only be a highly selective presentation of some of the vast range of studies of these processes of cross-fertilization. It is loosely structured in terms of a discussion of the significance of the role of social groupings, defined in terms of first race and then gender. However, as the examples make clear, neither race nor gender can be understood in isolation from each other, or independently of age, class or nation. The aim of this chapter is not to give a complete or comprehensive overview, but to provide a series of snapshots, to build up a dynamic, multidimensional view of the role of these groups in shaping consumer culture.

The studies show that there are cultural and political as well as economic complexities to the thesis of self-reflexivity: while the enjoyment of the capacity of calculated de-control – playfulness – may be characteristic of the new middle classes, it is not the only way in which the movement between the oppositions of being in and out of control or making choices is negotiated in the context of consumer culture. This chapter aims to show that participation in consumer culture is not necessarily a project of heroization, but instead may involve practices of appropriation, masquerade and imitation, creating tensions that disturb the legitimacy of the lifestyle associated with the new middle classes. In other words, the capacity to exercise consumer *choice* – and the implications of so doing – is shaped by, and shapes, the uneven history of consumer culture.

Commodity racism

The emergence of Euro-American consumer culture is closely linked to processes of transnational trade, imperialism and colonialism. Mimi Sheller (2003), for example, draws attention to the importance of the interlocking meanings of 'Carib' and 'cannibal' in the emergence of a multitude of forms of material and symbolic consumption, including ingestion, invasion, infection, appropriation and sacrifice, as well as various processes of destroying, possessing, using up and wasting away in exchanges between the Caribbean, Europe and North America. She argues that despite significant shifts in patterns of world trade and regimes of consumption over the last 500 years the significance of this transatlantic history must still be recognized. A crucial part of her argument is that the relation between Euro-American consumers and the Caribbean did not take place through importing slave-produced commodities or benefiting from wealth made on slave plantations alone. Not only things or commodities produced in the Caribbean were consumed, she says, but so too were landscapes, flora, fauna, cultures and visual representations: 'the accumulation of contemporary "Western" scientific knowledge, cultural innovation, and capital continues to be made viable by far-reaching global circuits of knowledge-production premised on the consumption of the landscapes, plants, foods, bodies, and cultures of the Caribbean and other "non-Western" places' (2003). These examples are forms of what she calls consumption 'at a distance' and they indicate the importance of the 'binding mobilities' of consumption.

Sheller outlines four phases of mobile consumption, each of which, she says, has shaped North Atlantic consumer relations with the Caribbean:

1 16th to 17th century: a period of 'discovery', piracy and 'bachelor' plantation, in which European migrants took land, collected plants,

and depicted a 'New World' of fruitful plenty, while Native inhabitants were dispossessed, enslaved, infected and killed. This period is associated with mercantilism as a specific early form of capitalism.

2 18th to 19th century: a period of rapid growth of the system of slavery in which Europeans consumed the products of the labour of enslaved human bodies in the coerced production of plantation commodities, while fighting wars of occupation. This period is associated with colonialism as a specific form of capitalist articulation with the periphery.

3 Mid-19th to mid-20th century: a period which saw the development of a colonial-industrial system of 'free labour' and capitalist plantation commodity consumption in which workers began to migrate in search of wages and metropolitan dwellers began to travel in search of exotic pleasures, while the United States exercised increasing military occupation in the Caribbean region. This system is usually associated with the period of empire and imperialism.

4 Late 20th century to today: a period of 'postindustrial' and 'postcolonial' service consumption in which fragments of industrial processes ('off-shore' export zones) occur in the Caribbean alongside new forms of service work (including high tech and financial services as well as tourism). Cultural commodification is linked to the explosion of tourism in the region, growth in the 'world music' industry, and new forms of informational capitalism. This is seen as a period of 'post-fordism' within capitalism. (2003: 29–30)

Focusing on the third phase outlined by Sheller, Anne McClintock (1994) identifies the emergence of what she calls 'commodity racism', as exemplified in Victorian forms of advertising and commodity spectacle: the imperial Expositions and the museum movement. According to McClintock, the commodity, abstracted from social context and human labour, was attributed with the civilizing work of empire. In 1899, an advertisement for Pears' Soap, claimed:

> The first step towards LIGHTENING THE WHITE MAN'S BURDEN is through teaching the virtues of cleanliness. PEARS' SOAP is a potent factor in brightening the dark corners of the earth as civilization advances, while amongst the cultured of all nations it holds the highest place – it is the ideal toilet soap. (Quoted in McClintock, 1994: 132)

The advertisement depicts an admiral, decked in pure imperial white, washing his hands in his cabin as his steamship crosses the ocean, en route to some outpost of the empire. Soap is represented as the cleansing agent of the imperial quest to bring 'light' to the 'darkest' corners of the earth.

In 1910, another Pears' soap advertisement is divided into two panels. The top panel shows a little black boy in a cast-iron bathtub about to be soaped and scrubbed by a young white nursemaid. In the panel below, her look of happy amazement registers the effects of what has evidently been a miracle. Where the soap has been applied, the boy's skin has changed colour from black to white. As McClintock notes, the selling point of both advertisements relies on a casual and taken-for-granted identification of whiteness with cleanliness and purity and of blackness with dirt and pollution. In the first advertisement, whiteness is associated with civilization, and soap is identified as its carrier. In the second, through the identification of whiteness with cleanliness and blackness with dirt, the rule of white civilization, administered by the white nursemaid, is likened to an act of charity and goodwill. That the success of this hygienic civilizing process is represented in the second advertisement as a miracle is premised on the assumption that races are characterized by fixed, natural or biological features, such as skin colour. The advertisement relies upon this for its 'comic' effect and its imagery reinforces social hierarchies between white and black through its association of these features with positive and negative values.

There are numerous other vivid examples of commodity racism in early twentieth-century advertising, especially in advertising for so-called Empire goods, including tea, coffee, cocoa and cotton. This racism is evident in, for example, the representation of black people as happy in servitude to white people, both in the fields and in the home, and in representations of black people as child-like or doll-like, and in the images of a feminine, mysterious or exotic otherness typically used to heighten a product's luxury or novelty appeal. In these and other ways racial differences became integral to the processes of selling and advertising things. However, the analysis of textual representations of race in advertising imagery is only a part of the broader project of documenting the historical relationship between race and consumption (McClintock, 1994; Ramamurthy, 1991; S. Willis, 1990; Gilroy, 1987, 1992, 1993; Hall, 1992).

Anne McClintock, for example, locates her discussion of advertisements in an analysis of changing economic practices. She argues that towards the end of the nineteenth century, economic competition between nations created a climate within which the aggressive promotion of products necessarily became ever more intense. It was this competition, she says, that contributed to the first real innovations in advertising and thus to the development of consumer culture. In 1884, for example, wrapped soap was sold for the first time under a brand name. This small event, McClintock argues, signalled a major transformation in advertising: items formerly indistinguishable from one another – soap sold simply as soap – came to be marketed by distinctive corporate signatures. Notable examples of these included Pears' and Monkey Brand – in Victorian culture, the monkey was an icon of metamorphosis, and therefore an apt choice to represent soap, with its alleged powers to transform nature (dirt, waste and disorder) into culture (cleanliness, rationality, industry).

Soap was also one of the first commodities to register a shift from myriad small businesses to the great imperial monopolies – in the 1870s, hundreds of small soap companies had made and distributed soap, but, by the end of the century, the trade was monopolized by ten large companies. McClintock suggests that while this shift was undergone by many commodities, soap had a special place in this economic transformation. This is because, she argues, branded soap was credited not only with bringing moral and economic salvation to the lives of Britain's great unwashed, but also with magically embodying the spiritual ingredient of the imperial mission itself. She writes:

> Soap did not flourish when imperial ebullience was at its peak. It emerged commercially during an era of impending crisis and social calamity, serving to preserve, through fetish ritual, the uncertain boundaries of class, gender and race identity in a world felt to be threatened by the fetid effluvia of slums, the belching smoke of industry, social agitation, economic upheaval, imperial competition and anticolonial resistance. Soap offered the promise of spiritual salvation and regeneration through commodity consumption, a regime of domestic hygiene that could restore the threatened potency of the imperial body politic and the race. (1994: 137)

More generally, she claims:

> Late Victorian advertising presented a vista of the colonies as conquered by domestic commodities. In the flickering magic lantern of imperial desire, teas, biscuits, tobaccos, Bovril, tins of cocoa and, above all, soaps beach themselves on far-flung shores, tramp through jungles, quell uprisings, restore order and write the inevitable legend of commercial progress across the colonial landscape. In a Huntley and Palmers' Biscuits ad, a group of male colonials sit in the middle of a jungle on biscuit crates, sipping tea. Towards them, a stately and seemingly endless procession of elephants, laden with more biscuits and colonials, brings tea-time to the heart of the jungle. (1994: 137, 142)

More than merely a symbol of imperial progress, it was as if soap became the *agent* of history itself. In contrast to this animation of products in the colonial context, representatives of the colonized people were depicted, not as historic agents, but as *frames* or *figures* for the exhibition of the commodity. In this way, the inclusion of a black person in an advertisement or other kinds of commodity imagery was not necessarily a reflection of, or an address to, a black person; his or her function in the image was to act as a cipher, enabling a white perspective on imperialism to be conveyed.

McClintock also addresses the complexity of the representation of race in relation to gender in advertising during this period. In the second example described above, for instance, the soap-as-commodity is represented as the active agent in carrying out the civilizing work of the Empire while the use to which the commodity is to be put – cleaning clothes, for instance – is figured as magic. She writes: 'The working-women, both black and white, who spend vast amounts of energy bleaching the white sheets, shirts, frills, aprons, cuffs and collars of imperial clothes are nowhere to be seen' (1994: 144). McClintock argues that the omission of women's labour attests to a fundamental dilemma in Victorian society: how to represent domesticity without showing women at work. This dilemma was a consequence of a widespread cultural anxiety about women and work. As women were driven from paid work in factories, shops and trades to private unpaid work in the home, domestic work became economically undervalued and the middle-class ideal of white femininity figured the proper woman as one who did not work for profit. Indeed, domestic work increasingly came to be represented as a labour of love towards the end of the nineteenth and the beginning of the twentieth centuries. In the meantime, the work of housewives and (largely female) domestic servants was either simply absent or represented as a magical process of transformation. The argument made by McClintock and others is that the representation of black people, while directed towards the creation of *white* subject identities, simultaneously marked these racialized identities (both black and white) in relation to a gendered hierarchy, in which masculinity was deemed superior to femininity. Both dimensions of commodity racism were fundamental to the emerging cultural forms of consumption.

McClintock locates these advertising texts in relation to a wider set of cultural shifts, and argues that such advertisements were part of what she calls the shift from 'scientific racism' – embodied in anthropological, scientific and medical journals, and travel writing – to '*commodity racism*'. She writes:

Commodity racism – in the specifically Victorian forms of advertising and commodity spectacle, the imperial Expositions and the
museum movement – converted the imperial progress narrative into
mass-produced consumer spectacles. Commodity racism . . . came to
produce, market and distribute evolutionary racism and imperial power
on a hitherto unimagined scale. In the process, the Victorian middle-
class home became a space for the display of imperial spectacle and the
reinvention of race, while the colonies – in particular Africa – became a
theatre for exhibiting the Victorian cult of domesticity and the reinvention of gender. (1994: 133)

The so-called Imperial and Colonial exhibitions she mentions here
were extremely popular marketing exercises sponsored by both
commercial companies, such as Liptons and other manufacturers
of tea, coffee, cocoa and various colonial goods, and the British
state. At their height in the 1920s, these exhibitions attracted up to
27 million people, offering them both the pleasures of funfairs and
education in the ways of the Empire through information displays
and exhibits. They are just one illustration of the broader social and
political climate in which the advertisements for soap discussed by
McClintock acquired their cultural appeal.

In her discussion of representations of race in consumer culture
at the end of the twentieth century (1990), Susan Willis argues that
there has been a shift away from the use of the representations of
natural or biological racial difference that predominated in commodity design, styling and advertising at the turn of the nineteenth
century. This is not to suggest that the earlier representations of
race described by McClintock have disappeared without trace. Until
recently, for example, a number of brands drew explicitly upon imperial and colonial iconography; examples include the long-standing
use of the image of an Indian woman uncomplainingly picking tea for
PG Tips and the use of the 'golly' or 'gollywog', a representation of
a black face which draws upon the stereotype of the happy dancing
minstrel with deliberately blackened skin and enlarged mouth, in
Robertson's jams and Trebor Black Jacks (Ramamurphy, 1991;
Chambers, 1992). And the use of quasi-imperialist modes of representation persists; Vron Ware, for example, describes the 'missionary
discourse' at work in the Body Shop's 'community trade initiative',
in which a white woman, in this case the Body Shop founder, Anita
Roddick, was figured as a saviour, providing a 'feminist green capitalism' which exoticized its natives whilst avoiding 'any kind of explanation for the way that the world has been degraded, environmentally,
politically [or] economically' (Ware, 1992: 243–8). However, Willis

argues that this kind of colonial imagery has largely disappeared, and in its place race is represented as a matter of *style*.

Stylization arises, Willis argues, as part of the *infinite seriality of commodification,* by which she means the combination of standardization and variation that she believes to be implicit in the commodity form.

Following Marx, Willis argues that there is an inevitable flattening out, a levelling out, of value in goods that are made to be exchanged on the market; they are all made to be exchanged for money, and money, as the abstract medium through which they are exchanged, squashes differences between political, moral and cultural values. At the same time however, the market requires novelty to stimulate demand, and as a consequence the imposition of the commodity form, that is, the production of goods for exchange on the market, is characterized by standardized variation, or repetition within certain limits. Race, Willis suggests, has been a primary figure or trope, through which this standardized variation or seriality has operated. In this way, understandings of race have been central to the development of consumer culture, not simply through the ways in which the category has been implicated in the economic processes of transnational capital, but also through its centrality to the understandings of stylistic difference which structure everyday understandings and use of goods.

For Willis, the seriality of commodification emerges in two apparently contradictory ways in the representation of race: on the one hand, the move towards sameness and, on the other, the pursuit of difference. Willis sees evidence of the first strategy in the production of black versions of white cultural goods, what she calls black replicants (see Keegan, 1992, for a discussion of the same tendency in advertising). One example of this phenomenon is the production of Jamaican, Hispanic and Chinese equivalents of Barbie, the white doll

[C]hildren today are granted instant global gratification in their play – immediate hands-on access to both Self and Other. Or so we are told by many of the leading fantasy manufacturers – Disney, Hassbro, and Mattel, in particular – whose contributions to multicultural education include such play things as Aladdin (movie, video, and dolls), G.I. Joe (male 'action figures' in black and white), and Barbie (now available in a variety of colors and ethnicities). Disneyland's river ride through different nations, like Mattel's Dolls of the World Collection, instructs us that 'It's a Small World After All.' Those once distant lands of Africa, Asia, Australia, and even the Arctic regions of the North Pole (yes, Virginia, there is an Eskimo Barbie) are now as close to home as the local Toys R Us . . . And lo and behold, the inhabitants of these foreign lands – from Disney's Princess Jasmine to Mattel's Jamaican Barbie – are just like us, dye-dipped versions of archetypal white American beauty. (Ducille, 1994: 48–9) first produced by Mattel, the toy manufacturers, in the 1960s. Black Cabbage Patch dolls have also been produced as copies of their white sister vegetables, as have more recently Bratz dolls.

In exploring this phenomenon of replication or the production of sameness further, Willis draws a parallel between what is happening in the production of toy dolls and certain developments in relation to their human counterparts – fashion models. She suggests that recent fashion displays are creating a 'new ethnicity' in which individuals who, in some way or other, represent all races in one are held up as ideals. She points to the use of 'beige' models in fashion shows and magazine features, and argues that their use indicates an attempt to erase the political significance of race. Another example – in the world of sport – might be the use of the statement 'I am Tiger Woods' by Nike in advertising imagery showing the golfer. In the case of fashion models, this racial homogenization is, Willis believes, paralleled by an attempted homogenization of gender through the use of androgynous-looking models. For Willis, this tendency raises the question of whether it is possible to give egalitarian expression to racial difference in a society in which whiteness is the norm against which all else is judged. She answers in the negative, arguing that when all the models are white, the black copy is reduced to a mirror. The implication that Willis draws from this is that the commercial representation of black people simply enables communication between white people. She writes, 'The black replicant ensures rather than subverts domination. The notion of "otherness", or unassimilable marginality, is in the replicant attenuated by its mirroring of the white model. The proliferation of black replicants in toys, fashion and advertising smothers the possibility for creating black cultural alternatives' (1990: 87).

A similar question arises in relation to the second tendency – the pursuit and celebration of difference for its own sake. This tendency is evident in the production of goods, images and identities that emphasize and multiply difference, including racial difference. One example that Willis gives here is the figure of the pop-star Michael Jackson. She suggests that Michael Jackson's persona was constituted by his very instability and changeability, by the rapid turnover of differences in his styles of self-presentation. She argues that this notion of transformation draws upon the historical figure of 'the blackface' or minstrel:

> On the one hand, it is the overt embodiment of the southern [American] racist stereotyping of blacks; but as a theatrical form blackface is a

metaphor of the commodity. It is the sign of what people paid to see. It is the image consumed and it is the site of the actor's estrangement from self into role. Blackface is a trademark and as such it can be either full or empty of meaning. (1990: 90)

Jackson brought this ambivalent image up to date. He was a toy transformer in human form, continually creating new identities for himself through the use of make-up, clothing, surgery and music. Indeed, Willis suggests that Michael Jackson's physical transformations *were* his trademark. Her argument is supported by an analysis of the video *Moonwalker*, in which a dozen or so incarnations of Jackson, from his childhood onwards, merge into one another, like so many roles or masks. Once again, Willis raises the issue as to whether this strategy makes difference meaningless and thus recuperates black alternatives. Her view is that the proliferation of representations of the difference of race and the celebration of the possibility of transformation devalues the meaning of what it is to be black, by relativizing it as just one more difference amongst others; everyone, it seems, is imagined to be equally 'raced'.

Identifying a common element in these two tendencies, Willis suggests that race is increasingly represented in consumer culture, at the level of fantasy at least, as a matter of style, something that can be put on or taken off at will. She is thus implying that one consequence of the stylization of consumption in contemporary consumer culture is a shift from understanding race as a biological or natural category to seeing race as a cultural or aesthetic category. It is a shift that has long historical roots. The examples discussed at the beginning of this section indicate that even at the end of the nineteenth century, there was a fascination with the power of commodities to 'change' races in Western societies. Soap was attributed the magical power of 'washing away' the colour of blackness. But this fascination was underpinned by a belief in the biological fixity of race; it was this that made many of the advertisements of the time humorous in intent. However, Willis argues that this fascination with the power of commodities to change racial identity has continued throughout the twentieth century, and has contributed to a shift in how racial identity is itself understood. She believes it has not removed racism, just transformed the terms of its operation.

The fantasy of the potential of commodities to change race is also evident in the publicity for Benetton, an Italian clothing company. In much of their promotional imagery, the young people used as models are colour-coded: that is, they are juxtaposed to bring out colour contrasts (Back and Quaade, 1993; Fernando, 1992; Franklin, Lury and Stacey, 2000). As in Benetton outlets, in which stacks of jumpers are folded and piled up so as to seem as if they are paint-colour charts, the overall effect of colour as the medium of the difference of fashion is enhanced through the graduations in tone, the suggested compatibility of hues and contrasts in tints created by the endless repositioning of one shade against another. The question such imagery seems to invite is, what colour is your skin going to be today? In an illustration for tights, for example, the viewer is confronted by a series of legs in profile, each slightly different in shape, completely encased in different-colour tights. The invitation to the viewer is to select a different colour at her whim. Skin colour, a key marker of race, is not simply displaced, but replaced and reworked as an act of choice. As Sonali Fernando writes, 'The legend United Colours (*sic*) of Benetton suggests a connection of skin colours and product colours, so that racial difference is commodified merely as a trope of product difference, within a self-styled commercial United Nations' (1992: 143). In this imagery, it is argued, a race is presented, not as a biological category, but as a matter of style, as a choice. The question arises, is this a choice that is equally available to all? In other words, what Willis describes as the two strands of seriality of the commodity, or what Appadurai calls 'the mutual effort of sameness and difference to cannibalize one another' (1993), may both have the effect of erasing the problem of racism.

The arguments presented so far show the ways in which images of black people and racial difference have historically been central to the development of expanded circuits of production and consumption of imperialism, especially in the development of new markets both in the colonies and within the imperializing nations themselves. It suggests that race is an important figure through which circuits of production and consumption and consumer culture itself have been organized. However, it has also been argued that although images of black people have a special part in this, their use does not necessarily indicate a concern with speaking about or speaking to black people. In other words, commercial images of black people have typically been used to facilitate commercial communication between white people. In relation to the USA for example, Gilroy notes the significance of consumer culture as an 'epoch-making context in which the Negro appeared not merely as an object, but as "as an object in the midst of other objects"' (2010: 8), while Fernando observes, 'As Black people in Britain . . . we live a paradox; we are both part of society . . . and excluded from it (largely voiceless, under-represented and under-addressed) – so that our relation to representation is in no way straightforward or fixed' (1992: 141–2). The implication here, then, is that the arguments discussed so far tell us very little about how not only the images but also the objects of consumer culture are actually used in the everyday activities of people to create raced identities, although they provide evidence to suggest that white people have been invited to use commodities to reinforce a sense of whiteness as superiority.

A number of writers have been concerned to show that consumption is not a passive process for black people, and that consumption activities are not fixed by producers and advertisers. In his early writings, Paul Gilroy documents 'the richness of cultural struggle in and around "race"' and identifies 'dimensions of black oppositional practice which are not reducible to the narrow idea of anti-racism' (1987: 154). He emphasizes the ways in which what Willis calls the seriality of the commodity is *opposed* in the consumption practices of black people, and explores how racial identities are sometimes composed by complex attachments to varieties, brands, styles and objects of consumption. He suggests that these attachments indicate that black people not only refuse the racism of many advertising images, but also that they create alternative understandings of race, through their participation in consumer culture. In doing so, he identifies the use of cultural goods such as clothes, films, books and music as especially important in the creation of these oppositional understandings.

One example of this is what Gilroy describes as the refusal and reversal of a white cultural economy of time and space; this is an economy in which the night-time is set aside as the period allocated for recovery and rest from work. The night-time, he argues, is assertively and provocatively occupied by black people for the pursuit of pleasure. Gilroy also suggests that in many black consumption practices, there is a refusal and reversal of the dominant white tendency to privatize consumption, to make it a matter of individual preference, carried out in the domestic sphere. In black culture, consumption is celebrated, not as a private or individual practice, but as a collective, affirmative practice in which an alternative public sphere is brought into being. He gives the example of music consumption: records are used as cultural resources in processes of creative improvisation in response to the requirements of specific public occasions – religious, political and cultural. This process of giving meaning to records takes different forms across different sites. So, for example, Gilroy points out that the record shop often acts as a popular cultural archive and repository of folk knowledge. He writes, 'It stores some of the key cultural resources of the racial group and provides an autonomous space in which the music, language and style that enable people to bring meaning and order to their social lives can be worked out and worked on' (1992: 136).

In the black dance hall, there is an orientation towards improvisation, spontaneity and live performance – the musical commodity is never finished, but always open to being reworked. Gilroy writes, 'records become raw material for spontaneous performances of cultural creation in which the DJ and the MC or toaster who introduces each disc or sequence of discs, emerge as the principal agents in dialogic rituals of active and celebratory consumption' (1987: 164). The rivalry between sound-system DJs over records is paralleled on the dance floors by intense rivalry amongst their followers, expressed in dance competitions. It is through such collective practices, Gilroy suggests, that the users of black music have managed to combine both a strong sense of fashion and a respectful approach to the historical status of their musical culture, which values its longevity and its capacity to connect them with their historical roots (1987, 1992). In this way, alternative understandings of race are sustained in black people's participation in consumer culture.

Gilroy argues that a further consequence of black people's participation in consumer culture is that they have played an important role in dissolving the distinction between art and life that has historically been a feature of European culture. On many occasions in black culture, listening to music is not just a cerebral process of contemplation as is typically the case in classical concerts, but also a bodily process of immersion in sound. Similarly, Kobena Mercer argues:

> If . . . postmodernity . . . refers to the dominant cultural logic of late capitalism, which 'now assigns an increasingly essential structural function to aesthetic innovation and experimentation' as a condition of higher rates of turnover in consumer culture, then any attempt to account for the gradual dissolution of boundaries between 'high' and 'low' culture, between taste and style, must reckon with the dialogic interventions of diasporic, creolizing cultures. (1994: 124)

Gilroy concludes by noting that the very terms of much contemporary analysis – production, circulation and consumption – obscure the complexity of race as a category of identity by artificially separating out different moments of meaning-making. Indeed, in these early writings, he argues that the term 'consumption' is especially problematic in this respect, since it emphasizes the passivity of its agents and plays down the value of its creativity as well as the political significance of their actions in understanding resistance in everyday life.

In his more recent writing, however, Gilroy develops an analysis that suggests that he thinks the interrelationships between race and consumption need to be further explored. So, for example, he draws attention to the fact that African Americans spend something in the region of $30 billion on cars and $9 billion more on related products and services, and that they constitute roughly 30 per cent of the car-buying public although they are currently only 12 per cent of the US population, to explore the intense associations of cars and freedom in black American culture. He suggests that 'the special seductions of car culture have become an important part of what binds the black populations of the overdeveloped countries to the most mainstream of dreams' (2010: 15). On the one hand, he argues, African American car cultures indicate that the official scripts of respectable domesticity and deferred gratification have been rejected. On the other, he suggests, they can also be taken as a sign that 'those dreams have already been surpassed – overtaken – by more powerful and reckless desires which can be examined through the predisposition to what the marketing literature calls "status purchasing"'(2010: 21). In these and other ways, he shows the continuing importance of what he calls 'transactions in blackness itself' (2010: 10) for the development of consumer culture.

Gender and the family economy

As noted in chapter 2, feminist writers have frequently had concerns about the use of the term 'consumption', especially when it is understood only as a response to (industrial) production. This is because of the significance they give to what is sometimes called the domestic mode of production or family economy. Within this framework, what is frequently termed consumption – the use of goods acquired through the market, for instance – is better understood as productive labour. As a consequence, while the so-called domestic revolution has been closely linked with the rise of consumer culture, this does not mean that women, historically the custodians of the domestic sphere, have been identified as the chief agents of consumer culture. This is because although women tend to have responsibility for the family economy, they are not usually in control of finances; nor do they make choices in relation to themselves alone. So, while women may have been the instruments of consumer culture, they have not necessarily been agents in its historical development.

Take the much-debated example of the activity of shopping. From the end of the nineteenth century onwards, the activity of buying came to be increasingly defined as worthy and significant, creating a new role for women as administrators of the home, directing consumption by their selection of the goods and services. So, for example, department stores – 'palaces of consumption' – were constructed as welcoming and inviting places for (middle-class) women in particular. At the Bon Marché in Paris, for instance, diaries, calendars, bulletins and even transport to the store were provided to encourage women to shop and feel at ease once they got there (Bowlby, 1985). However, while the activity of shopping carried out by upper- and middle-class women was seen as peculiarly feminine, it was not positively valued, but, rather, was constructed as irrational, fanciful and frivolous. Women shoppers were encouraged to think of themselves as being prone to become out of control, having an insatiable desire to buy. Managers of department stores helped create this perception through the way shoppers were treated once in the store. So, for instance, floor-walkers, men who escorted women around the store helping to 'control' their purchases, were common until the 1920s (Benson, 1986). Medical studies of the time purported to show sexual dysfunction as the cause of kleptomania or shoplifting in women. There were also attempts to rationalize housework in general and shopping in particular. So, for example, this period sees the introduction and growth of domestic science in schools, the proliferation of housework manuals, and a torrent of advice to housewives on how best to look after their home and family in, for example, women's magazines.

According to Janice Winship (1987), this aspect of the development of consumer culture can be seen as part of an attempt to co-opt the early demands of feminism and the desires of the growing number of women who were participating in paid work, and thus gaining some degree of economic independence. Indeed, sometimes shopping was explicitly presented as an alternative form of liberation, as, for example, when Mr Selfridge suggested that he was aiding the cause of women's emancipation in opening his department store! More recently, Betty Friedan, author of one of the first manifestos of second-wave feminism, *The Feminine Mystique* (1965), quotes, with outrage, an advertising executive who had a similar, although more obviously condescending, view of the implications of consumerism for women: 'Properly manipulated . . . American housewives can be given the sense of identity, purpose, creativity, the self-realization, even the sexual joy they lack – by the buying of things' (1965: 181).

More recently, their invitation to women to understand themselves as consumers in terms of feminine individuality is analysed by Winship by reference to the magazine *Options*, launched in 1982. This magazine was described in the publicity surrounding its launch as 'a magazine about choice', a choice which was later presented in terms of 'Better food, Better homes, Better fashion, Better living'. It is addressed to a reader who is invited to see herself as 'an entirely new breed of consumer', defined exclusively in terms of what she buys:

> She sees herself as the kind of woman who should have a calculator in her handbag, a stereo in her car, a note recorder in her office. She is the generation for whom video and telecom were made. Busy women with open minds who will take advantage to make work more efficient and play more fun. The first generation of women for whom freezers, dishwashers and microwave ovens are not luxuries but essentials. (*Options*, launch material, quoted in Winship, 1983: 47)

This is the new woman who can be independent *and* feminine, who can look attractive *and* create a fulfilling family and home life even when carrying out a demanding job.

The representation of consumption dominates this (and many other women's) magazine(s). Not only is about half of the magazine taken up by advertisements, but almost all the colour photography, both in advertisements and features, illustrates commodities of some kind. In feature articles and advertisements, the modern woman is represented as a superwoman, enjoying the skills and pleasures of consumption, not in a passive way, but by actively appropriating and reworking commodities to construct a lifestyle that expresses her *individuality*. Winship writes that in *Options*, 'the activities involved around consumption constitute a *creative skill* – the creation of a "look", whether with clothes, furnishings, food or make-up – which are both *pleasurable to do* and *to look at*' (1983: 48). The sphere of consumption is held up as the arena in which women can selectively choose 'options' to express her own unique sense of self by transforming commodities from their mass-produced forms into expressions of individuality and originality. The magazine provides optimistic encouragement to keep on trying, offering examples of women who have 'found themselves' through the adoption of an individualized lifestyle.

Winship argues that an important part of this latest stage in the representation of women in relation to consumption is the way in

which women are invited to view their own lives as their *own crea-tions*, and buy an identikit of different images of themselves created by different products. This latest stage in the constitution of women through consuming is linked by Winship to the growing importance of the *work of femininity*. Other writers too have argued that consumption practices have become an increasingly important source of the creation of a feminine self.

One instance of this is provided by the relation between notions of beauty and femininity. Winship argues that while beauty is not a new component of femininity, advertising in women's magazines has played an important part in redefining its meaning. She suggests that advertising has contributed to the idea that beauty is not a natural given – either absent or present – but instead is something that is achievable by any woman, though only through the application of the correct products. The way in which advertising has done this, according to Winship, is through its representation of women as 'the field of action for various products'. She points to the way in which, in advertisements, women's bodies are broken down into different areas as sites for the actions of commodities.

Winship suggests that advertising builds an anxiety that, unless women measure up, they will not be loved. They are set to work on an ever-increasing number of areas of the body, labouring to perfect and eroticize an ever-increasing number of erotogenic zones. Every minute region of the body is now exposed to scrutiny. Mouth, hair, eyes, eyelashes, nails, fingers, hands, skin, teeth, lips, cheeks, shoulders, elbows, arms, legs, feet – all these and many more have become areas requiring work. Winship sees this in terms of the imposition of a cultural ideal of feminine beauty and the multiplication of areas of the body accessible to marketing. It is the introduction of the idea that beauty is something that can be achieved, that it is something to be worked on, that Winship identifies as the work of femininity, and she suggests that consumer culture has been able to feed on and extend this work through its promotion of a multiplicity of products. Ros Gill, similarly, argues that there has been a shift in the definition of femininity such that it is defined as a bodily property rather than a social structural or psychological one. She writes:

> Instead of caring or nurturing or motherhood, it is now possession of a 'sexy body' that is presented as women's key source of identity. This is captured vividly in an advert for Wonderbra, which shows a young woman wearing only a black, cleavage-enhancing bra. Situated in between the breasts is the following slogan: 'I can't cook. Who cares?' – making the point that her voluptuous body is far more important than any other feminine skills or attributes she may or may not have. (2009: 97)

Winship further suggests that through the representation of beauty as an achievable goal of self-transformation through the use of commodities, women are constructed as consumers of *themselves as possessions or commodities*. John Berger makes the same point when he writes that, 'the publicity image steals [a woman's] love of herself as she is and offers it back to her for the price of the product' (1972: 134). Kathy Myers (1986) catches this contradictory nature of consumption for women by describing it as a kind of cannibalism. The point that is being made here is that women are both the objects, or signs, of representation in advertising and the market for the majority of products advertised. Women are thus simultaneously located at two moments of the cycle of commodity-exchange – that of a privileged sign in advertising and commodity aesthetics and the principal target market. They are also, in one sense, the principal protagonists in the moment of use of commodities. From this point of view, the emotionalization and aestheticization of housework – including, most importantly, the intensification of the work of femininity – is said to have contributed to the emergence of the distinctively stylized nature of consumer culture in contemporary society and the ideal of a possessive individual.

However, the extent to which women are active agents, in the sense of being in control of how to use commodities, whether they are self-possessed or possessed by others, is a controversial question. As noted above, for many writers, women's role in the development of consumer culture must be located in relation to the family economy. Here, it is argued, women are subordinated to men, through the expectation that they will carry out housework, including the work of femininity. To the extent that their use of commodities is not conducted for themselves, but for others, women may be seen, not as active consumers, but as bearers of a culture that they do not own. From this point of view the idea of a feminine individual promoted in magazines such as *Options* is a contradiction in terms. This line of argument suggests that women do not stand in the same relation to consumer culture as men. Myers writes:

> We, the audience, 'consume' meanings, and in so doing are able to interpret, complete the message of advertising. In the act of ingestion, we discover ourselves, find meaning in our lives and – crucially – pace our lives through the purchase of products. Arguably this is a process which men experience as well. But the crucial point . . . is that women are more vulnerable to the process because their upbringing and social expectations define them *as consumers and as images to be 'consumed' by the gaze of men*. Consumption, in this context, verges on cannibalism. (Myers, 1986: 137; my emphasis)

Other writers have seen the work of femininity in relation to what is sometimes called the institution of heterosexuality (Rich, 1981) and the ways in which women are sexually objectified by men. The argument here is that sexual relations between men and women are mediated through the construction of women by men as objects – in particular, as sex objects – and that such objectification helps to justify and sustain relations of domination and inequality between men and women.

Of course, this is a much contested argument, as issues of pleasure and desire are introduced alongside the complexities of self-presentation. Take the example of American Apparel. Their clothing has been described as undoing hyperfeminized modes of self-presentation, and flirting with a femme/butch aesthetic. But the same commentators also note:

At its most basic, there is the blunt fact that despite the stores selling men's clothes, the images are overwhelmingly of women. This, combined with how these women remain limited to specific types – young, relatively slim, femme – works to cast its porn references in a profoundly conservative light. That these sexualized and gendered dynamics of the promotional workplace function through a profound imbalance in power relations is, moreover, augmented by how the CEO constantly talks in interviews about his sexual relations with his female employees. (Moor and Littler, 2008: 716)

Relations of looking have been identified as a key aspect of the process of sexual objectification by a number of writers (Berger, 1972; Mackinnon, 1983; Mulvey, 1975), thus pointing to the importance of images and the art-culture system in this aspect of the development of consumer culture. John Berger, for example, developed an analysis of the nude in oil painting that suggests that there is a gendered contradiction at the heart of this genre of painting. This contradiction arose, he says, as a consequence of the fact that the painters and spectator-owners were usually men and the persons painted were usually women. The contradiction relates to the contrast between the individualism of the artist, the patron, the owner of the painting on the one hand and, on the other hand, the person who is the object of their activities, the woman who is treated as an object, a possession or abstraction. Berger suggests that this unequal relationship – between man as subject and women as object or possession of his gaze – is so deeply embedded in our culture, from high art to pornography to popular culture, advertising and everyday life, that it is possible to talk of a *male gaze*.

The operation of the male gaze means that women are conventionally depicted in quite different ways from men – not because the feminine body is different from the masculine body – but because the ideal spectator is always assumed to be male and the image of the female is designed to flatter him. Furthermore, so widespread is the process of objectification that men have come to be defined in terms of their actions, while women are judged in terms of their appearance. This has implications for the gendering of subjectivity. Men look at women. Women watch themselves being looked at. This, so Berger suggests, determines not only relations between men and women, but also the relation of women to themselves. From earliest childhood they have been taught to survey themselves continually, and so they come to consider themselves as objects or things. The use of commodities by women in, for example, the work of femininity, is thus shaped by their positioning as objects in relation to a male gaze. From this point of view, then, while women have been central to the development of consumer culture, this centrality is as much a consequence of their objectification as it is of their role as active consumers. This line of argument would thus also seem to imply that women, while fundamentally implicated in the development of consumer culture, have not been able to be active participants in its development. If women are denied the possibility of self-possession, and are unable to exercise ownership of their own selves, they cannot easily acquire other kinds of cultural capital either.

Other writers argue, however, that much of the work discussed so far presents an overly pessimistic view of the role of women in the history of consumer culture, and unfairly minimizes their role as active intermediaries in bringing about changes in consumption practices, overlooking the ways in which access to consumer culture may have provided resources for women in challenging gender inequality, including their objectification (Nava, 1992). This line of argument points out that, with the advent of the department store, for example, shopping lost its previous automatic association with purchase and further use, and was no longer simply the purchasing of predetermined requirements, but became an activity in its own right and, as such, provided an opportunity for women to explore their own desires, outside the confines of the home. Rachel Bowlby catches this moment in the title of one of her books: *Just Looking* (1985). This was the period that saw a dramatic increase in the use of transparent display windows, an improvement in the visibility inside stores with increased lighting, and a sense of theatrical excess in the display of items. As a result of these developments, stores can be seen to have provided a focus for women's fantasies, a site of entertainment, and a possible escape from the confines of domestic femininity. They provided a space within which (first middle-class and then working-class) women could participate in public life, in which they could experience some of the shocks, speed and spectacle of modernity, in which they could make brief encounters, and make 'unwise' purchases for themselves. Mica Nava writes, 'Consumption . . . has offered women new areas of authority and expertise, new sources of income, a new sense of consumer rights; and one of the consequences of these developments has been a heightened awareness of entitlement outside the sphere of consumption' (Nava, 1992: 166).

Yet the relation of women to consumer culture is highly uneven. Historically, while some groups have had the licence to 'look' openly, other groups, such as black people, have only been able to look illicitly. Carolyn Steedman (1998) has similarly argued that only some women are able to buy new fashions and styles for themselves, whilst others – working-class women especially – know that their desires have to remain subordinated to the needs of others, usually men and children. These points indicate that different groups of women have participated unevenly in the development of consumer culture, both implicated and excluded from cycles of production and consumption in contradictory ways. They also suggest that the adoption of simulation or masquerade, while it may be a feminine mode of fashioning the self, is cross-cut by class and race (see Tyler, 1991, for further discussion of this issue, also introducing questions of sexual difference).

A study that demonstrates this powerfully is that conducted by Debbie Weekes in a school in Birmingham in the Midlands in the UK (2002). She found that the black teenage girls she studied were asserting a claim to moral superiority and popular cultural status over white girls as a way of managing a tension between the enjoyment of the sexualization of their bodies in black popular culture and their desire to resist racist representations of black women as hypersexualized. The claim to popular cultural status involves a display of skill in dancing, fashion and hairstyling, supported by participation in consumer culture. This more active understanding of women's participation in consumption practices can be used to explain the emergence of the dynamic, ironic and self-conscious manipulation of style that is said to be characteristic of contemporary consumer culture. In this view, women are not only central to the stylization of consumer culture, but may stand to benefit from it, and can thus be seen as key cultural intermediaries.

More recent studies offer yet further complications, however, as they explore the implications of post-feminism and its links to consumer culture. Robert Goldman (1992), for example, discusses the emergence of what he calls 'commodity feminism', by which he means an attempt by advertisers to incorporate the cultural power and energy of feminism whilst simultaneously muting its critique, while Josée Johnston and Judith Taylor use the term 'feminist consumerism' (2008) to describe activities which have the potential to disrupt gender norms *within* consumerism, understood as 'a way of life dedicated to the possession and use of consumer goods'.

To explore what is involved in feminist consumerism further, Johnston and Taylor develop an analysis and comparison of the Dove Campaign for Real Beauty and a Toronto-based fat-activist organization that targets feminine beauty ideals called Pretty, Porky, and

Pissed Off (PPPO). Dove, a subsidiary of the giant Unilever company and the largest skin-care brand in the world, launched a Campaign for Real Beauty in 2004. This campaign used 'real' women, rather than professional models, for television and print advertisements featuring its new line of firming products, and engaged feminist critiques and concerns about beauty ideals in its advertising as well as participating in 'grass-roots' partnering to raise money for eating disorder organizations and Girl Scout programmes to build self-esteem. PPPO, a small, informal and non-commercial campaigning group, moved from street protests, in which activists handed out candy and questioned passers-by about their attitudes towards fat, to creating cabaret shows. They were focused on creating opportunities to resist consumerism, while recognizing the gender and class implications of fat bodies.

The analysis carried out by Johnston and Taylor suggests that the Dove campaign, 'while it contests narrow beauty codes, works within a hegemonic ideology of gendered beauty by refusing to challenge the idea that beauty is an essential part of a woman's identity, personhood, and social success and by legitimizing the notion that every woman should feel beautiful' (2008: 954). Indeed, Johnston and Taylor suggest that the campaign is best understood as a gender-specific marketing strategy to cultivate brand loyalty by using models and imagery that women can identify with while conveying an appearance of corporate philanthropy. Furthermore, they suggest that the apparently democratic ethos underlying the campaign – participation, voting on whether a woman is fat or fabulous – ignores the fact that beauty ideas and social respect are linked to inequalities of sex, race, class and body size. In contrast they believe that PPPO, while having a much more limited audience, offers a more ambivalent relationship to the idealization of women's physical beauty and recognizes the pain caused by beauty ideals for many women. They conclude: 'Consumer culture allows for, and encourages, individual difference but does not emphasize structural hierarchies or collective strategies for change' (2008: 959).

Ros Gill (2009) outlines the emergence of what she calls a post-feminist sensibility, which she says has the following characteristics: a shift from objectification to subjectification; an emphasis on self-surveillance, monitoring and discipline; a focus upon individualism, choice and empowerment; a marked sexualization of culture; and an emphasis on consumerism and the commodification of difference. This sensibility is exemplified for Gill by the 'makeover takeover' (Hollows, 2000) that dominates contemporary television. Beverley

Skeggs and Helen Wood (2004) argue that such shows produce 'new ethical selves' in which particular forms of selfhood are presented as solutions to modern life. They propose that the organization of taste is changing as it is increasingly mediated by the imperative to choose: 'Choice mediates taste, displaying the success and failure of the self to make itself, for instance in lifestyle programmes such as *Changing Rooms* (BBC), *House Doctor* (Channel 4) and *Better Homes* (ITV) where the domestic and thus the everyday is transformed through appropriating "better" taste' (2004: 206). This is an argument that suggests that the involvement of women in consumer culture as subjects – rather than or as well as objects – has not necessarily been beneficial for them. Instead, it suggests that it has contributed to new forms of individualism that have uneven and unequal implications.

Angela McRobbie further explores some of these complexities in her studies of young women today, asking in what sense they can be seen as 'top girls' (a phrase that deliberately draws on the British reader's likely knowledge of the highly successful fashion retail outlet, Topshop). She argues that young women are addressed by governments in 'advanced democracies' as having what she calls 'capacity', summed up in the (beauty retail chain) Body Shop phrase the 'can do' girl (Harris, 2004). She shows that young women are urged to become hyper-active across three key sites:

> Within the field of consumer culture this takes the form of the 'post-feminist masquerade' where the fashion and beauty system appears to displace traditional modes of patriarchal authority. Likewise the emergence of the 'phallic' girl appears to have gained access to sexual freedoms previously the preserve of men . . . The new sexual contract is also embedded within the fields of education and employment. Here too young women (top girls) are now understood to be ideal subjects of female success, exemplars of the new competitive meritocracy. (McRobbie 2007: 718)

Crucially, she points out that while such urgings attribute freedom and success to young women, actual success is predicated on punitive conditions, which are contributing to the undoing of feminism. She uses an advertisement for the magazine *Grazia* to make this point. The advertisement used the headline: '42% of women who ask for a pay-rise get one. 100% of them would probably celebrate with shoes.' She concludes:

> Consumer global citizenship predicated on hyper-activity, enthusiastic capacity and visible luminosity of youthful female subjects marks the

contours of the new dangers for women. By these means of contain-
ment in the landscape of spectacular femininity women are removed
once again from public life, the political sphere and from the possibility
of feminism. (2007: 734)

In this way, she suggests, participation in consumer culture contributes to the 'doing and the undoing' of gender in post-feminism.

This section has explored the two-way relationship between
changes in gender relations and changes in consumption. On the one
hand, it has identified a number of ways in which men and women
are very differently positioned in relation to consumer culture. On the
other, it has also considered the ways in which relations between men
and women, including the family economy and the objectification of
women, have contributed to the development of consumer culture,
through, for example, providing a specific context for the emotionalization and aestheticization of consumption.

There is considerable disagreement about the implications of this
two-way relationship for women themselves. Put crudely, this is a
question of whether women can be seen as the active intermediaries of consumer culture or simply the instruments or tools of its
development. However, even in the most pessimistic accounts of

the involvement of women in consumer culture, it is not intended to imply that women are passive in their consumption activities, for it is clear that they are not, but rather to point out that these activities tend to be carried out in sets of power relations which constrain women to act in certain ways. These power relations operate not only at the economic but also at the cultural and political level. Cultural resources for the creation of the identity of a self-possessed individual are not equally available to all, and in many, perhaps most situations, the value of a feminine identity remains limited.

In conclusion to this section, it may be suggested that it is in terms of the occupation of a paradoxical position, simultaneously subject *and* object of consumption practices, that women's role in the development of consumer culture is best recognized. Furthermore, in terms of developing an analysis of consumer culture these debates demonstrate that attention to gender opens up questions of pleasure, emotion and aesthetics in ways that have increasing importance in discussions of the contemporary economy. They also indicate that the development of consumer culture must be seen to have a number of interlocking histories, and cannot be understood in relation to a single overarching explanation or the activities of a single social group.

Conclusion

This chapter has described the importance of transnational exchanges for national cultures of consumption and the significance of uneven participation of different social groupings in consumer culture. It has pointed out that this unevenness is fundamental not incidental to the growth of consumer culture. The chapter has shown that not all individuals are in a position to exercise the capacity of calculated de-control or self-reflexivity, described as characteristic of the new middle classes in the last chapter, in the same way: members of different social groups have different relationships to this dimension of their identities. This is not surprising. Historians such as Steedman (2000) and Poovey (1998) have shown that ways of telling and knowing the self have always been unevenly distributed. The imperative to produce oneself in these ways relies not just on access to and control of symbolic resources, but also on knowing how to display one's subjectivity properly. And, as Bev Skeggs (2005) notes, while it may be up to the individual to 'choose' a repertoire of the self, if they do not have access to the range of narratives and discourses for the

production of the self in ways that are socially legitimate they may be held responsible for choosing badly, an irresponsible production of themselves. She writes:

> Choice does not merely represent a pre-formed self imbued with potential, rather it is a performative enactment of self; one that only some can

perform. Others do not have access to 'choice', all they can display is 'lack'; lack of access to the techniques for telling themselves and lack of access to the right culture; they cannot perform the good self because they do not have the cultural resources to do so. (2005: 974)

6

Brands: Markets, Media and Movement

Introduction

This chapter focuses on the rise and significance of branding in consumer culture. It outlines a brief history of branding, and introduces a couple of key perspectives. The aim, though, is not simply to introduce brands and branding, but also to open up the question of the relation between markets, media and consumer culture. The purpose is to show that the emergence of branding is part of a complex *mediation* of supply and demand, of what might be called a media or mediated economy, which has significant implications for the participation of consumers in the economy and also for consumer culture. Branding is thus introduced here as an example of changes in the economy that move away from a simple relation between production and consumption; indeed, branding practices indicate that not even the notion of a cycle or circuit of culture can capture the complexity of producer–consumer relations in the contemporary economy. The attention paid to branding here is thus a way of highlighting transformations in the forms, times and spaces of consumer culture, discussed elsewhere in terms of cycles or circuits of production and consumption, fluidization or prosumption.

> What is a 'brand'? A frequently cited epithet goes: a product is made in a factory; a brand is bought by a consumer. (Wang, 2008: 23)

But what does it mean to talk about a media economy or a mediation of the economy? In any dictionary there will be multiple meanings for the word 'medium': as something in-between or intermediate; a middle state or condition; a method or way of expressing something. The sense in which it is used in this chapter draws on all three meanings, but attention is focused on the third meaning – rather than seeing mediation as a neutral process, the expressive or transformative role of mediation is emphasized.

In some of the accounts presented in the chapter, mediation is understood in terms of the increasing role of markets and marketing – what is sometimes called marketization, *and* the increasing role of media or mediatization. Let me start by saying a little about both these terms. From a sociological perspective, marketization describes the expansion of arrangements for bringing buyers and sellers together for self-advantaging exchange. Of course, many individuals participating in markets do not actually want to put their interest above others, and do not act in terms of instrumental calculation. Nevertheless, marketization has intensified in recent years as part of what is sometimes called neo-liberalism (Harvey 2005). This is a politics which starts from the assumption that individual liberty and freedom can best be achieved by an institutional structure that supports strong private property rights, free markets and free trade. The implication of such a politics is that the state should not be involved in the regulation of the economy too much, but rather that it should use its power to preserve private property rights and the institutions of the market and promote those on the global stage. It typically involves an increasingly global fiscal policy through non-state institutions such as the International Monetary Fund and the World Bank, the deregulation of financial institutions, the redirection of public subsidies from services such as health and education, the deregulation of interest rates, and the liberalization of trade and foreign direct investment.

Mediatization refers to the increasing importance of information, image and media in the organization and expression of the economy, consumer culture and everyday life. Arguments about the growth in importance of mediation relate to broader theories of what has variously been called cognitive or knowing capitalism (Thrift, 2005) or an immaterial economy (Lazzarato, 2004) in which, as chapter 4 outlined, activity or productivity is no longer limited to the workplace but distributed *between* the producer and the consumer, and reaches outside the economy into everyday life. The emphasis on information, image and media provides a different vocabulary from that of symbolic exchange that has informed many discussions of the values, norms and beliefs of consumer culture. In this way it provides an alternative – or at least a supplementary framework for thinking about culture, and for the nature of our participation in culture, not so much perhaps in terms of interpretation but more and more in terms of operation, of 'doing' culture. As Nike would have it, the combined effect of marketization and mediatization is to make us 'Just Do It'.

Markets and branding

The phenomena that are now described as brands are diverse, and any attempt to define the brand is caught within conflicting frameworks and is able to call upon multiple histories, each of which gives branding a different origin. In many accounts, however, it is proposed that branding becomes a visible force in the organization of production and consumption in industrialized countries in the second half of the nineteenth century, and increases in significance – in fits and starts – over the following 150 years. Anne McClintock (1994), for example, suggests that during this period a climate was created within which aggressive competition between producers became ever more intense, due to the stretching of markets over national and international space, alongside the growth of national and international networks of circulation and distribution, as well as economic competition between nations. From the 1880s onwards, corporate logos were increasingly used to promote a whole range of mass-produced products such as Rowntree's Fruit Pastilles and Fruit Gums, Bassett's Liquorice Allsorts, Campbell's soup, H. J. Heinz pickles and Quaker Oats cereal. In 1886, in the USA, a medicinal product or 'nerve tonic' started being sold as Coca-Cola; as quickly as the late 1890s, it was being promoted as the 'national drink'.

In these early stages of development, brands were intended to allow the producer to speak 'directly' to the consumer through presentation, packaging and other media, a capacity that became increasingly important as markets grew rapidly. The development of corporate and product personalities was in part an attempt to replace the role of the retailer, the individual who had provided continuity and a trustworthy context for the consumer. But branding involves not simply a dis-intermediation of the role of the retailer, but also a re-intermediation in the development of brand logos, identities or personalities to speak for the product, to act as a guarantor of quality. Not surprisingly, this period is closely linked to emerging conflicts between manufacturers and retailers, and these conflicts – and alliances – have continued to be important ever since. For example, some supermarkets highlight the range of branded products they sell, while others develop their own brands.

The role of processes of mediation in economic life has since been intensively developed in the last 150 years, not least by the emerging discipline of marketing. It was through developments in techniques in communicating with – and acquiring knowledge about – the consumer that the discipline of marketing really began to emerge. While marketers were initially concerned only to describe the existing diverse ways in which products were brought to market – finding out what functions and firms were involved in making goods available to consumers – in a very short time they acquired a more active, interventionist role. There were, however, clear differences in the development of marketing in different countries, linked to the position of this new discipline in a complex of commercial practices (Bowlby, 1985, 1993; Nava, 1995; Winship, 2000). In the UK, in the early to mid-twentieth century, for example, the key form of retail organization was the trade association. In contrast, in the USA during this period, 'printed salesmanship', brand advertising and other early forms of non-price competition, were more commonly adopted as the acceptable means of market control. The postwar period also sees the rise of self-service systems in retail outlets, in which the 'silent salesman' of brands, promotion and packaging was increasingly able to coordinate selling (Bowlby, 2000).

By the 1950s and 1960s, the discipline of marketing was able to have a more active role in the coordination of production through its use of knowledge about the consumer, not only in the US and the UK but more widely. Thus, 1960 saw the publication of Theodor Levitt's manifesto for a global marketing revolution. A distinction between selling and marketing in terms of their relation to the consumer was crucial to his argument. Selling, he said:

> focuses on the needs of the seller, marketing on the needs of the buyer. Selling is preoccupied with the seller's need to convert his product into cash, marketing with the idea of satisfying the needs of the customer by means of the product and the whole cluster of things associated with creating, delivering and finally consuming it. (Quoted in Mitchell, 2001: 76–7)

The consolidation of the role of marketing was linked to the changing role of retail in the UK, as well as in the USA; no longer a passive activity, driven by the manufacturer, it was increasingly becoming a complex and aggressive activity in which information about the consumer was a pivotal resource. So, for example, major retailers were able to exert greater control of the supply chain through their use of information systems technology to coordinate and organize store management, logistics and the distribution chain. But the increasing legitimacy of marketing was also a consequence of internal developments: the abandonment of institutional economics by marketers and the adoption of a combination of quantitative techniques and behavioural sciences (Cochoy, 1998). On the one hand, the implementation of operations research and econometrics led to the birth of marketing science, a research stream that could model and optimize market activities. On the other hand, the importation of statistics, psychology and behavioural analysis gave birth to what came to be called 'consumer research'. This involves the use of economic, social and psychographic demographics to map the target market and describe this market in terms of lifestyle (see chapter 4).

The combined use of these methods secured a growing authority for marketers, an authority that legitimated an increasingly important role for marketing that in turn contributed to a greater emphasis on product differentiation. In this way, the development of marketing played an important role in the shift from Fordism to post-Fordism (see chapter 4). The idea put forward by marketers was that 'beyond prices, the result of competition depended on the management of the multi-dimensional aspects of products – above all, brands, services, packaging . . . one had to play on these many dimensions in order to shape the markets' (Cochoy, 1998: 213).

In the following years marketers found ways to show that products are not adequately defined by their functional properties alone; instead, they proposed that a product's potential existence extends beyond being a discrete physical good. So, for example, the pattern of customers' needs as identified through the use of the behavioural sciences in consumer research – in particular psychological theories of the self, such as Maslow's hierarchy of needs – were used to define a product's 'essence'. The 'nature' or 'essence' of products understood in this way was thus directly linked to a framing of the market in terms of consumers' perceptions, needs and practices as construed in the knowledge practices of marketers. The changes in product development and design that resulted from this shift in thinking about products thus contribute to the changes in the understanding and use of objects described by Knorr Cetina (2000) in her discussion of the open, incomplete and experimental nature of objects today.

Another key stage in the emergence of today's brand was a changed view of the producer–consumer relationship: no longer viewed in terms of stimulus-response, the relation was increasingly conceived as a relationship. This changed view was advocated most explicitly by the proponents of a new organizational model for advertising agencies, which put 'account planning' at the heart of the advertising process. This position was first developed by the London branch of J. Walter Thompson and the London agency Boase, Massimmi and Pollit, in the 1960s, and was taken up more generally only slowly, first by advertising agencies in the 1980s and then by design consultancies in the 1990s (Julier, 2000). In this model, the account planner, whose role is to act as a representative of the point of view of the consumer within an agency, coordinates the various other aspects of the advertising process. The role was designed to offer the client a view of the consumer's experience and to ensure that the identity of the brand was maintained throughout the execution of the advertising design or creative process (Julier, 2000: 19–20).

In the UK – and to some extent elsewhere – this move was associated with the rise of what was called 'creative advertising' in the 1980s and 1990s (Lash and Urry, 1994). This genre of advertising not only promoted the use of new forms of consumer research (especially lifestyle research, attitudinal and motivational research, and psycho-demographics), but also aimed to construct for consumers an imaginary lifestyle within which the emotional and aesthetic values of the product were elaborated (Nixon, 1996: 195). As Guy Julier notes, the methods adopted by market researchers enabled them to argue that they could interpret the desires of the consumer better than the consumer him or herself:

> A well-known example of this is in Sony's development of portable televisions. The American company General Electric had conducted a survey by judging people's responses to mock-up televisions to estimate demand for a small portable TV, the conclusion of which was that the 'people do not place a high value on portability of the television set' (General Electric quoted in Lorenz 1986: 34). By contrast, Sony looked at people's behavioural patterns at home and the number and type of channels available. Using this data they anticipated that a portable TV would actually suit changes in these patterns. Following the success of their portable TV, they then went on to do precisely the same with the video-cassette recorder, the Walkman personal stereo and the watchman flat-tube TV. Thus, lifestyle research for design consultancy becomes a form of cultural analysis, ethnography or design criticism itself. (Julier, 2000: 100)

From the 1970s onwards there was also a move away from the branding of stand-alone products to the branding of product ranges.

This process of product development is sometimes described in the marketing literature as 'brand extension'. By the 1980s and 1990s, there was also an increase in both the branding of services and in corporate branding, that is, the branding of a company rather than either particular products or services: 'Many of the brands that are emerging today are succeeding because they do not focus on a specific product, but instead communicate clear values which can extend across a plethora of different products and services' (Hart, 1998: 208).

At the same time, branding becomes increasingly central to the internal organization of firms, and brands come to have a dual role: in organizing the exchange between producers and consumers, and in organizing relations within the company itself, between employers and employees. This latter role is sometimes described as 'brand engagement' or 'internal marketing'. As the brand management company Interbrand puts it:

> A corporate brand stands for the relationship that an organization has with its employees, as much as it represents the relationship that it has with its customers through its product and service offerings. For a brand to come to life with customers, the organization must be internally aligned to deliver the brand promise through the organization's culture, reward systems, key success activities and structure. In other words, employees must 'live' the brand values in their day-to-day interactions. (Interbrand Insights, 2001: <www.Interbrand.co.uk>)

In the 1980s, a famous slogan for what was then called British Rail – 'We're Getting There' – was widely known to be as much a message to those who worked for this much maligned service as to its passengers (or customers as they have since come to be known). Elements of the visual identity of the brand British Rail were also part of an organizational strategy to change working practices. Brands thus came to be used as one of a growing number of devices to monitor and control the performance of employees, including productivity monitoring, video surveillance, and so-called active-badge systems. So, for example, a 'silver swallow' was part of the visual design identity produced for the InterCity rail service by the company Newell and Sorell in 1986, and was an element of the visual design identity that was applied to the trains as well as to literature and publicity. Employees were encouraged to 'earn' a 'silver swallow' badge as part of a drive to raise standards (Mollerup, 1997: 46–7).

By the last quarter of the twentieth century, then, a previously diffuse set of practices – including not only marketing but also distribution practices, media communication, product design, retail design, and point-of-purchase marketing among others – were becoming consolidated into an integrated approach to marketing and business strategy, and this is what is now known as branding (Moor, 2007). This process of consolidation was evident in the emergence of specific agencies, known as brand consultancies, and the institutionalization of brand management positions in private and public organizations. This increased prominence of branding fed into, and was fed by, other shifts in the economy, including the increasing significance of design-intensivity, flexible specialization, globalization and developments in media and communication technologies associated with the move to post-Fordism. It was also fed by shifts within the emergent branding and allied industries, including scepticism about the effectiveness of conventional advertising, the expanding role of product design, and developments in distribution and media technology, notably the Internet. At the same time, branding has become a matter of increasing public concern, in part because of the political activity associated with Naomi Klein's *No Logo* (2000) and other forms of consumer activism, but also because of the increasing use of branding by public and governmental organizations and the visibility of brands in public and commercial space (Moor, 2007).

In January 2008, the California-based Strategic Vision consultancy announced the results of extensive research into the racial aspects of the automobile market . . . Their press release is worth quoting at length:

> Differences that clearly stand out with African Americans are greater desires for success and the ability to show it. African Americans are much more likely to advocate vehicles that express their individuality and success to family and friends. Latinos have a greater concern for the impact on the environment while also exhibiting a greater desire to experience exhilarating driving and performance than others. Asian Americans have stronger demands for a balanced, complete vehicle performance and style that matches their lives. (Gilroy, 2010: 31–2)

By the last decade of the twentieth century, branding was no longer the responsibility of marketing departments alone, but permeated the organization of many companies. In 2000, a survey of 200 senior UK managers revealed that 73 per cent anticipated restructuring their companies, building the working structure of the firm around the brand (Manuelli, 2000, quoted in Julier, 2000: 193). This, of course, makes brand management a concern of management in general:

> How does the company make sure that there is a perfect match between values and behaviour? Products, buildings and machines – even ideas – can be copied, but the only unique elements in a company are its people. They constitute the soul of the brand. The first step to creating brand authenticity is therefore to ensure that its core values are clear and have been fully internalized by those who work within the company. That is not to say everyone has to be identical – that would be impossible and undesirable. But there should be certain values that they share *as part of their own core values*. (Marzano, 2000: 58; italics added)

In this regard, consider the ways in which the management of the brand informs the organization of workers and the work process through the mobilization of constructions of the market in terms of information about the consumer (as Bourdieu (1984) remarks, the act of classifying acts back on those who classify). The point being made here is that the creation of market hierarchies in terms of classifications of the consumer provides resources for techniques of control of the work process, and the incorporation, marginalization and exclusion of particular social groups *as* producers. This occurs as a consequence of the ways in which organizations of the market, in terms of consumer characteristics, behaviours and tastes, provide the resources for the definition of jobs, the organization of the work process, and competition between groups of workers as well as that between individual workers.

A striking example of [the redefinition of work of and the work process via branding] is to be found in the management literature that explicitly advises white collar employees to present themselves as brands (so-called personal branding). Consider how Tom Peters describes the project of becoming 'brand you' in *The Brand You 50: fifty ways to transform yourself from an "employee" into a brand that shouts distinction, commitment, and passion!* (1999). He outlines a number of exercises for those wishing to turn themselves into brands: make a personal brand equity evaluation; develop a one-eighth (or one-quarter) page yellow pages ad for brand you/me and co.; create an eight-word personal positioning statement; and devise a bumper sticker that describes your essence. As the back cover makes clear, Peters believes the choice

> to take up this opportunity is driven by the need for survival in a
> changing labour market.
>   'In today's wired world, you're distinct . . . or extinct. Survive,
> thrive, triumph by becoming Brand You!
>   'The fundamental unit in today's economy is the individual,
> a. k. a. YOU! Jobs are performed by temporary networks that
> disband when the project is done. So to succeed you have to think
> of yourself as a freelance contractor – Brand You! Someone who
> is savvy, informed, always learning and growing, who knows how
> to sell herself, and – most important – does work that matters.'
> (Lury, 2004: 35–6)

At the same time, the commercial success of the marketing management model outlined above has been such that the brand has been
extended in and beyond business through the invention of 'social
marketing'. In relation to business, this is an approach that proposes
that companies should acknowledge their 'strong social influence on
a society's sense of purpose, direction and economic growth' (Hart,
1998: 213).

> Since brands play such a fundamental role in society, we believe it is
> the responsibility of brand owners to begin to ask themselves more
> wide-ranging and searching questions: rather than ask a straightforward
> question such as 'Will it sell?' they must ask a series of more complex
> questions: 'Will it make a contribution to our customer's success?' 'Will
> it improve the customer's and society's well-being?' 'Does it add to our
> country's cultural stock or bring pride to our nation?' (1998: 213–14)

Outside business, it has involved a tendency for 'non-business'
organizations such as universities, political parties, charities, football
clubs, voluntary and campaigning groups, places, and individual
people to be presented as brands.
    As Cochoy (1998) notes, social marketing is oriented towards fun-
damental research, towards the study of the consumer for his or her
own sake as it were, rather than towards the study of the consumer for
the optimization of markets. And certainly the figure of the customer,
as consumer or user, is central to many recent attempts to recon-
struct institutions and practices in both the public and private sectors
(Keat, Whiteley and Abercrombie, 1994; du Gay, 1995). Indeed,
so widespread has the application of branding become – in relation
to governments, cities, faiths, charities, Web communities, financial services, education, new media and the public sector – that Liz

Moor argues for the need to 'decouple branding from simplistic ideas about 'commodification' and to reveal it instead as something more akin to a managerial technique or resource that seeks to use broadly 'cultural' . . . materials for a range of strategic ends' (2007: 88). Thus, charity branding may be used to recruit volunteers, to attract funding and to facilitate licensing agreements. In the public sector, branding may be used to establish legitimacy and reputation, but also to reshape citizens' perceptions of their relationship to government and their responsibility to act in particular ways. Indeed, it is possible to argue that some current branding techniques are not directly aimed at persuading consumers, but at sustaining persuasion as a mode of control: 'they work to colonize the lived experience of consumers in the interest of capital accumulation' (Hearn, 2008: 200).

Media and branding

This account of the history of branding has stressed the role of marketing, but there is a second line of development submerged here, which is to do with the significance of the media. Such accounts are important because they explicitly address the question of what kind

One problem for the agent trying to sell the stuffed shark was the $12m asking price. Another was that it weighed just over two tons and was not going to be easy to carry home. The 15ft tiger shark 'sculpture' was mounted in a giant glass vitrine and creatively named '*The Physical Impossibility of Death in the Mind of Someone Living*'. It had been caught in 1991 in Australia and prepared and mounted in England by technicians working under the direction of the artist Damien Hirst.

Another concern was that, while the shark was certainly a novel artistic concept, many in the art world were uncertain as to whether it qualified as art. The question was important because $12m represented more money than had ever been paid for a work by a living artist, other than Jasper Johns . . .

Why would anyone even consider paying this much money for the shark?

Part of the answer is that in the world of contemporary art, branding can substitute for critical judgement, and lots of branding was involved here. The seller was Charles Saatchi, an advertising magnate and art collector, who 14 years earlier had commissioned Hirst to produce the work for £50,000. At the time, the sum was considered so ridiculous that *The Sun* heralded the transaction with the headline: '50,000 For Fish Without Chips'. But Hirst intended the figure to be an 'outrageous' price, set as much for publicity it would attract as for the monetary return. (Thompson, 2008: 2)

of value is at issue in consumer culture. The interplay between marketing and media has been developed in recent accounts: of branding as icon (Holt, 2004); of branding as a new way of organizing production and managing consumption (Kornberger, 2010); of the brand as a new media object (Lury, 2004); and of branding as part of the mediatization of the economy (Arvidsson, 2006). At issue in the last two of these accounts is the role of the consumer in the creation of brand value: is the importance attached to representations of the consumer in professional branding practice matched by any real increase in consumer power? And what, to use terms derived from Bourdieu, are the new forms of cultural capital in a media economy, and under what circumstances, and how, can they be exchanged for economic capital?

For Doug Holt, what distinguishes a brand from a product is not simply a name, a trademarked logo, unique packaging, and perhaps

The case of Harvard's coming to brand consciousness in the early years of the new century is paradigmatic. The change was signaled by three things. First was the appointment of a new president, a noted economist well known as an enthusiast for globalization and keen to reposition Harvard in light of the globalized academic market. The second change was a set of moves to coordinate and intensify what had already become a plethora of initiatives to capitalize on the Harvard name, including private sector spin-offs to exploit patents and other forms of intellectual property. The third was an effort to globalize Harvard's reach technologically, by loosening undergraduate residency requirements, making course materials comprehensively available online, and launching a large-scale distance education programme . . .

The gamble of the new Harvard is that it might be possible to capitalize on the old form of ethos-and-nostalgia-driven reputation to acquire the excellence (e.g. via admission and SAT scores) not only to sustain the brand's value but also to replace the former with the latter as the basis of Harvard's claim to gold-standard status. (Wernick, 2006: 567)

When I coined the term 'nation brand' in 1996, it was in recognition of the fact that the reputation of places had become as important to their progress as the brand images of products and companies. I didn't mean that any country from Azerbaijan to Zimbabwe could build a Nike-sized brand if it could only raise a Nike-sized marketing budget: I was talking about brand image as a way of understanding the challenges faced by countries and cities, not proposing brand marketing as a way of fixing them. (Anholt, 2007: 57)

---

other design features, but a history of meaning that is 'filled with customer experiences' (2004: 3).

A brand emerges as various 'authors' tell stories that involve the brand. Four primary types of authors are involved: companies, the culture industries, intermediaries (such as critics and retail salespeople), and customers (particularly when they form communities). The relative influence of these authors varies over product categories. (2004: 3)

He goes on to focus on a particular type of brands – *iconic* brands, that is, those brands that consumers value as much for what they symbolize (once again, remember the emphasis in earlier commentaries on *symbolic* exchange) as for what they do.

> For brands like Coke, Budweiser, Nike, and Jack Daniel's, customers value the brand's stories for their *identity value*. Acting as vessels of self-expression, the brands are imbued with stories that consumers find valuable in constructing their identities. Consumers flock to brands that embody the ideals they admire, brands that help them express who they want to be. The most successful of these brands become *iconic brands*. (2004: 3–4)

Such brands, for Holt, are exemplars of what he calls 'cultural brands', that is, brands whose value resides 'in the specifics of the brand's cultural expression: the particular cultural contents of the brand's myth and the particular expression of these contents in the communication' (2004: 36).

In a book on brands (2004), I present an argument that contemporary branding has to be understood as a market device or market form that emerges at the intersection of a set of historical practices, including developments in graphic and product design and media, law and accounting, as well as in retail management and marketing.

The book argues that as a consequence branding, at least in its current form, must be understood as having multiple levels of existence, and cannot be reduced to advertising or brand image – or even its cultural content – alone. The book describes the brand as a new media object, that is, as an object that emerges at the convergence of media and computing. Such an object is performative, open-ended, distributed in time and space. It is a *dynamic platform or support for a variety of practices.*

The argument is that the brand emerged historically as a market device (Callon et al., 2007), that is, a device for the organization or management of markets. But I also draw a parallel with other media, to suggest that marketing functions in an analogous way to programming techniques in broadcasting and computing, especially in its deployment of the loop. So, for example, computer programmes make use of loops, which involve altering the flow of data through control structures in terms of operations such as 'if this/then that'. The suggestion I develop is that the marketing practices developed in the second half of the twentieth century may be seen as looping devices; they incorporate a representation of the activities of consumers in the processes and products of production and distribution. The marketing knowledge or information produced in this way is used to loop back and inform processes of brand product and process differentiation. Then, in turn, the resulting products and processes themselves become marketing tools, generating further information. The brand thus progresses or *emerges* in a series of loops, an ongoing process of product differentiation and brand integration. It is in this way, I suggest, that the brand is a device for organizing markets and a platform for products, activities and experiences. Exchange is no longer a repeated series of one-off exchanges, as it appears in commodity exchange, for example, but an ongoing relationship, in which consumers and their lives are entangled in a flow of commodities, services, promotion and events.

The role of the brand in organizing this movement or flow – in terms of a series of relations between products, services and events – is fundamental to my argument: that in marketing practices, the logo is able to secure the recognition of the brand as a constantly shifting series of associated products, services, events and experiences. Branding, from this point of view, can be described as the mediation of things (Lash and Lury, 2007), the mediation of commodities. There is a deliberate parallel here with John Ellis's description of television as the broadcasting of commodities (1992). In this argument, branding establishes relations between products in such a way that the consumer is caught up in a more or less open-ended relationship with it while commodities are organized in more or less continuous flows. In this way, then, branding contributes to what Lee calls 'the fluidization of consumption'.

> By one count, there are 15,000 Hello Kitty products. Sanrio receives 3% in royalties every time a company sells a product bearing a Sanrio character. From Sanrio's perspective, then, Hello Kitty has good reason to appear on and in stickers, coffee mugs, glasses, calculators, blankets, notebooks, phone cards, cameras, pocketbooks, watches, towels, pillows, toothbrushes, lunch boxes, pens, pencils, garbage pails, golf bags, boxer shorts, safes, luggage, scooters, and at Dai-Ichi Kangyô bank, bank-books and cash cards. (McVeigh, 2000: 229–30)

A further reason, I argue, that the brand is a new media object is because of the particular role it plays in the framing of communication between producers and consumers. In media theory, the terms 'frame', 'window', 'mirror', 'screen' and 'interface' are used in many discussions of media such as architecture, painting, cinema and computing. The most basic definition of the frame in media theory is 'a window that opens onto a larger space that is assumed to extend beyond the frame' (Manovich, 2001: 80); alternatively, the frame is said to separate 'two absolutely different spaces that somehow coexist' (Manovich, 2001: 95). The suggestion is that brands organize the activities of the market by acting as a dynamic frame or interface for communication. To elaborate: the interface – like the static frame of the window or mirror – is a surface or boundary that connects and separates two spaces, an inner and outer environment. So, for example, as a commercial interface, the brand is a frame that organizes the two-way exchange of communication between the inner and outer environments of the market in time and space, informing how consumers relate to producers and how producers relate to consumers. Kornberger expands this point, showing how brands 'expand the surface level' of an organization, attempting to put every internal function in touch with the external environment (2010: 21).

Importantly, the communication of the brand is not only to do with price, but also of emotion or affect, intensity and qualities. Relations become relationships, or at least they do if a brand is successful. However, although these exchanges are affective, dynamic and two-way, they are not direct, symmetrical or reversible. The interface of the brand connects the producer and consumer *and* removes or separates them from each other; it 'is revealing of some relationships, but it keeps others very well hidden' (Pavitt, 2000: 175).

A further element of this approach relates to the way in which branding practices stand at the convergence of media and computing. The role of information becomes central here, and it is worth noting the importance of what is called 'transactional data' in the growth of branding. Transactional data typically refers to data collected from consumers (sometimes without their knowledge) as a by-product of them doing something else, for example, shopping at the supermarket or making a purchase on a credit card. This data might be valuable because it may help companies to predict future behaviour, illuminate consumer tastes and preferences, or provide information that can be used to calculate the potential value (or lack of value) of a person's custom. The argument here is that media and computing technologies have greatly enhanced the productivity of data collection, in part because of their ability to generate and store new types and volumes of information or data, but also to cross-reference it with other types of data produced or collected elsewhere. Such developments provide the possibility that brand growth can be directed through processes of linking, adding, tagging and cross-referencing. For example, there are now quite well-established ways of measuring the 'engagement' of users with a website, using 'web analytics' tools that measure things like number of unique visitors, page views per visitor, time spent on site, total time spent per user, frequency of visits, depth of visits and 'conversions' (into sales). Tools include commercial proprietary devices such as Omniture and WebAnalytics, as well as the free service Google Analytics (<www.google.com/analytics>).

Brands are able to draw on this information to make themselves more valuable through their increased ability to intervene in and organize the types of social communication that unfold in electronic environments and to appropriate the information thus produced. With the rise of blogs and other social media, both as part of and beyond corporate and brand websites, the focus is now turning towards tools that can generate 'community insights' and measure, track and compare them, using 'community analytics'. So-called 'listening platforms', for example, allow brands to track discussions between users, identify key participants and even understand, albeit at a fairly simple level, the 'sentiments' being expressed. For example, Harvest Report Server 2.0, one of the key tools of this type, claims to 'deliver [. . .] value to your business by helping [you to] understand the value and sentiment of customer conversations . . . to analyze what they are saying and understand their tonalities' (<www.telligent.com/products/harvest-report-server>). It includes a 'dashboard' that provides scores on key indicators, as well as the 'data values' for particular dimensions of interaction and overall trends. Its 'sentiment detection' feature provides details about the 'overall tonality' of social media discussions on the site, identifying the key words or phrases producing the strongest positive or negative sentiment, as well as who is saying them (Lury and Moor, 2010).

The third approach to branding outlined here is that of Adam Arvidsson, whose analysis focuses directly on the economic and political implications of the relations between producers and consumers created by branding. His account is situated in relation to what he describes as 'informational capitalism', in which there is a blurring of the distinction between 'production' and 'consumption' that was central to industrial society. According to Arvidsson, informational capitalism involves: a blurring of work and leisure as a result of the extension of the capitalist production process to include phenomena that were formerly thought to belong to leisure, private life or the domain of circulation; an emphasis on an entrepreneurial production of a professional self; the development of an online economy, where flirtation, play and other forms of user interaction is what actually produces the content to which the sites in question sell access; and a new strategic importance of intellectual property rights and the appropriation and privatization of common resources, such as personal and genetic information and biodiversity. A brand does not refer to a simple commodity but to a virtual context for consumption; it stands for 'a specific way of using the object, a propertied form of life to be realized in consumption' (Arvidsson, 2005: 244).

At the heart of Arvidsson's analysis is the view that the workplace is no longer privileged as the place for the production of value: the direct exploitation of labour of workers is becoming less important as a source of profit, while the private exploitation of public or social knowledge is becoming more important. Branding is held up as a key example of this, since Arvidsson proposes that branding is a putting to work of communication through the mediatization of social life in general, and of consumption in particular. In order to develop this argument, Arvidsson emphasizes the historically changing environment of brands, notably the intensification of processes of mediation and re-mediation from as early as the middle of the twentieth century and intensifying in recent years. He points out that the distinction between advertising and media message is increasingly blurred. Examples of this blurring include the sponsorship of programmes by companies, advertorials in magazines and the use of product-placement in films. He also points out that advertising has lost (or perhaps never had much) capacity to persuade consumers; indeed, the industry's own research has undermined faith in the established linear sequential models of the communication process. At the same time, of course, there has been a continuing expansion and differentiation of television culture, and a growing use of home computers, video, computer games, the Internet and personal stereos. Earlier views of communication in the marketing industry tended to rely on the presupposition that consumers are more or less passive subjects to be moved by advertising through various behavioural stages, from product awareness to buying decision. But, Arvidsson says, marketers have increasingly become advocates of the view that consumers are active and reflexive.

In relation to this active, or reflexive, consumer, contemporary branding posits a different logic of value from that of the classic marketing approach: the 'semiotic logic of value' (Firat and Venkatesh, 1993, cited in Arvidsson, 2006). In this approach, *consumers value products according to the position they occupy in the flow of media culture*, and the relation between product, image and value has been reversed with the brand preceding the product. This shift is encapsulated in the description given by Phil Knight, the Nike CEO, that Nike is a marketing company and that its products are marketing tools. Furthermore, so Arvidsson argues, instead of a desire to keep up with the Joneses (a commonly used phrase that acknowledges the importance of what has been described sociologically as positional consumption), consumers are believed by brand managers to be more concerned with finding meaning in their lives (though a Bourdieusian analysis would suggest that the two cannot be separated). For example, British marketing expert John Grant suggests that the aim of 'the new marketing' is to seek to fill the 'great gaps of meaning that exist in people's life' and to propose brands as 'ideas that people can live by' (Grant, 1999: 15). Arvidsson concludes by saying that, 'Mediatized consumer goods have become a sort of medium by means of which new, less enduring and more "nomadic" forms of sociality can be constructed in response to the flexibility demanded by a transitory and complex environment' (2006: 77). So, for example, event-based marketing is now common and includes sponsoring existing music or arts events, as well as specially arranging events (Moor, 2003), such as, for example, Nike fun-runs and PlayStation club nights or art events.

It is communicative sociality, so Arvidsson argues, that underpins the new forms of value of what he calls informational capitalism. This

> The [advertising] agency's explicit concern with the affective dimensions of the person–product relationship has now become a central preoccupation of brand managers, especially within the fast-moving consumer goods industry . . . This preoccupation is succinctly formulated in the idea of Lovemarks. Lovemarks, according to Kevin Roberts, CEO Worldwide of Saatchi and Saatchi Advertising, are what represent the next step in the evolution of brands. Lovemarks are brands that are not simply respected and trusted, but loved . . . They signal an emotional connection and attachment to a brand that goes beyond reason – and for which a premium price can be charged. (Foster, 2007: 708)

is explicitly recognized by marketing and business studies proponents such as Prahalad and Ramaswamy, who argue that the 'interaction between the firm and the consumer is becoming the locus of value creation' (2004: 5). Communicative sociality is said to be encouraged by various kinds of brand events, including openings, launches, visits, specially arranged performances and happenings. As Arvidsson notes, this can result in the use of consumers as an external (and usually unpaid) form of both research and development and labour for a company.

Take the example of the Levi's 'Personal Pair'™ programme. This is a mass customization programme, introduced in 1995, in which a consumer's measurements are taken and entered into a computer. This information is sent directly to a factory and personally fitted jeans are produced and delivered on a pair-by-pair basis within two weeks, resulting in what Levi's describe as 'a genuine one-on-one relationship with our target consumers'. However:

> The programme is also important for another reason: size, style and colour preference details of each consumer can be stored and accessed, giving the company a wealth of valuable information about each Personal Pair consumer. Since these individuals tend to be some of the most motivated and loyal Levi's brand consumers, our ability to know who they are and what they want most provides us with a powerful way to ensure their continued engagement with the Levi's brand today and in the future. (Holloway, 1999: 71)

Consumers are here explicitly adopted as salespeople and as marketing tools.

Another much discussed example is the practice of cool-hunting and 'bro-ing' as developed by consultancies such as Sputnik, The L. Report and Bureau de Style. 'Bro-ing' is the name given to the practice of 'giving' prototype shoes and clothing to selected individuals in black inner-city neighbourhoods in New York, Philadelphia and Chicago by Nike marketers in order to evaluate their likely success (Klein, 2000: 72–5). In another example of the same strategy, in 1998, the Korean car manufacturer Daewoo hired 2,000 college students on 200 US campuses 'to talk up the cars to their friends' (Klein, 2000: 80). In another, some market researchers working for Nike asked schoolchildren to undertake research, by, for example, collecting and presenting evidence of 'their favorite place to hang out' (Klein, 2000: 94).

This stage in the development of branding has also contributed to the use of new techniques in retail management and retail design, 'theming', event-based and ambient-marketing sub-disciplines, in all of which the brand is staged as a performance or an event of some kind. This contributes to the development of reflexive environments or object worlds, the design of an environment to engage the whole human sensorium. So, for example, Niketowns are designed to encourage consumer activity in the space of the store: visitors are invited to try on shoes and clothing, test athletic equipment, watch videos, listen to music, and, in some stores, use an indoor basketball space. Other examples of dedicated retail stores that function as marketing spaces are the Sony showrooms that are located in global cities such as Tokyo, New York and Paris, all furnished with 'lifestyle settings' such as bedrooms, offices and lounges, in which consumers are encouraged to play with Sony products. 'Their behaviour and preferences are closely monitored by Sony staff. The showroom thus becomes a laboratory for analysing consumer reactions to different products. This information is passed on to Sony headquarters which then feeds into subsequent product research and development' (Julier, 2000: 106).

Some companies also attempt to create ties between consumers through social events. So, for example, Arvidsson notes that Harley Davidson (a brand also discussed by Holt) has been particularly successful in creating a feeling of community around the brand, defined by a particular 'biker ethos' where true biker status is contingent on participation in a branded Harley gathering. Motorola recently launched an interactive game called PartyMoto where users chat and SMS to acquire points from other users. These points eventually give them the community status required to enter the PartyMoto virtual nightclub, where they can assume a wide variety of characters.

Brand spaces – whether these be Nike or Prada superstore, or more mundane spaces like McDonald's or Starbucks – are designed to turn the physical environment itself into a branded context of action. The point here is to make consumers think of the brand as something that inspires loyalty, as a medium of communication.

More generally, as Michael Dell (of Dell computers) puts it, 'Our best customers aren't necessarily the ones that are the largest, the ones that buy the most from us, or the ones that require little help or service . . . Our best customers are those we learn the most from' (quoted in Mitchell, 2001: 230). Commentators such as Prahalad and Ramswamy propose that the roles of production and consumption, producer and consumer are converging in the co-creation of experiences that deliver 'unique' value to consumers. Others suggest that it is important to ask whether such co-creation is collaboration or co-option or even exploitation since, as Roberta Sassatelli puts it, 'modern consumers are asked to actively participate in the process of de-[and re-]commoditization, producing themselves as the source of value'.

> Value is: connecting with the world's passions.
> ('Creating New Value', *Coca-Cola Company 2002 Annual Report*, quoted in Foster, 2007: 708)

For Arvidsson, the purpose of such extended intervention is to make consumer practice add value to the brand. This can be done in two ways. First, the results of a relatively autonomous consumer practice can be appropriated and employed as an input into the actual production of the (next) branded commodity. Trend scouting is the example he gives of this. By means of ethnographic research and a network of informants, autonomous consumer innovations can rapidly be appropriated. The messaging practice among Japanese teenage 'thumb tribes' (*oyayubisoku*) contributed to developing the SMS function on Nokia and Sony phones. Through these and other cultural research techniques, he suggests, the everyday life of consumers is directly subsumed as a productive force.

> Video game code is deliberately left unlocked so that fans can rewrite and improve it. Boeing's new Dreamliner was designed in part in collaboration with 120,000 volunteers who signed up to help through the corporation's website. Facebook – a website based on user-generated content – is worth more than major manufacturing companies like Ford. (Mason, 2008: 4)

Second, contemporary brand management consists in providing and managing a context in which the productivity of consumers is likely to produce desirable experiences of, or relations to, the brand, that in turn reproduce and strengthen the standing of a desirable brand image. Such branded contexts are designed, he suggests, to anticipate a possible experience or relation, but they do not supply this as a ready-made object simply to be consumed. Rather, they presume productivity on the part of consumers. It is up to the consumer to fill in the blanks, to actually perform the value of the brand. One recent brand analyst describes this in terms of co-creation:

> rather than putting customers to work as more or less unskilled workers to further rationalize (Fordist) production processes and their focus on predictability, calculability, and efficiency, co-creation instead aspires to build ambiences that foster contingency, experimentation, and playfulness among consumers. (Zwick et al., 2008: 167)

Arvidsson puts it another way. He says brand management works with the freedom of the subject. The general point he is making is that brand management has become a matter of managing the productivity of consumer practices in ways that enhance brand value. Like many other forms of 'advanced liberal' governance; brands do not say 'You must!' but 'You may!' (Barry, 2001; Zizek, 1999). The 'use-value' of the brand to consumers consists in what they can make with it; what kind of person they can become with it, what kinds of social relations they can form around it. And what consumers 'just do' is what increases the exchange-value of the brand for brand managers and brand owners.

In this view, brand management is about managing investments of affect on the part of consumers – in the case of the beauty-care brand Dove, for example, the affect might be self-love and self-care – and

---

Over the past 100 or so years, the term 'brand' has undergone radical evolution from commodity, to product, to experience, to relationship, to this book's current usage – the interdependent living system of stakeholders. It's our view that a brand, rather than being an object of exchange, can be viewed as the sum total of relationships among stakeholders, or the medium through which stakeholders interact and exchange with each other. This dynamic is true for all stakeholders, not just for the stakeholder class we call 'consumers'. (Meyers, 2003: 23).

translating these into quantifiable estimates of attention that under-pin financial values, such as share prices (Arvidsson 2006: 73–4). For Arvidsson, consumers are contributing to brand equity: the communicative sociality of consumer activity – attention and affect – accumulated under the propertied symbol of the brand works as what he calls 'immaterial capital'. In other words, the 'surplus' value generated by branding is (at least in part) based on the 'surplus' sociality generated by consumers around the brand – a social relation, a shared meaning, an emotional involvement that was not there before:

> The source of brand value is thus the capacity on the part of consumers to create a social world through productive communication, to create a 'common' – in the sense of a shared resource – that gives substance to and 'realizes the promise' of the brand. In Maurizio Lazzarato's words, surplus value is based on the ability to produce surplus community. (2006: 87)

What Arvidsson is saying here is that in branding practices a greater amount of the value of commodities becomes based on activities that take place outside of the direct command of capital, in both self-organizing teams of contemporary knowledge-intensive workers and the productive practices of consumers.

One consequence of this concerns the way in which capital can control and realize economic value changes. One strategy adopted is to transform the nature of the consumer's relation to goods; as Robert Foster puts it, 'goods that consumers once owned are now effectively services that consumers lease on a continuing basis' (Foster, 2007: 719). The 'new economy', as he sees it, is not so much about the de-materialization of things into events, but the consequence of a shift from the permanent transfer of ownership to the ongoing rental of things: 'In buying branded goods, consumers pay again and again to recover the outcomes and means of their own productivity and subjectivity' (2007: 719).

At the same time the realization of economic value becomes increasingly linked to the imposition of technical standards or digital rights management technologies and intellectual property, including trademark, copyright and the laws of passing off (Coombe, 1998; Lury, 1993, 2004). Logos, for example, may be seen as a condensation of cultural capital or as image-properties. But while corporations are highly protective of the images that form the basis of this corporate cultural capital, they face a double-bind. On the one hand, the value of the logos depends upon their recognizability and thus requires constant use; on the other hand, the value can be dissipated by the logo's 'mis'-use. In order to protect their value, many corporations turn to the law courts. So, for example, the Disney Corporation is frequently involved in lawsuits to protect the exclusivity of its property rights, challenging the legitimacy of others to use its corporate cultural capital. It also adopts a whole set of procedures, including a prohibition against photography in the backstage of Disney World, to ensure that only copyright-perfect images are circulated for public consumption. In this way, the integrity of its logos is protected from uses that might undermine their potential to be realized as economic capital by Disney.

Nike's Air Force 1 is a basketball shoe that has been customized and re-released by the company themselves over 900 times since its launch in 1982. But this didn't stop 22 year-old Tokyo hip-hop DJ, Nigo, from creating his own version. Nigo . . . redesigned the Air Force 1 specifically for hip-hop fans, never intending it to be used as a basketball shoe . . . Nigo's fashion label, A Bathing Ape, which produces the shoes, is now a multimillion dollar streetwear brand with more than 16 stores in Japan, London and New York . . . There was a clear case of trademark infringement here, but Nike didn't sue Nigo, because it could see commercial value in what he was doing here. It recognized that his shoe wasn't detracting from the Air Force 1 brand, it was actually adding value. In music, good remixes make the original track more popular – the same thing was happening here. So instead of suing him, Nike looked at Nigo's remixed shoes, and created their own remixes in response, using a wider variety of materials and colours. They didn't view Nigo as a pirate, but as a competitor who pushed them to innovate. (Mason, 2008: 6)

Conclusion

The accounts presented above suggest that branding takes place in a context in which consumers' activities have become increasingly valuable for capital, and in which marketing has an expanded role in profiling this activity and feeding it back into the production process. Arvidsson focuses on the brand as a locus of new forms of valorization associated with informational capitalism, understood in terms of social communicativeness, that is, the ability of information to

---

More than a drugstore
Mexico's poor flock to discount chain for medical basics

By ELIZA BARCLAY
Houston Chronicle Foreign Service
    [. . .]
A long battle

In 1997, the [Mexican] Secretary of Health launched an effort to expand the market for generic equivalents of brand name drugs, which the multinational pharmaceutical firms like Eli Lilly and Roche resisted. At that point, those and other multinationals held 90 percent of Mexico's pharmaceutical market.

These multinationals waged a battle over patents for nearly a decade, but they were unable to restrict the dramatic growth of Farmacias Similares, which has reported a 420 percent jump in sales since 2000, according to the company.
    [. . .]
Despite their widespread use, [Farmacias Similares'] 'similar' drugs remain controversial. The secretary of health does not include any 'similar' generics in its basic catalog of drugs sold in public health institutions in Mexico and does not advocate their use. Mexico's pharmaceutical trade association, Canifarma, calls the generics sold at Farmacias Similares and other discount pharmacies 'interchangeable' because they don't have brand names. (<http://www.ontheroadin.com/baja/bajarvparks/mexico%20 news.htm>, accessed 7 April 2009)

---

be stored, networked, compiled and transferred. I situate the brand at the convergence of media and computing, suggesting that the brand communicates via an interface: which is able to both reveal and obscure, connect and separate producers and consumers. Moor makes the claim that the analysis of branding needs to look outside the economy as such, and consider the ways in which branding is being increasingly taken up by government and public bodies. All of these writers agree, however, that branding contributes to a new form of power and a new logic in consumer culture, one that operates in terms of an injunction not that you should, but that you may, or, as Andrew Barry (2001) describes it, a shift in the logic of discipline from 'Learn! You Must' to 'Discover! You May'. Baudrillard would describe this kind of brand power as obscene, while Bourdieu might

In July 2005, Internet news sites circulated stories about Sharad Haksar, a well-known commercial photographers based in the city of Chennai [India] . . . According to reports, Hindustan Coca-Cola beverages Private Ltd., a subsidiary of the Coca-Cola Company for whom Haksar had done work in the past, threatened Haksar with legal action on the grounds that he had caused '"incalculable" damage to the goodwill and reputation of the brand Coca-Cola' (Bhattacharya 2005). At issue was a large billboard that Haksar had placed in a busy area of Chennai. The billboard displayed a photograph of Haksar's that depicted a dry water-pump with four empty pots lined up next to it and waiting to be filled. In the background, painted white on a red wall, appear the words 'Drink Coca-Cola', the name of the soft drink written in its familiar, distinctive, and trademarked script.

  [. . .] The letter sent to Haksar by the law firm representing Hindustan Coca-Cola characterized the billboard as 'a deliberate attempt to bring disrepute to my client's global reputation built up by spending millions and millions of rupees and by its quality of product and service' (Bhattacharya 2005). Reputation – the public significance of the Coca-Cola brand – was thus unambiguously claimed as the exclusive creation and property of The Coca-Cola Company, regardless of the logical and material condition of reputation as an interactive or social process . . . So much for cocreating value. (Foster, 2007: 724)

describe it as obsequious. In all these accounts, there is an acknowledgement of the consumer as active, but the suggestion is that activity does not equal control: at the same time, the organization, valuation and ownership of this activity is becoming increasingly important as it is incorporated into a mediated economy.

[Hello Kitty] teaches us the need to focus not just on different tastes within a certain 'society'. . ., but also on diverse attitudes within the same individual. Such intra-subjective diversity is expressed, at least in the case of Hello Kitty, in two ways. The first is visible across generations. Through its marketing of Hello Kitty, Sanrio has made a concentrated effort to tie together within a single individual different modes of self-presentation that chronologically correspond to girlhood, female adolescence, and womanhood: 'cute', 'cool', and 'camp' . . .

A second type of intra-subjective diversity concerns ambivalent ideas held by the same individual about an item of pop culture synchronically (rather than chronologically). A notable number of individuals pointed out to me that though they do not really care for Hello Kitty, they feel they must act as if they do and 'take advantage of a ride (*binjô*, i.e. an opportunity)' in order to fit in . . . Not a few exchanges with correspondents went like this: 'So, since you dislike her so much, you don't buy any of her products, right?' Answer: 'Well, I don't like her, but perhaps I like her a little. I do have a Hello Kitty key chain and stationery.' (McVeigh, 2000: 226–7)

Head of Brand Management
Grade 7 – £48,360–£59,700

The Department for Work and Pensions is at the forefront of delivering the Government's social and economic agenda, affecting everyone within the UK. We combine pioneering policy work with delivery of essential services to the public. Helping individuals achieve their potential through employment and helping people prepare for later life are just two of our key aims. Communications is essential to achieving them.

We are looking for an outstanding Head of Brand Management to develop and deliver a brand strategy for the Department and its two delivery brands, the Pension, Disability and Carers Service and Jobcentre Plus.

This new role is a unique challenge and an excellent opportunity to help shape the future of brands that reach out to millions of people.

[. . .]

Closing date 15 September 2008
(Guardianjobs, Monday 12 September 2008, p. 11)

7

Consuming Ethics, or What Goes Around, Comes Around

Introduction

In chapter 2 it was noted that choice is often identified as a core value of contemporary consumer culture. What is usually meant is that *market* choice has become increasingly important. As Frank Trentmann puts it, the elevation of choice *as the right of a consumer rather than as the duty of a citizen* is tied to marketization (Slater and Tonkiss, 2001) and the politics of neo-liberalism (Harvey, 2005). In other words, what is being proposed is that the relation between the individual and the collective has come to be mediated by markets in more and more arenas of social life and that this is a key dimension of consumer culture.

Of course, as earlier chapters have indicated, many commentators insist that much of what is important about consumption is not addressed if there is too much of an emphasis on markets. Indeed, Miller goes so far as to suggest that studies of consumption need 'to rescue the humanity of the consumer from being reduced to a rhetorical trope in the critique of capitalism' (2001: 234). Nevertheless, a considerable amount of the literature on consumer culture focuses on marketization and the growth of a market society as the general political and moral environment in which individuals engage in consumption. As Barnett et al. put it:

> the historical development of systems of commodified social reproduction inevitably generated a set of questions about the relationship between how people want to live and how society should be organized. It is in this sense that consumption and consumerism are inherently 'ethical' or 'moral' realms of social practice. (Barnett et al., 2005: 26)

For this reason it is important to understand what a market is and what a market does in thinking about consumer choice.

In classical economy theory, market relations are anonymous and are, in principle, universal, that is, open to all. This has enabled representatives of neo-liberalism to claim that market relations support the freedom to choose and (global) democracy. But this formal universality (it is formal because not everyone is actually able to participate on the same terms) has enabled a paradoxical situation to emerge – one in which we are all, formally, free to choose, to choose who to be and how to be, and thus in some sense, removed from any sense of responsibility *to* or *for* others. This formal freedom also means that we are no longer the responsibility *of* others, for we have made our choice (and must lie in it!). But this only raises more questions. Can or should the exercise of choice be seen as an ethical act? Should it be linked to responsibility for ourselves and others? Or to responsibility for the environment? If it is to be so linked, how might consumer choice be exercised in such a way as to facilitate ethical decision-making? Or does choice become something other than choice – a decision, a duty, an obligation maybe – if it is linked not simply to selection between possibilities but to responsibility for the consequences of those selections? Can or should markets be organized to enable individuals as consumers to make responsible choices, and if so, how? Does it matter in what capacity we exercise the ability to choose? How do mechanisms of individual and collective choice differ? In short: what are the consequences of consumer choice for us as individuals or as (differently constituted kinds of) collectives?

The discussion of these and other questions is increasingly concerned with the implications of a dual process that Ronen Shamir describes in terms of 'the moralization of economic action and the economization of the political' (2008: 1). On the one hand, he argues, local, national and transnational authorities – including but not only those linked to the state – increasingly follow the logic of 'economic sustainability', while, on the other hand, commercial enterprises increasingly perform tasks that were once considered to be the exclusive concern of the state, or civil society. So, for example, business is held to be more routinely involved in the management of what were previously seen as 'externalities': companies develop community programmes, create executive positions to deal with human rights and install internal compliance systems – relating to green initiatives or equal opportunities – to enhance a 'value-oriented' culture both internally and in relation to multiple stakeholders.

Shamir points out that ideas about the moral corporation are spreading fast, giving the example of the growth of corporate social responsibility, often defined in relation to the claim that a company 'can do well by doing good' as a consequence of the growth of a 'market for virtue' (Vogel, 2006). But, Shamir argues, that responsibility is not confined to business: we are witnessing a move to neoliberal or economized 'responsibilization', a set of processes in which a whole variety of social actors are positioned to take responsibility for their actions. Significantly, for Shamir, responsibility – in contrast to obedience, or compliance with rules – implies care for one's duties and the application of values as a motivation for action. From Shamir's perspective, the effect of the dual processes of the economization of politics and the moralization of the economy is thus to dissolve the historically established distinction between economy and society.

This chapter and the next will consider this claim and outline some of the recent discussions of consumer culture that foreground these ethical and political questions and consider some of the historical and contemporary consumer movements that link consumption practices to a whole range of different kinds of politics.

Waste not, want not

It has become a common observation that rich nations consume – in the derogatory sense of use up – the rest of the world. This is not a new phenomenon; what is (relatively) new is the way in which this statement is formulated. On the one hand, this claim is now very often phrased in environmental terms: so, for example, it is frequently pointed out that consumption levels in Western Europe and North America exceed the bio-capacity – that is, not only the natural resources but also the waste-sink capacity – of their territorial reach, thus requiring a use of the resources and capacities of other parts of the world. On the other hand, what is also new is that the responsibility for this global and environmental inequity is awarded to individual consumers as a moral problem. As Gay Hawkins puts it, 'Before the emergence of environmentalism, the ethos of disposability framed waste as a technical rather than a moral problem, something to be administered by the most efficient and rational technologies of removal' (2006: 29).

Let's return to my bottle of . . . wine, or, since some time has passed, let's open a fresh one.

   . . . Now that I think about it, there must have been a jungle, a mountain range of externalities, currently obscured and invisible to me, that involved this object. That growing and fermenting of grapes . . . Topsoil loss, tractor exhaust, chemical fertilizer, insecticide sprays, the fuels involved in heating and distilling all that liquid . . . I'm not supposed to worry my pretty head about any of that, but you know something? I know that I am paying for it somehow. Those phenomena do impinge on me: legal, social, ethical, environmental, all of them. They're not pretty, and neither am I. They should inform my decision about whether I buy that bottle and integrate its contents into my body.

What goes around, comes around. (Sterling, 2005: 71, 72–3)

To consider the implications of this ethical address to consumers as individuals, let us consider the case of waste that Hawkins introduces. Waste – dirt, rubbish or matter out of place (Douglas, 1966) – is not, of course, unique to modern societies but a feature of all; what is of interest from a sociological point of view is what is regarded as waste and how it is treated. Recent histories of waste point to the role of the rise of an ethos of disposability in modern Euro-American cultures in providing the terms for distinctions between clean and dirty, useful and useless, and so on, and link it to the intensification of principles of efficiency, cleanliness and replaceability (Strasser, 1999; Hawkins, 2006). Strasser, for example, argues that the invention and use of a range of disposable paper products – including paper cups, straws and toilet paper – really began in the second half of the nineteenth century. But she notes the adoption of an ethos of disposability initially faced resistance as inefficient and wasteful. During the early twentieth century, however, the scope and scale of disposability was successfully extended and supplemented as economic rhetoric about efficiency and streamlined production entered the home, bringing with it an acceptance of the view that disposable things satisfied needs fast and effectively: 'Using disposable things was an indicator of one's commitment to new standards of cleanliness and efficiency. These objects conferred status on the user' (Hawkins, 2006: 27). But, so these writers argue, fundamental to this shift was also the expansion of mass consumption:

> The repetition of the ever new as ever the same, manifest in the fashion system and rapid turnover in style, shortens the life of the commodity and infuses person–thing relations with the logic of instant gratification. Commodity relations create a distinct temporality of desire that can be described as 'never present to the object but always future or past'. In other words, the pleasure of a purchase is always fleeting; the satisfaction of desire that the commodity promises is never complete. (Hawkins, 2006: 27)

The point being made here is that it was the drive to expand markets as part of the emergence of mass consumption that underpinned the ethos of disposability.

Certainly, waste is an increasingly visible problem: over the past thirty years, worldwide garbage output has increased rapidly, doubling in the USA alone (and the USA is responsible for 30 per cent of municipal wastes created by OECD member countries). Cans, bottles, boxes and wrappers now make up more than a third of US landfill space, and landfills are known to emit greenhouse gases, and leach hazardous chemicals and heavy metals into groundwater and soil. Waste incinerators emit 70 per cent of the world's dioxins, and pollute the air with toxic particulate matter and a host of gases that cause acid rain (Rogers, 2005). So, by most accounts, waste is an increasingly pressing problem.

Yet how is it that the consumer as individual is the one made to feel responsible for the problem of waste? To answer part of this question,

Heather Rogers traces the widespread use of the word 'litterbug' to
a 1950s 'Keep America Beautiful' campaign, partly financed by the
American Can Company, and notes that it was one of a number
of initiatives that put forward the view that individuals should take
responsibility for environmental degradation, with slogans such as:
'Packages don't litter, people do.' But, she asks, do individuals have a

> This bottle arrived in my possession seemingly stripped of conse-
> quences, but those consequences exist. Where is this bottle going,
> once I empty it? (Sterling, 2005: 74)

choice in the wastes they generate, and, in answer, redirects attention
to the ways in which processes of bringing goods to market, along
with the use of promotion, have contributed to the growth in packaging, describing this material as 'garbage waiting to happen'. In short,
Rogers argues that garbage is not a mere by-product that can easily
be dealt with by individuals as consumers. Instead, she says, waste is
designed into the workings of modern capitalism – a market system
that pathologically wastes resources. But what are the implications of
such a critique for making ethical consumer choices?

Consumer activism

There is a long history to consumer activism, in which consumers
have taken political action – individually and collectively, sometimes
in cooperation with producers and sometimes in opposition to them.
Tim Lang and Yiannis Gabriel provide an historical and sociological analysis of consumer movements as emerging in four waves:
cooperative consumers; value-for-money consumers; Nadarism; and
alternative consumers. Their aim is to highlight those 'people
and movements setting out to promote the rights, consciousness and
interests of either all or particular groups of consumers' (2006: 39).
They point out the waves they identify parallel the history of industrialization. So, for example, the Cooperative Movement – the prime
example of Lang and Gabriel's first wave of consumer activism – took
off in its modern form in Rochdale, in north-west England, 1844, at
the height of industrialization in the UK. Its founding principle was
'self-help by the people' and it made no distinction between members
as consumers and as producers. Cooperation was put forward as an
alternative principle to the competition of capitalism. The movement
has not disappeared, but has grown and diversified: in loose terms,
the cooperative movement is one of the largest organized segments
of civil society across the world – in the fields of health, housing and
banking among others. Cooperative communities are now widespread, with one of the largest being the Mondragon Cooperative
Corporation in the Basque Country in Spain. There are 700 million
people signed up to co-ops in more than 100 countries.

The second wave of consumer activism identified by Lang and Gabriel is the emergence of 'value-for-money' consumer groups, which emerged in a modern form in the 1930s, but built upon US consumer initiatives in the late nineteenth and early twentieth centuries, such as the National Consumers League which had sixty-four branches in twenty states in 1903. Initially, such groups were focused on limiting the power of emergent powerful corporations, but gradually transformed into organizations that sought to enable consumers to get the best from the market, rather than trying to undermine the market through cooperative action or political agitation and lobbying. More recent organizations that can be considered in this way include the UK Consumers' Association. This association aims to make the market more efficient, championing the role of the consumer within it. This is conceptualized in terms of helping the consumer make the right choice by providing independent information about products and services, as indicated by the title of its magazine, *Which?* This had a 700,000 subscriber list in the mid-1990s. The association continues but it has declined somewhat more recently, in part because it faces increased competition in advising the consumer from a welter of consumer websites, but also because of its relative conservatism when set alongside third and fourth waves of consumer activism.

The third wave described by Lang and Gabriel is largely specific to the USA: Naderism. The namesake of this movement is Ralph Nader, who helped expose the failings of the car industry in a campaign called 'Unsafe at Any Speed', in 1965. Nadar went on to set up the Center for Study of Responsive Law and the Project for Corporate Responsibility in 1969. By the 1990s there were twenty-nine organizations under the Nader umbrella whose common concerns were a distrust of corporations, a defence of the individual, a demand that the state protect its citizens, and an appeal for Americans to be citizens not just consumers. This movement did not really get taken up in other countries, which have instead seen a series of alternative campaigns that comprise Lang and Gabriel's fourth wave. These began to emerge slowly in Europe in the 1970s and accelerated in the 1980s. Green consumerism was initially the most influential of these campaigns in both Europe and North America, but the early 2000s has seen the growth of so-called ethical consumption, which will be discussed in more detail below. While there is no single organization or campaign heading up this movement, Lang and Gabriel describe it in terms of a reaffirmation of the moral dimension of ethical choice. While Lang and Gabriel's account of the history of ethical consumption is widely shared, it should be noted that there is a long history of the state calling upon the citizen to act ethically as a consumer alongside these civil, voluntary and campaigning groups. Moreover, it is now not only alternative or third-sector organizations that call into being 'the consumer' as a moral and political subject, but also corporations.

The case of Fairtrade is especially interesting here, because it functions as a brand itself in many respects (see fairtrade.org. uk; ptree.co.uk; pan-uk.org; ethicalconsumer.org). The Fairtrade Foundation, a charitable organisation, does not produce goods, but promotes the use of a Fair Trade mark or label (this, like many other logos, is a graphic representation of a person) for products which meet standards of fair trade. It was set up by CAFOD, Christian Aid, New Consumer, Oxfam, Traidcraft Exchange, and the World Development Movement, who were later joined by the Women's Institute (Britain's largest women's organisation). Sales of fair trade foods have grown rapidly in recent years. Fairtrade brands now account for 14% of the total UK roast and ground coffee market, and there are more and more products available under this label: sugar, wine, honey, fruits, juices, snacks and biscuits, chilli peppers and meat as well as tea, coffee and bananas. The Co-op, Safeway and Sainsbury's supermarkets have even started their own fair trade lines, while Starbucks and Costa Coffee also have Fairtrade sub-brands. World-wide sales of fair trade products are thought to be close to $300 million a year (Vidal, 2003: 8; quoted in Lury, 2004: 138)

Ethical consumption

Over the last two or three decades, there has been a significant increase in the number and visibility of initiatives and movements campaigning around such issues as fair trade, corporate social responsibility, green and sustainable consumption – the fourth wave described by Lang and Gabriel above (see also Nicholls and Opal, 2005; Connolly and Prothero, 2008; Littler, 2009). These include fair trade or ethical finance or trading organizations (for example, Oxfam, Traidcraft, Body Shop); lobby groups (for example, the Soil Association); consumer boycott campaigns (for example, anti-Nestlé, Stop Esso); and 'no-logo' anti-globalization campaigns (for

From: "Personalize, NIKE iD"
To: "Jonah H. Peretti"
Subject: RE: Your NIKE iD order o16468000

Your NIKE iD order was canceled for one or more of the following reasons:
1) Your Personal iD contains another party's trademark or other intellectual property
2) Your Personal iD contains the name of an athlete or team we do not have the legal right to use
3) Your Personal iD was left blank. Did you not want any personalization?
4) Your Personal iD contains profanity or inappropriate slang, and besides, your mother would slap us.

If you wish to reorder your NIKE iD product with a new personalization please visit us again at www.nike.com

Thank you, NIKE iD

From: "Jonah H. Peretti"
To: "Personalize, NIKE iD"
Subject: RE: Your NIKE iD order o16468000

Greetings,

My order was canceled but my personal NIKE iD does not violate any of the criteria outlined in your message. The Personal iD on my custom ZOOM XC USA running shoes was the word "sweatshop."

Sweatshop is not:
1. another's party's trademark,
2. the name of an athlete,
3. blank, or
4. profanity.

I choose the iD because I wanted to remember the toil and labor of the children that made my shoes. Could you please ship them to me immediately.

Thanks and Happy New Year, Jonah Peretti

From: "Personalize, NIKE iD"
To: "Jonah H. Peretti"

Subject: RE: Your NIKE iD order o16468000

Dear NIKE iD Customer,

Your NIKE iD order was canceled because the iD you have chosen contains, as stated in the previous e-mail correspondence, "inappropriate slang." If you wish to reorder your NIKE iD product with a new personalization please visit us again at nike.com

Thank you, NIKE iD

From: "Jonah H. Peretti"
To: "Personalize, NIKE iD"
Subject: RE: Your NIKE iD order o16468000

Dear NIKE iD,

Thank you for your quick response to my inquiry about my custom ZOOM XC USA running shoes. Although I commend you for your prompt customer service, I disagree with the claim that my personal iD was inappropriate slang. After consulting Webster's Dictionary, I discovered that "sweatshop" is in fact part of standard English, and not slang.
   The word means: "a shop or factory in which workers are employed for long hours at low wages and under unhealthy conditions" and its origin dates from 1892.
So my personal iD does meet the criteria detailed in your first email.

Your web site advertises that the NIKE iD program is "about freedom to choose and freedom to express who you are." I share Nike's love of freedom and personal expression. The site also says that "If you want it done right . . . build it yourself." I was thrilled to be able to build my own shoes, and my personal iD was offered as a small token of appreciation for the sweatshop workers poised to help me realize my vision.
I hope that you will value my freedom of expression and reconsider your decision to reject my order.

Thank you, Jonah Peretti

From: "Personalize, NIKE iD"
To: "Jonah H. Peretti"
Subject: RE: Your NIKE iD order o16468000

Dear NIKE iD Customer,

Regarding the rules for personalization it also states on the NIKE iD web site that "Nike reserves the right to cancel any personal iD up to 24 hours after it has been submitted." In addition, it further explains: "While we honor most personal iDs, we cannot honor every one.

Some may be (or contain) other's trademarks, or the names of certain professional sports teams, athletes or celebrities that Nike does not have the right to use. Others may contain material that we consider inappropriate or simply do not want to place on our products. Unfortunately, at times this obliges us to decline personal iDs that may otherwise seem unobjectionable. In any event, we will let you know if we decline your personal iD, and we will offer you the chance to submit another." With these rules in mind, we cannot accept your order as submitted. If you wish to reorder your NIKE iD product with a new personalization please visit us again at www.nike.com

Thank you, NIKE iD

From: "Jonah H. Peretti"
To: "Personalize, NIKE iD"
Subject: RE: Your NIKE iD order o16468000

Dear NIKE iD,

Thank you for the time and energy you have spent on my request. I have decided to order the shoes with a different iD, but I would like to make one small request. Could you please send me a color snapshot of the ten-year-old Vietnamese girl who makes my shoes?

Thanks,
Jonah Peretti

example, against Nike, Gap, McDonald's, etc.) (Barnett et al., 2005: 26–7). In short, ethical consumption emerges in a broad spectrum of practices, organizations and initiatives, and addresses a wide range of issues, including working conditions, fair trade, animal welfare, human rights and environmental concerns.

It is also important to recognize the role of an increasingly reflexive economy (Callon 1998; Callon, Meadel and Rabehariosa, 2005) in such developments. Take the case of American Apparel, for example. This is a privately owned company that produces all its goods under one roof and that promotes itself as both 'brand-free' and 'sweatshop-free'. Liz Moor and Jo Littler (2008) argue, however, that it should be seen as an example of a reflexive company insofar as it represents itself as both engaging with popular knowledge of the problems of post-Fordism and as a partial solution to those problems. They point to the way in which the company deploys a series of material, symbolic and visual props to create an effect of openness and transparency which inverts the sweatshop mode of production by rendering visible aspects of production usually kept out of view, and by representing itself as a 'community of workers and consumers'. They note that this relates to trends emphasizing the 'traceability' of products as well as to more general use of notions of 'provenance' as a marketing tool. They also emphasize the ways in which the company establishes a reflexive environment for consumer choice. So, for example, they describe the large glass panels at the front of stores, the 'amateur' photography on its walls, the see-through plastic bags in which customers carry their purchases, the black and white lettering of the logo, as well as its unfussy sans serif font. The walls of stores, they note, are typically whitewashed and clothes displayed on long, free-standing clothes rails and IKEA-style shelving: 'These design features give the impression that one is not in a shop so much as a warehouse or art gallery, which in turn creates the sense of a comparatively unmediated encounter with the product' (2008: 705). They suggest that in consequence 'informational' functions of transparency become blurred with its emotional or aesthetic ones: 'By encoding an aesthetic of transparency in these ways, the brand appears to offer itself up to an unprecedented level of consumer scrutiny, although in fact what is available for scrutiny, and what remains hidden, is very highly controlled' (2008: 705–6). They conclude by suggesting that American Apparel is an example of a company whose activity can be seen as simultaneously extending and exploiting the terrain of ethical consumption by affording a very particular environment for forms of consumer reflexivity.

A number of writers have sought to describe and explain the fourth wave of consumer activism in other ways. One point a number of writers make is that this wave goes beyond a 'consumer rights' focus, which emphasizes the right to safety, the right to information, the right to choose, and the right to be heard and so on (Sassatelli, 2007: 184). As Sassatelli points out, such rights-based approaches adopt an atomistic, individualistic notion of choice, and frequently employ commoditized information-type measures, tools and devices that follow an instrumental logic. In contrast, many 'alternative', 'ethical' or 'critical' modes of consumption do not assume that choice is always good and simply needs to be exercised more carefully or even that choice should be a private issue. As she puts it, 'the dominant attitude is not that of the renunciation of consumption . . . but that of a re-evaluation of what it is to consume' (2007: 186–7).

It is worth acknowledging the importance of the term 'ethical' at this point, rather than, for example, either 'political' or 'moral'. Jo Littler suggests that 'ethical' has emerged as the favoured term because it appears to be less prescriptive as a consequence of its emphasis on modes of conduct and draws attention to a notion of 'mutual social responsibility' without enforcing a single morality (Littler, 2009: 5). It is also suggested that it is a sufficiently general term to include both what are called deontological approaches, that is, approaches which emphasize people acting according to their moral stances by doing the 'right' thing, and so-called consequentialist approaches, that is, approaches that privilege the 'good' done, that is, focus on the outcomes and consequences of actions (Barnett and Land, 2007).

A further point that a number of writers are keen to make is that attention to 'ethical consumption' should not obscure the complex ethical dimensions of ordinary consumption. For example, rather than assuming that ethical consumption is a self-reflexively conscious practice set off against non-ethical consumption, Barnett et al. (2005) are keen to emphasize that everyday consumption practices are always already shaped by and help shape certain sorts of ethical dispositions. They say that everyday consumption routines are *ordinarily ethical*. As they put it, if 'ethical' is taken 'to refer to the activity of constructing a life by negotiating practical choices about personal conduct, then the very basics of routine consumption – a concern for value for money, quality, and so on – can be seen to presuppose a set of specific learned ethical competencies' (2005: 28).

Similarly, Kim Humphery (2009) identifies the ethical dimension of everyday consumption practices as a central paradox of consumption in industrial and post-industrial societies: namely, that alongside a seemingly unstoppable propensity to consume in many industrial and postindustrial societies there often exists a powerful collective distaste for consumerism. He describes a variety of different processes feeding into this paradox. These include high levels of non-commodified activity, which exist alongside increasing consumer expenditure. And here he points to a multiplicity of alternative economic activities and spaces, beyond or in a contradictory relationship with a profit-oriented consumer capitalism, many of which are informed by the values of subsistence, care and community. He also points out that, faced with an imperative to become consumers, people often 'stand back' from the market, feel anger at its encroachments, refuse to participate in it or, at the very least, question its relevance to other aspects of their lives. He describes this as an everyday process of imagining an 'outside-ness' in relation to a potentially dominating consumer culture, of distancing at the level of thought, if not always of practice.

> An innovative mobile phone app could create a new generation of ethical shoppers by allowing them to check a company's social responsibility rating and environmental credentials.
>
> Barcoo, developed by a group of young Germans, allows customers to point their phones at the barcode on products in shops and find out information such as how environmentally friendly a company is and even how it treats its staff. (Connolly, 2010: 17)

Significantly, Humphery also attends to actual consumer practices, and is not willing to dismiss these practices in terms of manipulation, addiction or pathology of some kind or other. Instead, he puts forward an understanding of consumer practices in terms of three interlinked processes: enforcement, enablement and routinization. What he means by the first of these, enforcement, is that individuals are systematically impelled to live, work, consume and over-consume in certain ways; that is, the options available to individuals as subjects of capitalist economies are limited. So, for example, he suggests that we are all, to varying degrees, compelled to work at certain jobs and for certain hours, to shop in various places, to consume various kinds of products and services, and to organize our lives in particular ways, and suggests that such constraint is collectively lived and evaded. But enforcement is not the only reason he gives for our participation in consumer culture: participation, he says, is enabling. Commodities facilitate life, functionally and symbolically. He believes the role of commodities as objects of desire and pleasure is overstated in many accounts, but that nevertheless it is important to recognize the communicative uses and embodied satisfactions of commodity. Nor, he suggests, can we deny that life is essentially material; it is necessary, he argues, to confront the 'thingy-ness' of material commodities themselves. The third process he identifies is routinization. Routine – or habit – is crucial, he says, in comprehending how contemporary everyday life is structured in ways that continually commodify. In large part routinization works through the socio-technological systems and material objects with which Western individuals in particular must interact. These systems and objects frame everyday practice; in a sense, he says, they have an agency to direct us to certain forms of consumption which then become simply routine, habitual aspects of living – and which lead individuals on to further types and levels of commodity acquisition and use. Here, he refers to the work of Elizabeth Shove, who, as will be discussed in chapter 9, shows that consumption occurs in systems that continually develop, and that in the process reshape particular conventions and expectations of, for example, cleanliness, comfort or convenience across generations.

Once the ordinary ethical dimension of consumption is recognized, the key issue is how that dimension becomes the object of explicit policies, campaigns and practices of 'ethical consumption'. Or, to make this point another way, it becomes important to focus on how ethical consumption campaigns actively aim to transform everyday ethical consumption practices in some way or other. As Barnett et al. put it, 'Individual dispositions to choose . . . are worked up, governed, and regulated by an array of actors who make possible certain forms of individualised conduct' (2005: 29). And, as they go on to point out, attempts to influence people's consumption habits depend on a series of highly mediated strategies for governing complex *assemblages* of individual conduct, collective action, technologies, spaces and discourses.

Amongst these strategies, Barnett et al. point to the key role of campaigning organizations, policy-makers, and businesses that explicitly aim to facilitate the adoption of ethical consumption practices by consumers. They suggest that these bodies have developed strategies that can be thought of as so many devices for turning 'oughts' into 'cans'. They further argue that such strategies have resulted in the emergence of a particular form of governing the self in and through consumption. For Barnett et al., strategies of ethical consumption are thus also ambivalently implicated in a broader process of generalizing a particular model of what it is to be ethical: 'This model combines an emphasis upon individual choice with a sense of responsibility to others, so that ethical action is easily defined in terms of a choice made to accept a widened scope of responsibility towards both human and non-human others *and to act upon that acceptance through one's identity as a consumer*' (2005: 30; my emphasis). The point they are making here is that strategies of 'ethical consumption' do not simply bring to light already existing ethical dispositions but also invent new ones.

The example Barnett et al. focus on to explore how ethical consumption is actively brought into being is the organization Traidcraft, which describes itself as 'the leading fair trade organization in the UK'. The initial sales of the organization's products of around £1 million in 1982 increased to over £12 million in 2003, with further rapid growth in more recent years, as the fair trade movement itself has grown. Traidcraft was, for example, a leading member of the consortium that launched CafeDirect, which in turn was followed by TeaDirect, CocoDirect and Geobars. The branding of these products emphasizes the strong ethical intention inscribed in their development – to cut out unfair trading by 'middlemen' through 'direct' connections that link up across different spaces, thereby articulating a caring for 'distant others'. Barnett et al. note that individuals are encouraged to be involved in the activities of this organization in various ways, including: the display of products as the credentials of fair trade consumerism in the home and workplace; the giving and receiving of products and cards, especially at Christmas; and the organization of and participation in special events at which Traidcraft products may be sold, such as arts and crafts exhibitions, cookery demonstrations, school fairs, and church events (Barnett et al., 2005: 39–40).

Barnett et al. make a number of interesting points about this case of ethical consumption. On the one hand, they suggest that organizations such as Traidcraft that encourage different kinds of participation are more effective than strategies that simply provide information about a product. Information-based strategies, they suggest, contribute to a set of oppositions between active consumers and passive recipients, lead to an excessive sense of responsibility (since individuals cannot easily act on the information provided), and have the effect of flattening power relations by presenting responsibility as falling equally on individualized actors. As they put it:

> There are two related problems with this model of moral agency. On the one hand, by focussing on the responsibilities of individuals (rather than various collective actors) . . . it produces an excessively stringent account of ethical conduct. On the other hand, by privileging knowledge as the key factor motivating responsible conduct, it tends

to underplay a range of other considerations that might play a role in shaping people's dispositions towards others, and the world around them. (2005: 25)

In contrast, they argue, Traidcraft articulates an ethical obligation ('I ought to'), *and* provides a practical means of translating this into actual conduct ('I can do'). Importantly, it also allows a narrow sense of individualized ethical responsibility to be transformed into a practice of collective, political responsibility.

On the other hand, so Barnett et al. argue, the activities of Traidcraft also display a basic contradiction between the means and ends of ethical consumption insofar as the practical devices through which an ostensibly universal responsibility is made possible are also a means of socially and culturally differentiating certain classes of people from others. This differentiation arises since the conditions of access to Traidcraft products, occasions and activities is socio-economically and culturally uneven. In their analysis, the power relations that are part of ethical consumption practices such as those of Traidcraft rely upon deploying distinctively cultural forms of 'self-government', such as practices aimed at the cultivation of moral consciousness, of self-control and of self-display. Such forms of moral agency are not natural, so they suggest, but are rather themselves characteristic of class-based neo-liberal forms of (self-)governmentality.

Similar arguments are put forward by a number of other writers. So, for example, Paul Cloke and others (2005) develop the term 'moral selving', and Jo Littler refers to 'sanctimonious shopping', to point to those consumption practices adopted self-consciously by individuals to enhance their moral standing and show their responsibilities to others. Daniel Miller observes that commodities are becoming a medium for objectifying and performing values and morals (1998), while Connolly and Prothero (2008) emphasize the links to processes of individualization and the growth of feelings of individualized responsibility. In other words, it is suggested that even ethical consumption is implicated in the politics of neo-liberalism to the degree that the display of an ethical self is becoming an imperative; a kind of 'compulsory individuality', it has to be displayed as a sign of social responsibility, self-governance and morality (Skeggs, 2005). Alternatively, however, it can be argued that the growth of grassroots community groups, local farmers' markets (Seyfang, 2009) and downshifting trends (Ghazi and Jones, 2004) go beyond this emphasis on the individual, and challenge the individualizing implications of consumer choice mediated by the market, creating new forms of collective ethical activity.

This is not a plastic bag

The question of exactly what is involved in ethical consumption has been explored by other writers too. Let us return to the case of waste, and in particular plastic bags. In China, plastic bags are known as white pollution, while South Africans call them the 'national flower', and in India sacred cattle choke on them. In a number of countries they have recently becomes the focus of a variety of consumer activism initiatives.

> Figures from Wrap, the government's waste and resources programme, show that whereas 870m single-use plastic bags were handed out in the UK in May 2006, the figure for May 2009 was down to 450m – a 48% reduction, and 4,740 tonnes to send to a landfill against 8,890 tonnes in May 2006. (Vidal, 2009: 9)

Gay Hawkins (2009) draws out two contrasting approaches to the politics of plastic bags. First, she discusses the politics and ethics of the campaigns to eliminate plastic bags that have become a common fixture in countries where environmentalism is highly organized. She describes such 'Say No' campaigns as using a range of scientific information about environmental impacts to frame plastic bags as hazardous, expose their material afterlife and extend the ethical imagination of the shopper. She notes that these campaigns reveal 'disposability' as a myth, and establish a network of connections and obligations between ordinary habits and the purity and otherness of nature. In this way, she says, the bag becomes capable of generating not only environmental concern but also guilt. Guilt, she argues, following the work of Foucault, is the product of a range of techniques of the self that have come to constitute distinct styles of subjectivity. Along the same lines as Barnett et al., she argues that such campaigns assume that to be a consumer now means cultivating particular modes of reflexivity. It means developing special ethical techniques and capacities and making the self into an object of ethical attention. She writes:

Say No campaigns run by governments or environmental NGOs show how plastic bags have become implicated in processes of moral self-regulation and conscience, how circuits of guilt, self-reproach and virtue have become enfolded with ordinary acts of shopping. And how, in activating techniques of conscience, the plastic bag participates in shaping an environmentally aware subject. (2009)

> Britain has become a nation of guilty greens – people who admit they do not do enough to fight climate change – according to a Guardian/ICM poll . . . While almost everyone claims to have made some effort to live environmentally-friendly lives, almost two-thirds also say they could do more. (Glover, 2009: 1)

In her view, such campaigns are important but have serious limits. She draws on the work of William Connolly (2005) to argue that conscience and other code-driven moral techniques are crude, blunt tools for coping with the world. The tendency of such campaigns to ground moral and political actions in categorical imperatives of human mastery and self-certainty makes them blind to the ambiguous and disturbing aspects of many choices. The moral weight of codes can too easily turn obligation into duty, guilt and resentment. In contrast to these approaches, she puts forward an alternative that proposes that the 'materiality' of plastic bags always exceeds moral framings. What does she mean by this?

Hawkins develops an approach in which subjects and objects are not assumed as fixed oppositions but as products of their relating, as co-constituted, a view that she says is at odds with the assumption of human mastery and self-certainty that is implicit in neo-liberal forms of governmentality. Her argument is that while she might agree that the world would be a better place without plastic bags, the moral imperative to refuse them denies the complexity of contexts in which they are encountered and the diversity of responses bags generate:

> There is no possibility that plastic bags might move us or enchant us or invite simple gratitude for their mundane convenience; that they might prompt us to behave differently . . . By letting plastic bags 'have their say' . . ., it is possible to open up a different line of thinking about the relations between ethics, politics and the environment. (2009; available at: <http://www.australianhumanitiesreview.org/archive/Issue-May2009/hawkins.htm>)

To illustrate this possibility, Hawkins focuses on a recent advertisement for Adidas in which a small boy roams through an unidentified

South American slum collecting plastic bags. He pulls them out of garbage bins, he grabs them blowing about in the wind, collecting as many bags as possible. Finally, he is shown crawling through a fence into an open space and fashioning something out of the bags: a football, made by bundling bag after bag into a sphere. As he kicks his plastic bag creation triumphantly into the air, the Adidas logo comes up with the slogan – 'nothing is impossible'. Of course, she observes, it might be interesting – and some would say appropriate – to carry out an analysis which explores the ways in which the advertisement mystifies or obscures relations of global inequality for the purposes of brand image. But instead Hawkins chooses to focus upon the representation of the material capacities of the bags as an example of how the animation of things in advertisements can show the liveliness of matter. So she says: 'These plastic bags are not inert environmental hazards nor are they appealing to conscience. They don't problematize nature or bad habits. They simply make us aware of how plastic bags can be both resistant and useful.' What is important about this approach from her point of view is that unlike 'Say No' campaigns, the plastic bags of her analysis are not moralized intermediaries prompting techniques of conscience, but a practical resource for invention and innovation. As she puts it: 'The reality they perform resonates with everyday experiences of plastic bags: their mundane convenience, their light and malleable form, their sticky persistence.'

The first mode of political intervention – the 'Say No' campaigns – give what Hawkins calls 'excessive primacy' to humans and the subject–object distinction. The only power attributed to the bag in this analysis is to remind humans of their political agency, to confirm their capacity to act on a world of objects and non-human stuff 'out there', to say 'No' to plastic bags. This is the freedom to choose (or to reject), a kind of agency Hawkins identifies with the formation of the neo-liberal subject. She argues that there is a valorization of voluntarism in this approach in which things only matter to the extent they reveal human will and mastery. In the second analysis, the bags are an example of the complex entanglements of humans with matter. This approach, she suggests, has the potential to call up a different kind of ethics; the representation of the possibility of 'cooperation' between the boy and plastic bags short-circuits guilt and makes human subjects open to 'the thing-power potentiality of plastic materiality'. Central to Hawkins's analysis is the proposal that matter – things, stuff, maybe even waste – can disrupt normal moral codes and reveal other affordances and realities. She writes: 'For it is precisely in these minor practices, like being responsive to the plastic

Introduced just over 25 years ago, the ugly truth about our plastic bag addiction is that society's consumption rate is now estimated at well over **500,000,000,000 (that's 500 billion)** plastic bags annually, or almost **1 million per minute.**

Single-use bags made of high-density polyethylene (HDPE) are the main culprit. Once brought into existence to tote your purchases, they'll accumulate and persist on our planet for up to 1,000 years.

Australians alone consume about 6.9 billion plastic bags each year, that's 326 per person. According to Australia's Department of Environment, an estimated 49,600,000 annually end up as litter.

In 2001, Ireland used 1.2 billion disposable plastic bags, or 316 per person. An extremely successful plastic bag tax, or PlasTax, introduced in 2002 reduced consumption by 90%.

According to *The Wall Street Journal*, the U.S. goes through 100 billion plastic shopping bags annually. An estimated 12 million barrels of oil is required to make that many plastic bags.

Four out of five grocery bags in the US are now plastic.

Plastic bags cause over 100,000 sea turtle and other marine animal deaths every year when animals mistake them for food.

In a dramatic move to stem a tide of 60,000 metric tons of plastic bag and plastic utensil waste per year, Taiwan banned both last year.

According to the BBC, only 1 in 200 plastic bags in the UK are recycled.

According to the WSJ Target, the second-largest retailer in the U.S., purchases 1.8 billion bags a year.

As part of Clean Up Australia Day, in *one day* nearly 500,000 plastic bags were collected. Unfortunately, each year in Australia an estimated 50,000,000 plastic bags end up as litter.

The average family accumulates 60 plastic bags in only four trips to the grocery store.

Each high quality reusable bag you use has the potential to eliminate an average of 1,000 plastic bags over its lifetime. The bag will pay for itself if your grocery store offers a $.05 or $.10 credit per bag for bringing your own bags.

Windblown plastic bags are so prevalent in Africa that a cottage industry has sprung up *harvesting* bags and using them to weave hats, and even bags. According to the BBC one group harvests 30,000 per month.
(<http://www.reusablebags.com/facts.php?id=4&display=print>, accessed 27 August, 2009)

bag suggesting that you jump high, that bags can shift perception and suggest experiments with new practices, or make us think again about our relations with them.' She wants to try to acknowledge the ethical significance of rubbish without generating moral righteousness or resentment. She also recognizes the value of drawing attention to the different kinds of ethical affordances offered by different kinds of things, different materialities; not all things have the same ethical potential in the same way.

What is being pointed to here is a consumer ethics – perhaps a politics – in which the socio-technical networks that form around commodities variously enable consumers to address matters of concern (Latour and Weibel, 2005) and to constitute themselves as publics. As Robert Foster (2007) notes, such publics often emerge around 'corporate externalities' – that is, the costs and unwanted consequences of a corporation's doing business, including, in the case of plastic bags, environmental issues.

This study by Hawkins is part of what have variously been described as object-centred or at least object-oriented approaches, and includes the work of Michael, Knorr Cetina and others, discussed in chapters 2 and 3. These approaches start from the assumption that it is helpful to consider the role of objects and the environment when considering the question of whether and how individuals make choices and typically investigate subject–object relations, without assigning specific capacities to one or the other. A second example of this approach – Noortje Marres's study of the use of electricity meters as part of green politics (2009) – will also be discussed here.

Marres starts by asking the question: 'Why would one let a smart electricity meter into one's home?' As she notes, a host of freelance writers, environmentalists and technology enthusiasts have taken it upon themselves in recent years to provide extensive answers to this question on the Web and in other publicity media. Most of them are careful to note the advantages and disadvantages of this household addition, pointing out the potential disquiet caused by a sizeable display in the living room that provides constant updates of money spent and CO2 emitted as a result of routine domestic activities, such as boiling the kettle or watching the television. But, on the whole, she notes, these writers tend to praise smart meters for their ability to inform people *in an engaging way*. 'When people can see how much energy and money they are saving when they switch off the TV rather than leaving it on standby, they immediately become more engaged in the whole issue of energy efficiency' (<http://news.bbc.co.uk/1/hi/sci/tech/4754109.stm>).

Marres argues that in such practices smart meters are being self-consciously deployed as devices of political engagement. Thus, while smart electricity meters could be criticized for keeping people's attention focused on 'little things in the household', such as how much energy their toaster uses, they are also, in the blogs she studied, ascribed the ability to involve people in large and complex issues. But Marres does not presume the nature of this engagement; instead, she explores what it involves and finds that people ascribe to these devices the ability, not just to 'inform' them about domestic energy use, but to turn a familiar domestic setting into an interesting place.

What interests Marres here is the way in which these accounts indicate a fusing of the activities of political involvement and material entanglement. So she notes that objects such as smart electricity meters have the capacity to disrupt the distinction between being involved and being merely implicated, and in doing so, they complicate our understanding of the relation between knowing, choosing, having and doing. In this sense, they disrupt the taken-for-granted terms of political involvement as one of a subject who is a rational and autonomous individual and challenge the conventional understanding of objects as having predictable effects. She notes that the green blogs she studied not only attribute powers of engagement and the ability to implicate people in environmental issues to everyday objects and practices, but also identify 'problems' with this mode of involvement. Thus, many green blogs provide lists of things that happen that make domestic subjects complicit in environmentally damaging wastefulness: water tanks that heat water even when you take a cold shower, aluminium wrappings that push up the carbon footprint of chocolate Easter eggs, and 'our crap tea-making skills [that] are emitting a lot of pointless carbon'.

Marres observes that not only do such lists of environmentally dubious routines and practices indicate the 'uncontainability' of life, but also the costs involved in engaging with environmental issues by material means. Thus, some of the blogs enumerate the pathologies the authors started suffering from after embarking on green living exercises, including weirdness ('your house smells of vinegar') to fixation problems ('I know there is anecdotal evidence across the web that people who have meters installed [. . .] becom[e] obsessive about it'), to the problem of getting lost in triviality ('there have been plenty of silly little changes this month – like altering the margins on my Word documents, eating ice cream in a cone rather than a cup and shaving in the sink'). Marres suggests that these comments can be interpreted as an indication that green living experiments de-stabilize everyday habits and, relatedly, that they rob people of their sense of proportion, making them unable to differentiate between big and small issues, more and less important matters of concern. Advocates of 'nudges' (see chapter 8) might suggest that some of the green devices described in such accounts have such effects because they are not well-designed, but Marres's study suggests they are evidence, not of some 'thing' not working, but of the inevitable – sometimes rewarding, sometimes annoying, sometimes engaging – instability of subject–object–environment relations.

Conclusion

This chapter briefly outlined some of the history and forms of ethical consumption. It noted the variety of these forms, showing that practices of consumption have provided an important arena in which people have demonstrated their capacity to act ethically. It has also emphasized the importance of mediation by agencies, human and non-human, in the working up of ethical consumption as a field of social action. Some writers, including, for example, Humphery, propose that ethical consumption has the potential to contribute to the emergence of social justice not only within but also across national boundaries. He does this by developing an idea of a performative notion of justice – not only to self and other, but what he calls 'other others', such as animals and the environment.

One of the most important issues for commentators on this history, however, is not only what kind of ethics is put into practice, but also how or whether such forms of ethical behaviour rely upon or privilege a particular – and perhaps unhelpful – conception of the individual and associated understanding of human agency. As Barnett et al. put it:

> If consumption is . . . one of the key practices through which models of individual subjectivity as a modality of choice are currently assembled, then ethical consumption is, in a certain sense, parasitical on this broader array of processes. It might then be a means through which people consume particular conceptions of what it is to be ethical – ones that turn upon notions of accepting one's responsibilities and obligations. (2005: 44)

Many of the writers discussed above are, in one way or another, critical of the ways in which the individual is positioned as responsible for the ill-effects of mass consumption in contemporary consumer

culture, suggesting that they should instead be attributed to the economic and political power systems that drive consumption. Some
writers, such as Hawkins, go so far as to suggest that a truly radical
consumption practice must challenge the privileging not only of ideas
of the individual sovereign consumer, but also the privileging of the
human.

8

Consumer Culture, Identity and Politics: When Are You (Not) a Consumer?

Introduction

Why study consumer culture? This book suggests that not only is consumer culture interesting and sociologically significant in its own right, but also that consumer culture can act as a lure to think about other contemporary concerns. How do we live in the economy? What is the relationship between economy and society? What kinds of relations with objects do we have and what kinds of relations with objects do we want? What are the relations between having, doing and being? How do objects make meaning? Are objects changing? When we choose, are we responsible for ourselves as individuals, or for the effects of our choices on others, and if so, for which others? What is the difference between owning and possessing something?

To try to answer these and other questions, the book has investigated the phenomenon of consumer culture from a number of angles. Chapter 1 considered the view that consumer culture should be seen as an important contemporary manifestation of Euro-American material culture. One consequence of adopting this approach is that the importance of exploring the interrelationship between economic and cultural aspects of material goods or objects in the organization of all societies is highlighted. One of the issues it raises, however, is whether the organization of this relationship in terms of symbolic exchange is equally important in all societies, or whether and how other kinds of communication are involved. Chapter 2 introduced a number of approaches to the analysis of systems of exchange, while chapter 3 outlined perspectives that explore how materiality and meaning are combined in material culture. Chapter 4 emphasized the series of interlinking circuits of exchange that exist in contemporary

Euro-American societies, and focused on the shift from Fordism to post-Fordism as a way of demonstrating the complexities of these relationships. Particular attention was given to the role of class, habitus and cultural intermediaries. Other aspects of these inter-linking circuits were explored in chapter 5 – especially those relating to race and gender. The conclusion of these chapters was that reflexivity, or self-fashioning, is not the only way in which personal and collective identities are brought together in consumer culture. Consumer culture does not simply contribute to the emergence of a self-fashioning, self-possessed individual, but rather to multiple forms of identity and (un)belonging. Chapter 6 used the example of brands to explore the impact of techniques of marketing and the rise of media in the emergence of global flows and the incorporation of consumer activities in the economy, complicating any notion of a one-way relationship between production and consumption. Chapter 7 addressed the ethical dimension of consumer culture, and raised the question of what kind of politics can encompass the non-human. One conclusion about the nature of consumer culture emerging from across these chapters is that it is a culture of exchange, mobility and circulation, of transnational movement and transformation of ideas, people and things. This is a notion of consumer culture that confirms that consumption must be understood as transformation rather than use.

The central claim in chapter 1, however, was that in today's consumer culture the figure of the consumer has become a 'master category of collective and individual identity' (Trentmann, 2006b: 2). This is the view that contemporary consumer culture is an instance of material culture in which personal and collective identities are organized through consumption practices. This final chapter tries to address this claim head-on by considering ways in which consumer culture may be held to have come to provide sources of identity and to have contributed to the emergence of a cultural politics of consumption. This will be done through, first, an exploration of the role of consumer culture in the creation of 'the reflexive individual' as a form of identity and, second, in relation to contemporary forms of cultural politics. This second section of the chapter will address the relationship between consumer culture and collective identity, forms of sociality and sources of community and solidarity. The third and final section of the chapter will look at how changes in relations between objects and subjects are transforming the category of consumer, and how occupying this category shapes identity by transforming relations between individuals and collectives.

Consumer culture, the individual and the exercise of will

A series of advertisements for the lager Schlitz, in the 1990s, displayed the contents of the rubbish bins of a number of celebrities. In one advertisement, the text notes: 'we can figure out . . . that she's into health food, owns a dog and gets sent stacks of scripts. She also drinks Schlitz.' What else can the viewer figure out? Is the display of the final detritus of consumption to be read as evidence of identity? Is garbage, the husks of a personal selection of consumer goods, to be understood as a self-portrait? What kinds of identity are made available to us – or maybe required of us – by our participation in consumer culture?

> Along this route, we are also required to adjust the way we understand commodities. These automobiles were products, but we have already seen that they could also be conspicuously productive . . . It bears repeating: they were the ur-commodity, and as such they help to periodise capitalism as it moves into and leaves its industrial phase . . . In doing so, the curved, reflexive surfaces they provide can show us our distorted selves. Their hold over us reveals how particular objects and technologies can become, in effect, active, dynamic social forces in the material cultures of everyday life. Their power compels acknowledgement of the conditions under which technological resources can acquire the characteristics of historical agents and social actors. (Gilroy, 2010: 30)

These are difficult questions to answer, not least since participation in consumer culture is both uneven and contradictory. However, a study carried out by Peter Lunt and Sonia Livingstone in 1992 provides one way of answering this question. The study aimed to explore the hypothesis that consumer culture provides the conditions within which most people work out their identities. In order to do this, they directly asked people about how consumption informed their everyday life in an in-depth postal survey with 279 respondents, a series of 9 focus-group discussions and a series of 20 interviews to provide material for the construction of individual life-histories. The general finding of the study was that people's involvement with consumer culture is such that it infiltrates everyday life not only at the level of economic decision-making, social activities and domestic life, but also at the level of meaningful psychological experience. It affects the construction of identities, the formation of relationships and the framing of events.

However, this finding, of the widespread significance of consumer culture for personal identity, does not mean that everyone is a shopaholic. Rather, Lunt and Livingstone's study suggests that it is possible to divide people up into different groups, according to their shopping habits. They identify five such groupings:

Alternative shoppers   12 per cent
These people use the alternative market buying second-hand books, clothes and attending jumble sales. They seem to stand outside the pressures and pleasures of modern consumer culture. They find little pleasure in shopping.

Routine shoppers   31 per cent
These people shop on the high street whenever they need something, but seem disengaged from consumer culture. They rarely buy on impulse and do not use the alternative market. They find little pleasure in shopping. Shopping is a routine activity.

Leisure shoppers   24 per cent
These people come closest to the stereotype associated with consumer culture ('I shop therefore I am'), enjoying a range of shopping experiences, enjoying window shopping and using consumer goods in their social relationships as rewards, promises and bribes.

Careful shoppers   15 per cent
These people find shopping fairly pleasurable, but seem to be careful shoppers, enjoying the use of the products they purchase rather than the process of selecting them. They avoid the alternative market and are moderately economical in their shopping habits.

Thrifty shoppers   18 per cent
These people find some pleasure in shopping, especially enjoying shopping for clothes, food, presents and shopping with the family compared to window shopping. They are thrifty, shopping around for the best buy, waiting for the sales for expensive purchases. They use all forms of the alternative market to buy goods.

(Adapted from Lunt and Livingstone, 1992: 89–94)

Rather than assuming that everyone is preoccupied with shopping, then, what Lunt and Livingstone mean when they say that people's identities are constituted in relation to consumer culture is that their identities are bound up with the negotiation of a set of oppositions deriving from consumer culture. These oppositions include:

cash	credit
simplicity	complexity
budgeting	borrowing
institutional control	individual responsibility
necessities	luxuries
being careful	having pleasure
second-hand	new
control	loss of control

(Adapted from Lunt and Livingstone, 1992: 149)

Like Humphery (whose work was discussed in chapter 7), Lunt and Livingstone are keen to stress the variety and complexity of the views people hold in relation to consumption, and point out that most people formulate a set of strategies or rules to guide their consumer decisions. They suggest that these strategies are motivated by the desire for control over the social environment; and that they have a strong rhetorical component, expressing people's aspirations, hopes and fears as well as their actual practices. The rules are a way of negotiating the oppositions between opportunity and danger, freedom and responsibility, pleasure and the moral order. Lunt and Livingstone identify the following common strategies or rules of resistance:

(i) make appropriate social comparisons – do not think a good is a necessity for yourself just because someone else has it;
(ii) follow guiding principles – follow abstract principles of consumption which provide a framework for taking numerous specific decisions;
(iii) adopt coping actions;
(iv) maintain self-control;
(v) follow warnings.

These everyday rules or resistances are seen by Livingstone and Lunt to be a response to the push and pull of the oppositions at work in consumer culture.

But how are these oppositions identified? Lunt and Livingstone suggest that certain objects characteristic of consumer culture – such as, for example, the credit card, the cash dispenser or the shopping mall – act as key symbols in the setting up and negotiation of these oppositions.

The credit card, for example, was frequently attacked by their interviewees as a symbol of decline, although most people interviewed had

> The cash dispenser
> The modern wayside shrine – never mind rewards in heaven: a moment's devotion produces cash upfront right now! Drawbacks: sin punished by having your card eaten, and pilgrimages to find a machine in working order. (Kohn, 1988a: 180)

at least one themselves. The card symbolized a perceived lack of self-control and a perceived loss of traditional community feeling. More generally, the credit system was seen as a major source of loss of individual control, satisfying the desire for ownership of possessions but leading to a lack of self-discipline. Put simply, there was a notion that the so-called traditional values of thrift, prudence and patience were being replaced by personal debt, avarice and impatience (epitomized by the character Gordon Gekko in the film *Wall Street* who claims, 'Greed is good'). Yet, so Lunt and Livingstone argue, credit cards are responsible for only a very small proportion of personal credit in Britain (remember they were writing this in the early 1990s). They thus conclude that it is the *symbolic meanings* of the credit card that are really significant in defining these oppositions, and point to the relation between these symbolic meanings and anxieties about personal or self-identity, especially the dimension of identity to do with control or lack of control.

The significance of these symbolic meanings is linked to what Helga Dittmar (1992) describes as a fundamental contradiction in contemporary understandings of self-identity: the idealism–materialism paradox. In describing this paradox, Dittmar points out that the dominant Western ideal of personal identity is that it is unique and autonomous, uninfluenced by other people and socio-cultural surroundings. Idealistically, then, personal identity should be independent of material context in the sense that *we are who we are no matter what we possess*. Yet, as she notes, this view is in apparent conflict with the fundamental axiom of contemporary consumer culture: that identity is defined through the exchange, possession and use of goods (the subtitle of her book is 'To have is to be'). From this perspective, the arguments put forward by Featherstone and others – that members of the new middle classes have developed a reflexive relation to self-identity – is a magical resolution of this paradox. Insofar as the link between possession and identity can legitimately be defined as one of play, the paradox can be made to disappear: possessions can be used to express, transform even create identity, but this creation is not to be taken seriously – it is only play – and thus does not contradict the belief that we are who we are no matter what we possess. Indeed, as Featherstone notes, in the context of the lifestyle of the new middle classes, to take the link too seriously would be to reveal oneself as vulgar, a person without discrimination, style or taste.

However, while the new middle classes may have sought to legitimate this magical solution to the idealism–materialism paradox in the elevation of their taste as a playful lifestyle choice, the manipulation of the dimension of self-control by other groups has not so easily been accepted as playfulness. The (mythical) figure of the 'abnormal consumer' or 'addictive personality' indicates the extent of public anxiety about the consequences of the unchecked spread of a calculated de-control of emotions beyond the enclaves of the new middle classes. As Dittmar points out, the magical solution to the idealism–materialism paradox as identified by Featherstone obscures a situation in which:

> the argument that all are much freer to acquire the lifestyle – and thus identity – of their choice runs the risk of slipping into an imaginary world of equal opportunities, and thus of becoming a rhetoric that all are equal, even if some remain more equal than others. (1992: 201)

It is thus a magical solution that is potentially the site of much political conflict.

Life politics

This view that the individual can fashion him- or herself through the exercise of will has a parallel in the view put forward by some academics and some politicians that we live in a society in which the individual has become an important site of political change. One representative of this view is Anthony Giddens (1991, 1992), a sociologist who was a key advisor to the Third Way of New Labour in the 1990s. Giddens locates the significance of the notion of identity in contemporary society in relation to a movement away from *emancipatory politics* to *life politics*. Emancipatory politics in its various forms is seen by Giddens to be concerned with releasing people from the constraints of traditional social positions – of class, gender, race and age – by breaking down hierarchies. Consumer culture is seen by some as an important process in this breakdown, or at least in the refiguring of these hierarchies, through the resources it offers for a more flexible relationship between the individual and self-identity.

Life politics, in contrast to emancipatory politics, is said to be a politics of self-determination. The protests, campaigns, strikes and rallies associated with emancipatory politics were an attempt to reveal the invasion of people's everyday lives by social and political forces of domination and exploitation. Life politics is said to work at a different level. It concerns a *reflexive* relation to the self in which the individual is less concerned with protesting about the actions of others than with taking control (that phrase again) of the shape of his or her own life through the negotiation of self-identity. Giddens writes that life politics 'is a politics of self-actualisation in a reflexively organised environment, where that reflexivity links self and body to systems of global scope' (1991: 214). What he is arguing here is that each of us is increasingly expected to organize our lives in relation to the question 'How shall I live?', and seeks to answer that question in day-to-day decisions about how to behave, what to wear and what to eat. As it has become possible for the individual to construct personal identities in a reflexively organized environment, so identity has become a social issue, a topic for public debate, and a site of political contestation and change. Note the importance Giddens attaches to the environment here: he is not talking about changes brought about by the individual him- or herself, but changes in the organization of environments that enable – perhaps compel – self-reflexivity.

Prominent examples of this life politics are the emergence of the so-called 'green consumer' in the late 1980s and the lesbian, gay and queer subcultures that are linked to the buying power of the so-called 'pink pound'. So, for instance, the emergence of the green consumer can be seen in terms of a reflexive process, in which a variety of different actors and intermediaries within the green consumer field of action, including environmental groups, retailers, product manufacturers, market researchers, consumer groups and government departments, are brought together, each of them representing the green consumer and the nature of green consumer action in different ways. As Giddens points out, in relation to his notion of life politics, individual choices in particular local situations have increasing global relevance, which, in turn, highlights ethical decision-making. This was clear in Connolly and Prothero's study of green consumers (2008). In their interviews they found that individuals understood their local choices in relation to far-off places, contributing to doubts about whether their choices were indeed 'the right ones': 'But I do think the biggest problem in the world is the imbalance between the vast numbers of poverty stricken people and the affluent West, and is our lifestyle moral?' (Helen, quoted in Connolly and Prothero, 2008: 131). Connolly and Prothero conclude that 'individuals are left with a sense of *I know that I should and can do something, but I don't know what is the right thing to do*' (2008: 133).

Giddens argues that consumer culture contributes to a reflexive understanding of identity, insofar as it provides many of the resources with which individuals fashion their own personal and political identities. He and other writers (see Beck, Giddens and Lash, 1994) have pointed out that the aestheticization of everyday life that is part of consumer culture can be seen as an important part of such an altered world, as an enhancement of the material environment in such a way as simultaneously to numb and excite the senses. Indeed, the process of aestheticization is sometimes held to have culminated in 'total environments', such as theme parks, holiday worlds or tourist bubbles, small, enclosed, self-contained worlds that overload the senses. For Giddens, the modern condition entails both opportunities and dangers for the individual. The material conditions within which and in response to which we form our identities are not always benign. They afford possibilities for personal development and they threaten that development – increased freedoms go hand in hand with increased responsibilities.

But is this reflexive relation the same for all individuals? Do we all have access to the same freedoms and suffer from the same responsibilities? Is consumer culture an adventure playground for everyone? A number of arguments suggest that it is not. One of these points to the fact that a significant proportion of the populations of even Euro-American societies live in poverty. While, as chapter 1 pointed out, economic deprivation does not necessarily mean that an individual will not participate in consumer culture, it clearly sets some limits on the nature of that participation.

Let us return to the example of the credit card to explore this argument further. Since Lunt and Livingstone completed their study, the levels of personal debt (including but not only credit card debt) have grown significantly in the UK and the USA. This is in part because of the ways in which the economy was deregulated in the 1980s and 1990s. During this period, many economists and government policy-makers were not concerned about rising personal debt levels, seeing them as a natural (even desirable) outcome of lower inflation and nominal interest rates. In other words, growing debt levels amongst individuals in all socio-economic groups were seen as contributing to growth in national economies (a kind of democratization of debt!). However, others held a more pessimistic view. Montgomerie (2007), for example, argues that the widespread use of what was called asset-backed securitization – typically the use of homes as 'security' for loans – created an increased supply of credit available for lending based on access to streams of revolving debtors that was not adequately secured. In addition, she suggests that people with static or only slowly increasing incomes created a new form of demand for consumer credit, what she describes as 'defensive consumption', that is, consumption that was perceived as a necessity, but was only such because of the increased availability of credit. The argument here is that the centrality of consumer culture in society provided sufficient cultural justification for increasing consumption despite static incomes for many if not most wage-earners. She describes the combination of these processes as 'the financialization of consumption'. What was new about this was 'the integration of the future income and spending habits of households into financial market expansion' (2004: 21). In this way, individual consumer choices and domestic economies came to be much more closely tied up – for better or for worse – with the global financial economy.

Significantly, writing even before the recent upheaval associated with the crisis in the economy, Montgomerie argued that the most significant impact of the financialization of consumption was on lower-income groups. She shows that lower-income groups incurred the largest increases in debt (relative to their income).

> For instance, the targeting of university students and low-income households shows how declining state support, flexible employment and stagnant wage growth have led to increased borrowing. Both groups were targeted by consumer credit marketing because they produce large profits based on their inclination to revolve debts. University students come from predominantly wealthy backgrounds, but dwindling state subsidies, rising tuition costs, their minimal income while in school, limited employment opportunities after graduation coupled with outstanding student loans, means they are more likely to revolve debt. Credit card companies claim they focus on university students because relationship marketing with the young will ensure brand loyalty. Growing evidence suggests it is their household resources, specifically their parents' and student loans' ability to prevent default, which make them suitable risks. Plus, the frequent revolving of debt makes them extremely profitable. (2004: 20)

She thus concludes that the financialization of consumption has had most impact on groups such as students and low-income groups who are least able to cope with the consequences.

A number of other writers have focused on the perceived overlap – and mutual reinforcement – between the political discourse of neo-liberalism and some aspects of consumer culture. It is important to point out that neo-liberal policies have not been adopted uniformly in Europe or even in the United States (Harvey, 2005). Nevertheless, their influence is such that they are seen to have provided an economic and political context in which the exercise of choice by individuals has come to be a political necessity for most people. But critics of neo-liberalism suggest that more individual choice does not necessarily lead either to greater agency for (most) people or to a more democratic system. In response to the perceived negative effects of the emergence of what has been called 'consumer-spectator-citizenship' (Sennett, 2007), there has developed a critique of neo-liberalism because of its emphasis on commodity choice as a field of individual power and as a vehicle for the expression of identity.

Neo-tribalism

A further approach to the question of how to understand the relations between choice, self-reflexivity and consumer culture is *neo-tribalism*. This is an approach that has been proposed by a number of writers, including Maffesoli (1991, 1993) and Bauman (1990, 1992a and b), although, in these two cases, with rather different political conclusions. Both adopt the concept *neo*-tribalism to describe the groupings arising in contemporary society as a variant of the tribal life described by 'classical' anthropologists.

> What makes the 'tribes' one joins by purchasing their symbols superficially similar to the real tribes is that both set themselves apart from other groups and make a lot of fuss about underlining their separate identity and avoiding confusion; both cede their own identity to their members – defining them by proxy. But here the similarity ends and a decisive difference begins: the 'tribes' (let us call them henceforth *neo-tribes* to prevent misunderstanding) could not care less about who proclaim themselves members. They have no councils of elders or boards or admission committees to decide who has the right to be in and who ought to be kept out. They employ no gatekeepers and no border guards. They have no institution of authority, no supreme court which may pronounce on the correctness of members' behaviour. (Maffesoli, 1993: 206–7)

Whether excluded or included, membership of the pre-modern tribe was seldom a matter of individual choice; in contrast, neo-tribes are formed by a multitude of individual acts of self-identification. Maffesoli claims:

Overall, within massification, processes of condensation are constantly occurring through which more or less ephemeral tribal groupings are organized which cohere on the basis of their own minor values, and which attract and collide with each other in an endless dance, forming themselves into a constellation whose vague boundaries are perfectly fluid. (1991: 12)

Neo-tribes are said to be marked by their fluidity: they are locally condensed and dispersed, periodically assembled and scattered. They are momentary condensations in the flux of everyday consumer life and, in this sense, less enduring than the reflexivity described by Giddens; however, while they are fragile, ephemeral and unstable, they command intense emotional or affective involvement from their fickle members. Maffesoli writes:

> it is no longer possible to say that any aspect of social life, not cookery, nor attention to appearance, nor small celebrations, nor relaxing walks, is frivolous or insignificant. In so far as such activities may provide a focus for collective emotions, they constitute real underground movements, demands for life which have to be analysed. 'Banal' forms of existence may, from a utilitarian or rationalist perspective, serve no purpose but they are full of meaning, even if it tends to get worn away in practice. (1991: 8)

The inner organization, aims and aspirations of neo-tribes are unimportant, argues Maffesoli; their existence is the only purpose they need. Membership does not require an admission procedure; neo-tribes exist solely through individual decisions to sport the insignia of tribal allegiance. They persevere only thanks to their continuing seductive capacity; they cannot outlive their power of attraction.

Maffesoli's theory is borne out in East Asia where market segmentation in tribal terms has taken on a life of its own. Maffesoli's *tribus* has splintered into tiny subdivisions, each half a generation apart, in places like China, Taiwan, Hong Kong, and Japan. Not surprisingly, neo-tribes in China, such as the bobos, DINKs, and Ifs, are now considered rather conservative in their taste, because as the established social elites, they are not as cool as their successors, the neo-neo-tribe (*xin xinrenlei*) – Asia's hottest market segment . . . They have a symbiotic existence with high-tech communication gadgets. Their threshold for irreverence is immeasurable. And with less money than the bobos, they are no easy prey for mainstream consumerism. (Wang, 2008: 202)

Maffesoli further argues that the existing sociological categories of class, gender, race and age are no longer adequate to describe these groups, which are short-lived and 'transversal', operating *across* existing categories and *along* fluctuating and short-lived networks of affinity, interest and neighbourhood. Individuals move between these groupings incessantly, modifying their behaviour, outlook and identity as they move. However, the individual is not isolated, but is part and parcel of an emotional geography of places – sports stadia, concert halls, shopping malls – which are invested with the emotion that previously characterized sacred sites. Neo-tribes are to be understood in terms of aesthetics, a recognition, Maffesoli suggests, that points to 'the importance of the "immaterial" in the very heart of the "material"' (1991: 11).

The role of aesthetics, Maffesoli argues, is visible in the practices of *self-fashioning* adopted in contemporary tribes, practices in which the individual fashions or creates his or her own self-identity as if it were an artwork. So, for example:

> Whether trendy exercises in sensory isolation, or various forms of body-building, or jogging, or Eastern techniques of one sort or another, the body is being constructed as a value, even to the extent of its epiphany . . . Note, however, that even in its most private aspects, the body is being constructed only in order to be seen; it is theatralized (sic) to the highest degree. Within advertising, fashion, dance, the body is adorned only to be made into a spectacle. (1991: 18–19)

For Maffesoli, these practices of self-fashioning do not result in greater individuation or privatization, but, rather the 'functions of aggregation and reinforcement which I call *sociality*' (1991: 19).

In contrast to Maffesoli, Bauman sees the phenomenon of neo-tribalism, which he describes superficially in very similar terms to Maffesoli, to have very different political implications, tending to argue for the 'unambiguously individualistic impact of the neo-tribal phenomenon' (1992b: 25). Bauman argues that the individual – increasingly detached from his or her membership of the social categories of class, gender, race and age – is engaged in the tribal scene in a privatized relationship of fluctuating freedom and dependence in a desperate search for community. While membership of neo-tribes appears to be a matter of choice, the way of life they offer is, in fact, prescribed: 'If the neo-tribes themselves do not care to guard their entry, there is someone else who does: *the market*' (Bauman, 1992b: 27).

Rather than being a source of new forms of sociality, of collective belonging and association, Bauman believes that neo-tribes are an adaptive response to the disaggregation of sociality and the resulting confusion this creates for the increasingly isolated individual faced with contradictory advice from a bewildering array of experts on how to care for the self. 'Tribes are simultaneously refuges for those trying in vain to escape the loneliness of privatized survival, and the stuff from which private policies of survival, and thus the identity of the survivor are self-assembled' (1992b: 25).

He argues that not only do 'fear campaigns' promote specific products of expert knowledge (in the form of diets, exercise programmes, fashion and beauty advice, psychological profiling, and so on), but the contemporary cult of specialists diffuses feelings of helplessness and incompetence which produce a need for the continual assistance of 'people in the know'. He writes:

> Neo-tribalism is an indispensable complement of a habitat in which private survivals are serviced by the variegated and often contradictory advice of experts . . . The choice, however, is a daunting task, as the hierarchies of relevance suggested by the experts servicing different problem areas are hardly ever compatible. It is in this difficult yet indispensable matter of choice that tribes perform a crucial function, as they sanction global *lifestyles*, each offering its own structure of relevances . . . For the individual, joining a tribe means adopting a peculiar lifestyle; or, rather, the road to a coherent lifestyle leads through the adoption of tribally sanctioned structure of relevances complete with a kit of totemic symbols. (1992b: 25)

For Bauman, neo-tribalism thus encourages a process of individualization by supporting an ethos of survivalism. This is an ethos which 'can be put to socially destructive as much as to socially creative uses. More often than not, it is put to uses that are both destructive and constructive' (1992b: 12). Bauman suggests that the lifestyle of survivalism is one in which the individual is encouraged to take responsibility for him- or herself *as* an individual. The resources of self-identity – health, beauty and taste – are managed for individual profit. This view is in contrast to that adopted by Maffesoli, for whom the opposition between the individual and the social is being *fused* in 'the confusional societal' of neo-tribalism (1993: 4). For Maffesoli, individuals no longer have functions accruing from their social position, but roles acquired through the reversible practices of self-fashioning, roles which enable the feeling of participating in a general representation or spectacle, and thus 'privilege the grasping of the whole' (1993: 4).

Complaints about apathy and depoliticisation are as old as politics itself. They are the stock-in-trade of activists who celebrate the golden age of political culture in some earlier moment – 1945, 1968 or whenever. But the past decade has witnessed a massive loss of confidence in what many held to be the bedrock of formal democracy. Faith in government, in the credibility of politicians, in the power of governments to do anything, has hit an all time low . . .

Is there really nowhere to go but the shops? . . .

What needs saying at this stage is that our conception of politics must be prised open . . . Today's consumer culture straddles public and private space, creating blurred areas in between. Privatised car culture, with its collective red nose days and sticker for lead-free petrol; cosmetics as the quintessential expression of consumer choice now carry anxieties over eco-politics. These are the localised points where consumption meshes with social demands and aspirations. So the above cannot be about individualism *versus* collectivism, but about articulating the two in a new relation that can form the basis for a future common sense. (Mort, 1989: 40–1)

To some extent, the notion of neo-tribalism describes well the outcome of the processes described here for social life, although the use of the term 'neo-tribalism' can be criticized for the similarity between its reliance upon racialized notions of 'the primitive' or 'animalism' and commercial techniques for the appropriation of a racialized authenticity. It can thus be seen as the academic equivalent of the painted faces – black and white – employed by Benetton to sell its jumpers. However, many commentators would argue that neo-tribalism is really only accurate to describe the consumption practices of some young people, and even then only in relation to some products and services, not all.

Nevertheless, the notion of neo-tribalism is interesting insofar as it highlights the question of whether consumer culture is undermining the basis of group-belonging in contemporary society. As noted above, Featherstone suggests that the potential offered to individuals in consumer culture to fashion themselves is sometimes assumed to be undercutting any sense of belonging to social groups, and some interpretations of Maffesoli and Bauman's description of neo-tribalism would suggest that they both support this view. However, the same writers who have problems with Giddens's account of self-reflexivity also suggest that this view is wrong. Alan Warde, for example, asserts the continuing importance of group solidaristic considerations in the choice and development of lifestyles: 'Though necessarily aware of the styles associated with neo-tribes, the consumer chooses the group as much as, and probably more than the style; and membership of the group commands a certain path through the enormous number of commodities on sale. Belonging comes before identity' (1994: 70). However, it may be that it is neither that belonging comes before identity nor that identity comes before belonging, but that belonging and identity are done together.

It is this latter claim that has been developed in this book. Roberta Sassatelli also supports this point of view. She argues that people have increasingly come to ground their humanity in being different from the 'objectivity' of things, that is, they have sought to distinguish themselves from the perceived passivity, docility and transience of the many objects that surround them. She suggests that subjects perform their identity through commodities as difference from commodities (2007: 150). But more than this, she says, 'modern consumers are asked to actively participate in the process of de-commoditization, producing themselves as the source of value'. This is important as she is proposing that part of what it is to be a subject in consumer culture is not simply having actively to choose, but having to choose in ways that enhance your identity as a source of value.

An example of this is provided by the practices of self-branding, which is described by Alison Hearn as 'the self-conscious construction of a meta-narrative and meta-image of self through the use of cultural meanings and images drawn from the narrative and visual codes of mainstream culture industries' (2008: 198). Hearn argues that work on the production of a branded self involves creating a detachable, saleable image or narrative, which effectively circulates cultural meanings, and leads to a construction of self as a site for the extraction of value. Sassatelli also goes on to argue, however, that the individual subject is not free in this performance – on the contrary, the subjectivity required by consumption is a binding or restrictive individuality. As she puts it: 'To adequately perform their social roles as consumers, actors must thus find a point of balance between indifference to commodities and the search for difference as an end in itself' (2007: 149). She recognizes that the realization of that difference is more or less possible, more or less valuable for members of different groups: 'autonomous choice is clearly coded by gender, class and race, in so far as certain categories of people (women, the poor and racial minorities in particular) are perceived as closer to bodily desires and nature, thus being considered as less able to display a self-possessed self'.

ID: identifying and identified

In this final section, the implications of recent developments in consumer culture for how individuals come to occupy the category of the consumer are explored a little further. These developments complicate the idea of a decision or choice as the locus or site of self-making, and so provide alternative ways to understand the dynamics of consumer culture and its implications for identity. They do this by focusing on the organization of the material and economic environment of consumer culture, and seek to address the symbolic or cultural capacity of such environments reflexively to create consumers.

> Who, dear reader, do you think you are? Do you think your mind is capable of independent judgment and largely directs the course of our rational, conscious self? Do you believe you are in control of your life?
> . . . research into our brains . . . [suggests that] people are useless at making choices. We are lazy, myopic, and much of our decision-making is made by unconscious habits of the mind which are largely socially primed. (Bunting, 2009: 27)

It has long been acknowledged that there is an ambiguity in the use of phrases such as 'making up your mind' to describe the process of making a choice. Rachel Bowlby (1993) identifies a number of different ways in which the phrase 'making up your mind' is understood; they include:

(i)   supply a lack, as in phrases such as 'make up the difference' or 'make up for lost time';
(ii) add something, with a positive connotation of enhancement or adornment, ending in a situation in which someone is 'made up' (in contrast to the first meaning, which merely involves the avoidance of something negative);
(iii) putting together pieces;
(iv) to invent, with a buried connotation of fictionality.

The multiplicity of these meanings illustrates the complexity of the processes by which decisions are made or choices taken; all attest to the difficulties and uncertainties involved in making choices. Is making up one's mind an inventive process, part of the artificial making up of an imaginary whole person out of bits and pieces? Or is it the decisive, rational, goal-oriented act of the sovereign individual? That these processes are being made ever yet more fraught, so Eve Sedgwick (1994) suggests, is a consequence of the ways in which *sites of volition*, or sites for the exercise of the will, are being multiplied in contemporary consumer culture. Here she is pointing, like Giddens above, to the importance of the sites or environments in how decisions are made.

Sedgwick's argument is that the multiplication of sites in the fields of exercise, health, therapy, diet, love and sexuality has led to a widespread anxiety in society about the exercise of individual will. This anxiety is expressed in the fear that we are all living in the shadow of the threat of becoming addicts of some kind or another. In the past, the concept of addiction – of losing the capacity to exercise one's will and being under a compulsion to act – was defined in relation to a special category of substances, so-called foreign or noxious substances, alcohol or drugs. In this way, Sedgwick makes links between the cultivation of will, the need to uphold boundaries and the project of Empire. Certain substances were believed to be dangerous because they were seen to break down the individual's 'natural' capacity to regulate his consumption reasonably. The danger was attributed to the substance. But now, it seems, addiction can be applied to consumption of almost any kind of substance (see also Cronin, 2004a).

Food, for example, is a substance to which, it is believed by some, one can now be addicted; and you can also be addicted to activities – to exercise, to keep fit, to relationships, to sex and, of course, to shopping. Moreover, one can be addicted not only to too much of a substance such as food – in which case, you might be invited to attend an Overeaters Anonymous self-help group – but also to its refusal, as anorexics are said to be, or to its controlled ingestion, as in the case of those following diets. As the number of activities to which one can be addicted grows, it seems that even trying to control addiction can be addictive. As Sedgwick wryly notes: 'Within the last year, there has even been a spate of journalism on the theme that the self-help groups and books that have popularized this radical critique of addiction, and that promote themselves as the only way out of it, may themselves be addictive' (1994: 133). Even some advertisements employ the rhetoric of addiction, as in the Nike campaign,

'Encyclopedia of Addictions', which included images of individuals carrying out a range of activities with the text 'I am addicted to things that are good for me. I am addicted to things that are bad for me' (Cronin 2004).

Sedgwick suggests that, since it is no longer the substance that is identified as the locus of danger, then it must be the relation between the individual and the substance or the activity, *the individual exercise of will itself*, that is being identified as dangerous in contemporary society. She concludes that the pervasiveness of the vocabulary of addiction to describe almost any activity is an indication that the assertion of will – making up one's mind – has become increasingly problematic in contemporary Euro-American societies, and explains this in terms of what she calls the especially 'resonant relations' between problematics of addiction and those of the consumer phase of international capitalism. All of us, she suggests, are caught between the 'twin hurricanes' of 'Just Do It' and 'Just Say No'. Ann Cronin (2004a) takes this argument one stage further when she suggests addiction has in some sense become normalized.

One response to anxieties around whether people exercise choice 'properly' currently being developed by behavioural economists is *Nudge: Improving Decisions About Health, Wealth and Happiness* (2008) by Richard H. Thaler and Cass R. Sunstein. This book proposes that 'better' decisions could be made if individuals are gently pushed in the right direction, through the use of 'cognitive nudges' or prompts in the environment. This view is informed by an interpretation of the recent findings of studies about the way the brain works by psychologists and neuro-scientists. Such studies, Thaler and Sunstein say, indicate that individuals have two cognitive systems: one that is automatic, that is uncontrolled, effortless, associative, fast, unconscious and skilled, and another that is reflexive, that is, controlled, effortful, deductive, slow, self-aware and rule-following. Much decision-making, Thaler and Sunstein argue, takes place automatically rather than reflectively and, as such, can be changed by nudging, or directing the brain's automatic cognitive system in particular ways. They thus propose that political strategy should focus on the design of what they call 'choice architecture'.

Thaler and Sunstein acknowledge some of the potential problems with such a proposal, but argue that 'Choice architects can preserve freedom of choice while also nudging people in directions that will improve their lives' (2008: 252). Such an approach, they argue, provides the basis for (a new, improved) 'Third Way', or libertarian paternalism. Others, however, suggest that the obvious dangers of

Dollar a day. Teenage pregnancy is a serious problem for many girls, and those who have one child, at (say) eighteen, often become pregnant again within a year or two. Several cities, including Greensboro, North Carolina, have experimented with a 'dollar a day' program, by which teenage girls with a baby receive a dollar for each day in which they are not pregnant. Thus far the results have been extremely promising. A dollar a day is a trivial cost to the city, even for a year or two, so the plan's total cost is extremely low, but the small recurring payment is salient enough to encourage teenage mothers to take steps to avoid getting pregnant again. And because taxpayers end up paying a significant amount for many children born to teenagers, the costs appear to be far less than the benefits . . .

Filters for air-conditioners; the helpful red light. In hot weather, people depend on air conditioners, and many central air-conditioning systems need their filters changed regularly. If the filter isn't changed, bad things can happen; for example, the system can freeze and break down. Unfortunately, it is not easy to remember when to change the filter, and not surprisingly, many people are left with huge repair bills. The solution is simple; people should be informed via a red light in a relevant and conspicuous place that the filter needs to be changed . . .

No-bite nail polish and Disulfiram. People who hope to change certain bad habits might want to buy products that make it unpleasant, or painful, to continue to indulge those habits. Through this system, the Reflective System can choose to discipline the Automatic System through products that tell the Automatic System: Stop!

Several products accomplish exactly this task. Those who want to stop biting their nails can buy bitter nail polishes such as Mavala and Orly No Bite. A more extreme version of this concept is Disulfiram (antabuse), which is given to some alcoholics. Disulfiram causes alcohol drinkers to throw up and suffer a hangover as soon as they start to drink. For some people suffering from chronic alcoholism, Disulfiram has had a strong and positive effect as part of a treatment program. (Thaler and Sunstein, 2008: 234–5) such a strategy, such as unacknowledged or hidden manipulation by those in positions of power, and lack of openness, outweigh its possible benefits.

A further set of reasons for thinking that choosing is not so simple has come from those approaches arguing that what it is to be a subject is created in relations with objects. The approaches that develop this view are as various as theories of practice, actor network theory and studies of science and technology; in each case, the argument is that agency – the capacity to act – does not emanate from subjects but is rather produced in practices or relations between subjects and objects. For this reason, it is always important in these approaches to see how agency is distributed and where and how it can be attributed, fixed and owned in either subjects or objects, and to consider how environments are organized to enable agency to be made visible, whether this is as, for example, rational decision-making, choice or entanglement, and as free or forced, unthinking or ethical practices.

These approaches – including what has been called a *theory of practice* approach to consumption (Warde, 2005; Shove, 2007) – suggest that the notion of freedom of choice has always been misleading. This approach aims to avoid either individualist or totalizing explanations, emphasizing instead plural and flexible pictures of the constitution of social life. It does not dramatize the dilemmas of choosing, but instead situates choice in the context of everyday life. From this point of view, consumption is not, by itself, a practice, but is, rather, a moment in almost every practice, and, so it is argued, it is the organization of practices – not personal choice – that steers consumption: 'Practices, rather than individual desires, we might say, create wants' (Warde, 2005: 137). It is further suggested that it is a contemporary increase in practices – the multiplication of enthusiasms and interests sometimes described as cultural omnivorousness – that explains the increase in things defined as part of a 'normal and decent life' rather than consumer demand. This view is consistent with an approach to consumption that stresses the routine, ordinary, collective, conventional nature of much consumption. It attends less to individual choices and identity and more to the collective development of modes of appropriate conduct in everyday life. As one of the key advocates of this approach puts it:

From this angle the concept of the 'consumer', a figure who has bewitched political and social scientists as well as economists evaporates. Instead the key focal points become the organization of the practice and the moments of consumption enjoined. Persons confront moments of consumption neither as sovereign choosers nor as dupes. (Warde, 2005: 146)

A further approach which foregrounds the organization of practices in terms of human and non-human, interpersonal and technical, relations is illustrated by a study of the current popularity of showering, a practice chosen for study, in part, because of its significance in relation to the environmental politics of water provision. Rather than looking at how people come to acquire showers or the cultural significance of shower appliances, Hand, Shove and Southerton consider showering as a set of socio-technical practices: 'looking at how complexes of bathroom technology interest with repertoires of meaning and with conventions of propriety and procedure' (2005). So they explain the increasing popularity of showering in terms of the development of domestic infrastructures of water and electricity provision, changing practices of cleansing, restoration, presentation and pleasure linked to changes in societal and self-governance of bodies, and, finally, the temporal organization of daily life. Here the claim is that 'speed' and 'convenience' are important in explaining both the ascendancy of showering and the decline of bathing. They argue, however, that none of the histories – of infrastructure, of governance, of the organization of temporality – is sufficient on its own. Instead, their analysis shows the importance of a specific interconnectedness or arrangement between cultural and technical histories, which is both constitutive of, and a consequence of, the practice of showering itself. In their view, their study outlines the limitations of an environmental politics that focuses on individual consumers. In place of such an emphasis, the authors advocate attention to the study of how practices become normal and how they change in understanding what and how we consume:

> As we have shown, people do not really 'use' energy or water. Instead, resources are consumed in the course of accomplishing important and valued practices like those of showering, or of heating, cooking, watching television or whatever . . . From an environmental point of view, there may well be opportunities to intervene and modify both the process and the outcome of the de- and re-routinization (Elzen et al., 2004). To take advantage of these or even to identify them requires a different way of thinking about the limits and possibilities of environmental policy. (2005)

As chapter 7 also pointed out, ethical consumption practices increasingly draw attention to the mobilization of publics constituted in commodity networks connecting diverse actors (human and non-human) across vast distances. In such a politics, the category of consumer as an individual identity is not a useful starting point.

Such arguments point to internal divisions in the notion of the category of the consumer as identity, such as the tension between being identified as a consumer by others, including companies, marketers, and government, and self-identifying as a consumer. It is not inevitable, of course, that being identified as a consumer – that is, being addressed as a consumer – will lead to the adoption of the identity of a consumer. The accounts above suggest that consumption is carried out routinely by people who are *not identifying* as consumers at all, and as such are a valuable corrective to the view that people self-consciously act as consumers whenever and however they consume something. However, the power of an address to the consumer does not necessarily depend on its conscious acceptance. Other developments discussed elsewhere in the book – including the use of RFIDs, branding, the use of data transaction management techniques, web analytic devices and geo-demographic software – indicate the increasing importance of media and information in shaping today's consumer culture. They provide a very different environment for the formation of individual and collective identities, and suggest that the value of consumption practices is increasingly being realized not (only) by people but (also) by corporations, in ways that do not necessarily involve subjective identification and are not always recognized by individuals themselves, but that nonetheless still augment the centrality of the category of the consumer to the organization of social life. They provide a new context for a cultural politics of value in consumer culture.

At the same time, as noted in chapter 2, a number of writers have begun to challenge the importance of the category of the consumer altogether. Writers such as Gabriel and Lang identify what they call a fundamental paradox between 'the ubiquity of the consumer in contemporary discourses' and 'the virtual impossibility of generalizing about consumers' (2008: 322). The consumer, they argue, is unmanageable, both as a concept, since no one can pin it down to one specific conceptualization at the expense of others, and as an entity, since attempts to control and manage the consumer lead to the consumer mutating from one persona to another. Other writers, such as Ritzer and Jurgenson, suggest that the centrality of the consumer to contemporary culture is being replaced by the prosumer (2010), while Naomi Klein, author of *No Logo*, argues that politics must move beyond notions of identity altogether (2000). She says that her generation of university students were 'media narcissists' who focused on identity politics but left issues of social inequality untouched. While recognizing the importance of all these points, this book has argued that what needs to be acknowledged is that the power of the figure of the consumer is due to it working at the level of 'an identity, audience [and] category of analysis' (Trentmann, 2006b: 2) simultaneously. It is for this reason that it continues to be central to thinking about consumer culture.

Conclusion

The claim that has been explored in this final chapter is that consumer culture is a particular form of material culture in which the capacity to exercise consumer choice has become central to personal or self-identity. From this point of view, it is interesting to note – as pointed out in chapter 7 – that some aspects of both the contemporary ethos of anti-materialism and green politics are often intertwined with an individualized politics of consumption in which choice becomes implicated in morality. This suggests that even in activities that are critical of how one exercises choice – either by choosing to purchase one good rather than another, or by choosing not to purchase certain goods at all – the nature of such choice is taken as an indication of who one is. This implies that 'consumer choice' is indeed one of the most important means by which our society thinks about individual agency and autonomy, and makes judgements about individuals. From this point of view, the sociological significance of consumer culture is to be found in the fact that the individual is not judged by him- or herself or by society in terms of how well they carry out their duty or responsibility in relation to some wider collective or external morality ('the family', 'the community', 'the greater good of all' or 'God's will'), but in terms of how well they exercise their capacity to make a (consumer) choice. It is no surprise, then, that what it is to choose has itself become the subject of study in this and many other books. However, what this concluding chapter has also argued is that the nature and conditions of choice must also be addressed if the significance of its centrality to self and collective identity is to be adequately assessed.

In general terms, the argument developed in this book is that what it is to be middle or working class, to be a man or a woman, to be black or white, or to be young or old is a particular kind of reflexive relation to self and this relation has been and is being transformed or reorganized by consumer culture. The view that emerges is thus that different kinds of relation to the self, enabled by consumer culture, inform *specific* kinds of belonging to the social groupings of class, gender, race and age. This is an argument that suggests that consumer culture provides a specific context for the development of novel relationships between self-identity and group membership, and that this context is interpreted, reflexively, in various ways by different social groups. In this sense, social groupings, rather than being displaced, are being reworked in the diverse processes of making or assembling the self that are characteristic of contemporary consumer culture. This suggests that questions of difference, struggle and inequality will not disappear, but will surface in struggles between social groupings in different ways, including a politics and ethics of consumption, which consider questions of access, participation and ownership, changing forms of materiality and the politics of identity. As the processes of self-assembly or putting the self together are transformed in the practices of consumer culture, the coordinates of the social field are transformed: not flattened but redrawn.

Bibliography

Abercrombie, N. 1991: 'The privilege of the producer'. In R. Keat and N. Abercrombie (eds), *Enterprise Culture*. London: Routledge, 171–86.

Abercrombie, N. 1994: 'Authority and consumer society'. In R. Keat, N. Whiteley and N. Abercrombie (eds), *The Authority of the Consumer*. London: Routledge, 43–57.

Abercrombie, N. 1996: *Television and Society*. Cambridge: Polity.

Abercrombie, N., Hill, S., and Turner, B. 1986: *Sovereign Individuals of Capitalism*. London: Allen and Unwin.

Abercrombie, N., and Warde, A. 1988: *Contemporary British Society: A New Introduction to Sociology*. Cambridge: Polity.

Abrams, M. 1961: *Teenage Consumer Spending in 1959: Middle Class Boys and Girls*. London: London Press Exchange.

Adkins, L. 1995: *Gendered Work: Sexuality, Family and the Labour Market*. Buckingham and Bristol: Open University Press.

Adorno, T. 1974: *Minima Moralia: Reflections on a Damaged Life*. London: NLB.

Adorno, T., and Horkheimer, M. 1979: *Dialectic of Enlightenment*. London: Allen Lane.

Amin, A., and Goddard, J. (eds) 1986: *Technological Change, Industrial Restructuring and Regional Development*. London: Allen and Unwin.

Amin, A., and Thrift, N. (eds) 1994: *Globalization, Institutional and Regional Development in Europe*. Oxford: Oxford University Press.

Anderson, M., Bechhofer, F., and Gershuny, J. 1994 (eds): *The Social Economy of the Household*. Oxford: Oxford University Press.

Ang, I. 1991: *Desperately Seeking the Audience*. London: Routledge.

Anholt, S. 2007: 'Africa needs brand aid', *Monocle*, 6/1 (September): 56–7.

Appadurai, A. 1986 (ed.): *The Social Life of Things*. Cambridge: Cambridge University Press.

Appadurai, A. 1993: 'Disjuncture and difference in the global cultural economy'. In B. Robbins (ed.), *The Phantom Public Sphere*, Minneapolis, MN: University of Minnesota Press, 269–97.

Arvidsson, A. 2005: 'Brands: a critical perspective', *Journal of Consumer Culture*, 5/2: 235–58.

Arvidsson, A. 2006: *Brands: Meaning and Value in Media Culture*. London and New York: Routledge.

Back, L., and Quaade, V. 1993: 'Dream utopias, nightmare realities: imaging race and culture within the world of Benetton advertising'. *Third Text*, 22: 65–80.

Barkham, P. 2008: 'The big McMakeover', *G2, The Guardian*, Monday 28 January: 6.

Barnett, C., and Land, D. 2007: 'Geographies of generosity: beyond the "moral turn"', *Geoforum*, 38/6: 1065–75.

Barnett, C., Cloke, P., Clarke, N., and Malpass, A. 2005: 'Consuming ethics: articulating the subjects and spaces of ethical consumption', *Antipode*, 37/1: 23–45.

Barry, A. 2001: *Political Machines: Governing a Technological Society*. London: Athlone.

Baudrillard, J. 1983: *Simulations*, trans. P. Foss, P. Patton and P. Beitchman. New York: Semiotext(e).

Baudrillard, J. 1988: *Selected Writings*, ed. M. Poster. Cambridge: Polity.

Baudrillard, J. 1996: *The System of Objects*, trans. J. Benedict. London: Verso.

Bauman, Z. 1987: *Legislators and Interpreters: On Modernity, Postmodernity and Intellectuals*. Cambridge: Polity.

Bauman, Z. 1990: *Thinking Sociologically*. Oxford: Blackwell.

Bauman, Z. 1992a: *Intimations of Postmodernity*. London: Routledge.

Bauman, Z. 1992b: 'Survival as a social construct'. *Theory, Culture and Society*, 9: 1–36.

Beck, U., Giddens, A., and Lash, S. 1994: *Reflexive Modernization*. Cambridge: Polity.

Belk, R. W., and Coon, G. S. 1993: 'Gift giving as agapic love: an alternative to the exchange paradigm based on dating experiences', *Journal of Consumer Research*, 20/3: 393–417.

Bennett, O. 1991: 'Selective memory', *Creative Review*, 56/24 (November): 55–6.

Benson, R. and Armstrong, S. 1994: 'These people know what you want'. *The Face* (July): 54–6.

Benson, S. P. 1986: *Counter Cultures: Saleswomen, Managers and Customers in American Department Stores*. Urbana and Chicago, IL: University of Illinois Press.

Berger, J. 1972: *Ways of Seeing*. London: BBC Books.

Berland, J. 1992: 'Angels dancing: cultural technologies and the production of space'. In L. Grossberg, C. Nelson and P. Treichler (eds), *Cultural Studies*. New York and London: Routledge, 38–50.

Bhabha, H. 1990 (ed.): *Nation and Narration*. London: Routledge.

Bhabha, H. 1994: *The Location of Culture*. London: Routledge.

Bhattacharya, C. S. 2005: 'Cola behind empty pots? Coke thirsts for a fight – no water, no problem?', *Telegraph* (Calcutta; July 17).

Bird-David, N., and Darr, A. 2009: 'Commodity, gift and mass-gift: on gift-commodity hybrids in advanced mass consumption cultures', *Economy and Society*, 38/2: 304–25.

Boltanski, L., and Chiapello, E. 2007: *The New Spirit of Capitalism*. London: Verso.

Bourdieu, P. 1977: *Outline of a Theory of Practice*, trans. R. Nice. Cambridge: Cambridge University Press.

Bourdieu, P. 1984: *Distinction: A Social Critique of the Judgement of Taste*. London: Routledge and Kegan Paul.

Bowlby, R. 1985: *Just Looking: Consumer Culture in Dreiser, Gissing and Zola*. New York and London: Methuen.

Bowlby, R. 1993: *Shopping with Freud*. London: Routledge.

Bowlby, R. 2000: *Carried Away: The Invention of Modern Shopping*. London: Faber and Faber.

Branigan, T. 2008: 'The real Olympics competition: Nike and Adidas claim China's heroes', *Guardian* (Monday 18 August): 23.

Braverman, H. 1974: *Labour and Monopoly Capital*. London: Monthly Review Press.

Breton, A. 1969: *Manifestos of Surrealism*, trans. R. Seaver and H. R. Lane. Ann Arbor, MI: Ann Arbor Paperbacks, University of Michigan Press.

Brooker, E. 1993: 'Ticking over'. *Guardian Weekend* (9 October): 36–8.

Bunting, M. 2009: 'In control? Think again. Our ideas of brand and human nature are myths', *Guardian* (24 August): 27.

Callon, M. 1998: (ed.) *The Laws of the Markets*. Oxford: Blackwell.

Callon, M., Meadel, C., and Rabehariosa, V. 2005: 'The economy of qualities'. In A. Barry and D. Slater (eds), *The Technological Economy*. London: Routledge, 28–51.

Callon, M., Millo, Y., and Muniesa, F. (eds.) 2007: *Market Devices*. Oxford: Blackwell.

Campbell, C. 1989: *The Romantic Ethic and the Spirit of Modern Consumerism*. Oxford: Blackwell.

Campbell, C. 1996: *The Myth of Social Action*. Cambridge: Cambridge University Press.

Cannon, D. 1994a: 'The desire for the new: its nature and social location as presented in theories of fashion and modem consumerism'. In R. Silverstone and E. Hirsch (eds), *Consuming Technologies: Media and Information in Domestic Spaces*. London: Routledge, 48–67.

Cannon, D. 1994b: *Generation X and the New Work Ethic*. London: Demos.

Castells, M. 1977: *The Urban Question: A Marxist Approach*. London: Edward Arnold.

Castells, M. 1996: *Rise of the Network Society*. Chichester: Wiley.

Chambers, E. 1992: 'Blackness as a cultural ikon', *Ten-8*, 2/3: 122–7.

Chua, B. Huat. 1992: 'Shopping for women's fashion in Singapore'. In R. Shields (ed.), *Lifestyle Shopping*. London and New York: Routledge, 115–36.

Clifford, J. 1988: *The Predicament of Culture*. Cambridge, MA, and London: Harvard University Press.

Cloke, P., Johnson, S., and May, J. 2005: '"Discourse of charity" in the provision of emergency services for homeless people', *Environment and Planning A*, 37/3: 385–402.

Cochoy, F. 1998: 'Another discipline for the market economy: marketing as performative knowledge and know-how for capitalism', in M. Callon (ed.) *The Laws of the Markets*. Oxford and Malden, MA: Blackwell, 194–221.

Connolly, K. 2010: 'Mobile phone barcode app to help ethical shoppers', *Guardian* (1 April): 17.

Connolly, J., and Prothero, A. 2008: 'Green consumption: life-politics, risk and contradictions', *Journal of Consumer Culture*, 8/1: 117–45.

Connolly, W. 2005: *Pluralism*. Durham, NC: Duke University Press.

Coombe, R. 1998: *The Cultural Life of Intellectual Properties: Authorship, Appropriation and the Law*. Durham, NC: Duke University Press.

Coupland, D. 1992: *Generation X*. London: Abacus.

Coupland, D. 1993: *Shampoo Planet*. London: Simon and Schuster.

Cowan, R. 1983: *More Work for Mother: The Ironies of Household Technology from the Open Hearth to the Microwave*. New York: Basic Books.

Cowe, R. 1994: 'The high street fights back', *Finance Guardian* (24 December): 32.

Cronin, A. 2004a: *Advertising Myths: The Strange Half-Lives of Images and Commodities*. London: Routledge.

Cronin, A. 2004b: 'Regimes of mediation: advertising practitioners as cultural intermediaries?', *Consumption, Markets and Culture*, 7/4: 349–69.

Dant, T. 1999: *Material Culture in the Social World*. Buckingham: Open University Press.

Dant, T. 2008: 'The pragmatics of material interaction', *Journal of Consumer Culture*, 8/1: 11–33.

Debord, G. 1977: *Society of the Spectacle*. Detroit: Black and Red.

de Certeau, M. 1988: *The Practice of Everyday Life*. Berkeley and Los Angeles, CA, and London: University of California Press.

Delphy, C. 1984: *Close to Home*. Cambridge: Hutchinson.

Delphy, C. and Leonard, D. 1992: *Familiar Exploitation: A New Analysis of Marriage in Contemporary Western Societies*. Cambridge: Polity.

Denegri-Knott, J., and Molesworth, M. 2010: '"Love it. Buy it. Sell it": Consumer desire and the social drama of eBay', *Journal of Consumer Culture*, 10/1: 56–79.

Dennis, K., and Urry, J. 2009: *After the Car*. Cambridge: Polity.

Dittmar, H. 1992: *The Social Psychology of Material Possessions*. Hemel Hempstead: Harvester Wheatsheaf.

Douglas, M. 2002: *Purity and Danger: An Analysis of Concepts of Pollution and Taboo*. London: Routledge.

Douglas, M., and Isherwood, B. 1979: *The World of Goods*. London: Allen Lane.

Dowling, R. 1993: 'Femininity, place and commodities: a retail case study'. *Antipode*, 25/4: 295–319.

Ducille, A. 1994: 'Dyes and dolls: multicultural Barbie and the merchandising of difference', *differences*, 6/1: 46–68.

Du Gay, P. 1995: *Consumption and Identity*. London: Sage.

Eco, U. 1984: 'A guide to the neo-television of the 80s', *Framework*, 25: 18–27.

Elliott, R. 1994: 'Addictive consumption: function and fragmentation in post-modernity', *Journal of Consumer Policy*, 1: 159–79.

Ellis, J. 1992: *Visible Fictions: Cinema, Television, Video*. London: Routledge.

Elzen, B., Geels, F. G., and Green, K. (eds) 2004: *System Innovation and the Transition to Sustainability*. Cheltenham: Edward Elgar.

Enninfirl, E. 1994: 'On the street: the future of fashion discussed by the creative upstarts who are influencing its cutting edge'. *i-D* (October): 36–40.

Evans, C., and Thornton, M. 1989: *Women and Fashion: A New Look*. London and New York: Quartet Books.

Ewen, S. 1976: *Captains of Consciousness: Advertising and the Social Roots of the Consumer Culture*. New York: McGraw Hill.

Ewen, S. 1988: *All Consuming Images: The Politics of Style in Contemporary Culture*. New York: Basic Books.

Ewen, S., and Ewen, E. 1982: *Channels of Desire*. New York: McGraw-Hill.

The Face, 1988: 'Designer everything', *The Face* (September): 154.

Featherstone, M. 1991: *Consumer Culture and Postmodernism*. London: Sage.

Fernando, S. 1992: 'Blackened images', *Ten-8*, 2/3: 140–7.

Fine, B., and Leopold, E. 1993: *The World of Consumption*. London: Routledge.

Firat, A. Fuat and Alladi Venkatesh. 1993: 'Postmodernity: the age of marketing', *International Journal of Research in Marketing*, 10: 227–49.

Forty, A. 1986: *Objects of Desire*. London: Thames and Hudson.

Foster, R. J. 2007: 'The work of the new economy: consumers, brands, and value creation', *Cultural Anthropology*, 2/4: 707–31.

Franklin, S., Lury, C., and Stacey, J. 2000: *Global Nature, Global Culture*. London: Routledge.

Friedan, B. 1965: *The Feminine Mystique*. Harmondsworth: Penguin.

Friedman, J. 1991: 'Consuming desires: strategies of selfhood and appropriation', *Cultural Anthropology*, 6/2: 154–64.

Friedman, J. 1994: Introduction. In J. Friedman (ed.), *Consumption and Identity*. Newark, NJ: Harwood Academic Publishers, 1–23.

Gabriel, Y., and Lang, T. 2008: 'New faces and new masks of today's consumer', *Journal of Consumer Culture*, 8/3: 321–40.

Gad, T., and Rosencreutz, A. 2002: *Managing Brand Me: How to Build Your Personal Brand*. New York: Momentum.

Gaines, J. 1988: 'White privilege and looking relations – race and gender in feminist film theory', *Screen*, 29/4: 12–27.

Game, A., and Pringle, R. 1984: *Gender at Work*. London: Pluto Press.

Ganes, M. 1993: *Symbolic Exchange and Death*. London: Sage.

Garnham, N. 1990: *Capitalism and Communication: Global Culture and the Economics of Information*. London: Sage.

Garon, S., and Maclachlan, P. L. 2006: (eds) *The Ambivalent Consumer: Questioning Consumption in East Asia and the West*. Ithaca, NY: Cornell University Press.

Gates, H. J. Jr. 1992: 'The black man's burden'. In G. Dent (ed.), *Black Popular Culture*. Seattle, WA: Bay Press, 75–83.

Gershuny, J. 1978: *After Industrial Society*. London: Macmillan,

Gershuny, J. 1983: *Social Innovation and the Division of Labour*. Oxford: Oxford University Press.

Ghazi, P., and Jones, J. 2004: *Down-shifting: The Guide to Happier, Simpler Living*. London: Hodder and Stoughton,

Gibney, Jr., F., and Luscombe, B. 2000: 'The redesigning of America', *Time*, 26 June: 48–55.

Giddens, A. 1991: *Modernity and Self-Identity*. Cambridge: Polity.

Giddens, A. 1992: *The Transformation of Intimacy*. Cambridge: Polity.

Giesler, M. 2006: 'Consumer gift system', *Journal of Consumer Research*, 33: 283–90.

Gill, R. 2009: 'Supersexualise me! Advertising and "the midriffs".' In F. Attwood (ed), *Mainstreaming Sex: The Sexualization of Culture*. London: I.B. Taurus, 93–111.

Gilroy, P. 1987: *There Ain't No Black in the Union Jack*. London: Unwin Hyman.

Gilroy, P. 1992: 'Wearing your art on your sleeve', *Ten-8*, 2/3: 128–39.

Gilroy, P. 1993: *The Black Atlantic: Modernity and Double Consciousness*. London: Verso.

Gilroy, P. 2010: *Darker than Blue: On the Moral Economies of Black Atlantic Culture*. Cambridge, MA: Harvard University Press.

Glover, J. 2009: 'Britain admits it is not green enough, reveals poll', *Guardian* (1 September). Available at: <http://www.guardian.co.uk/environment/2009/sep/01/climate-change-poll>.

Godelier, M. 1999: *The Enigma of the Gift*, trans. N. Scott. Cambridge: Polity.

Goldman, R. 2002: *Reading Ads Socially*. New York and London: Routledge.

Graeber, D. 2001: *Towards an Anthropological Theory of Value: The False Coin of Our Own Dreams*. London: Palgrave Macmillan.

Grant, J. 1999: *The New Marketing Manifesto*. New York: Texte.

Hall, S. 1992: 'What is this "Black" in Black popular culture?' In G. Dent (ed.), *Black Popular Culture*. Seattle: Bay Press, 21–37.

Hamer, D., and Budge, B. 1994: *The Good, the Bad, and the Gorgeous: Popular Culture's Romance with Lesbianism*. London: Pandora.

Hand, M., Shove, E., and Southerton, D. 2005: 'Explaining showering: a

discussion of the material, conventional and temporal dimensions of practice', *Sociological Research Online*: <http://www.socresonline.org.uk/10/2/
hand.html>.

Hardt, M., and Negri, T. 2001: *Empire*. Cambridge, MA: Harvard University
Press.

Harris, A. (ed.) 2004: *All About the Girl: Culture, Power and Identity*.
Abingdon and New York: Routledge.

Hart, S. 1998: 'The future for brands'. In S. Hart and J. Murphy (eds),
Brands: The New Wealth Creators. Basingstoke and London: Macmillan
Business, 206–14.

Hartman, 2007: 'Ikeaization of France', *Public Culture*, 19/3: 483–98.

Harvey, D. 1989: *The Condition of Postmodernity*. Oxford: Blackwell.

Harvey, D. 2005: *A Brief History of Neoliberalism*. Oxford: Oxford University
Press.

Haug, W. F. 1986: *Critique of Commodity Aesthetics*. Cambridge: Polity.

Hawkins, G. 2006: *The Ethics of Waste: How We Relate to Rubbish*. Oxford:
Rowman and Littlefield Publishers.

Hawkins, G. 2009: 'More-than-Human Politics: The Case of Plastic Bags',
Australian Humanities Review, 46 (May). Available at: <http://www.aus-
tralianhumanitiesreview.org/archive/Issue-May-2009/home. html>.

Hayles, N. K. 2009: 'RFID: human agency and meaning in information-
intensive environments', *Theory, Culture and Society*, 26/2–3: 47–72.

Hearn, A. 2008: 'Meat, mask, burden: probing the contours of the branded
self', *Journal of Consumer Culture*, 8/2: 197–217.

Hebdige, D. 1979: *Subculture: The Meaning of Style*. London: Methuen.

Hebdige, D. 1987: *Cut'n'Mix: Culture, Identity and Caribbean Music*.
London: Methuen.

Hebdige, D. 1988: *Hiding in the Light: On Images and Things*. London:
Routledge.

Hewitt, R. 1986: *White Talk – Black Talk: Inter-racial Friendship and
Communication amongst Adolescent*. Cambridge: Cambridge University
Press.

Hirsch, F. 1977: *The Social Limits of Growth*. London: Routledge.

Hirschman, E. C. 1992: 'The consciousness of addiction: toward a general
theory of compulsive consumption', *Journal of Consumer Research*, 19
(September): 155–79.

Holloway, R. (1999): 'Levi Strauss: focus on the legend . . . and record-
breaking global sales'. In F. Gilmore (ed.), *Brand Warriors*. London:
HarperCollins Business, 63–78.

Hollows, J. 2000: *Feminism, Femininity and Popular Culture*. Manchester:
Manchester University Press.

Holt, D. 2004: *How Brands Become Icons: The Principles of Cultural Branding*.
Cambridge, MA: Harvard Business Review.

Humphery, K. 2009: *Excess: Anti-Consumerism in the West*. Cambridge:
Polity.

Humphrey, C., and Mandel, R. (ed.) 2002: *The Market in Everyday Life: Ethnographies of Postsocialism*. Oxford and New York: Berg.

Huyssen, A. 1986: *After the Great Divide: Modernism, Mass Culture and Postmodernism*. London: Macmillan.

Jameson, F. 1991: *Postmodernism, or, the Cultural Logic of Late Capitalism*. London: Verso.

Jefferson, T., and Hall, S. (eds) 1976: *Resistance Through Rituals: Youth Subcultures in Post-war Britain*. London: Hutchinson.

Jhally, S. 1987: *The Codes of Advertising*. New York: Frances Pinter.

Jhally, S. 1989: 'Advertising as religion: the dialectic of technology and magic'. In I. Angus and S. Jhally (eds), *Cultural Politics in Contemporary America*. New York: Routledge, 23–47.

Johnson, B. 2009: 'Why did Big Brother remove paid-for content from Amazon's Kindles?', *Guardian*, Technology Section (23 July): 1.

Johnston, J., and Taylor, J. 2008: 'Feminist consumerism and fat activism: a comparative study of grassroots activism and the Dove Real Beauty campaign', *Signs*, 33/4: 941–66.

Julier, G. 2000: *The Culture of Design*. London: Sage.

Julier, G., and Moor, L. (eds.) 2009: *Design and Creativity: Policy, Management and Practice*. Oxford and New York: Berg.

Keegan, R. 1992: 'Distilling the essence', *Ten-8*, 2/3: 148–9.

Kellner, D. 1983: 'Critical theory, commodities and the consumer society', *Theory, Culture and Society*, 3: 66–84.

King, B. 1989: 'The burden of Max Headroom', *Screen*, 30/1&2: 122–38.

Klein, N. 2000: *No Logo*. London: Flamingo.

Knorr Cetina, K. 1997: 'Sociality with objects: social relations in postsocial knowledge societies', *Theory, Culture and Society*, 14/4: 1–30.

Knorr Cetina, K. 2000: 'Post-social theory'. In G. Ritzer and B. Smart (eds), *Handbook of Social Theory*. London: Sage.

Kohn, M. 1988a: 'The cash dispenser', *The Face* (September): 180.

Kohn, M. 1988b: 'The pink pound', *The Face* (September): 132.

Kopytoff, I. 1986: 'The cultural biography of things: commoditization as process'. In A. Appadurai (ed.), *The Social Life of Things*. Cambridge: Cambridge University Press, 64–94.

Kornberger, M. 2010: *Brand Society. How Brands Transform Management and Lifestyle*. Cambridge: Cambridge University Press.

Labi, A. 2000: 'Wheelie good fun', *Time* (26 June): 62.

Lamont, M. 1992: *Money, Morals and Manners: The Culture of the French and the American Upper-Middle Class*. Chicago, IL: University of Chicago Press.

Lang, T., and Gabriel, Y. 2006: *The Unmanageable Consumer*. London: Sage.

Lash, S. 1990: *The Sociology of Postmodernism*. London: Routledge.

Lash, S., and Lury, C. 2004: *The Global Culture Industry: The Mediation of Things*, Cambridge: Polity.

Lash, S., and Urry, J. 1987: *The End of Organized Capitalism.* Cambridge: Polity.

Lash, S. 1994: *Economies of Signs and Spaces.* London: Sage.

Latour, B., and Weibel, P. (ed.) 2005: *Making Things Public: Atmospheres of Democracy.* Cambridge, MA: MIT Press.

Lazzarato, M. 2004: 'From Capital-Labor to Capital-Life', *Ephemera: Theory and Politics in Organization,* 4/3: 187–208.

Lee, M. 1993: *Consumer Culture Reborn: The Cultural Politics of Consumption.* London: Routledge.

Leiss, W. 1976: *The Limits of Satisfaction.* Toronto: Toronto University Press.

Leiss, W., Kline, S., and Jhally, S. 1986: *Social Communication as Advertising: Persons, Products and Images of Well-being.* New York: Macmillan.

Le Roux, B., Rouanet, H., Savage, M., and Warde, A. 2007: 'Class and cultural division in the UK', *CRESC Working Paper no. 40.* Available at: <http://www. cresc.ac.uk/publications/papers.html>.

Lévi-Strauss, C. 1963: *Totemism,* trans. R. Needham. London: Merlin Press.

Lipsitz, G. 1994: 'We know what time it is: race, class and youth culture in the nineties'. In A. Ross and T. Rose (eds), *Microphone Fiends: Youth Music and Youth Culture.* London and New York: Routledge, 17–28.

Littler, J. 2009: *Radical Consumption: Shopping for Change in Contemporary Culture.* Buckingham: Open University Press.

Low, G. Ching-Liang 1989: 'White skins/black masks: the pleasures and politics of imperialism', *New Formations,* 9 (winter): 83–103.

Lunt, P., and Livingstone, S. 1992: *Mass Consumption and Personal Identity: Everyday Economic Experience.* Buckingham and Bristol: Open University Press.

Lury, A. 1994: 'Advertising: moving beyond the stereotypes'. In R. Keat, N. Whiteley and N. Abercrombie (eds), *The Authority of the Consumer.* London: Routledge, 91–102.

Lury, C. 1993: *Cultural Rights: Technology, Legality and Personality.* London: Routledge.

Lury, C. 2002: 'Style and the perfection of things'. In J. Collins (ed.), *High-Pop: Making Culture into Popular Entertainment.* Oxford: Blackwell, 201–24.

Lury, C. 2004: *Brands: The Logos of the Global Economy.* London: Routledge.

Lury, C., and Moor, L. 2010: 'Brand valuation and topological culture'. In M. Aronczyk and D. Powers (eds), *Blowing Up the Brand: Critical Perspectives on Promotional Culture.* New York: Peter Lang Publishing, 29–52.

MacAlister Hall, M. 1992: 'A nation of shoppers', *Observer Magazine* (13 December): 16–29.

Mac an Ghaill, M. 1989: *Young, Gifted and Black.* London: Routledge.

Mack, J., and Lansley, S. 1985: *Poor Britain.* London: George Allen and Unwin.

McKendrick, N., Brewer, J., and Plumb, J. H. 1982: *The Birth of a Consumer Society*. London: Europa.

McClintock, A. 1994: 'Soft-soaping empire: commodity racism and imperial advertising'. In G. Robertson et al. (eds), *Travellers' Tales: Narratives of Home and Displacement*. London: Routledge, 131–55.

McCracken, G. 1988: *Culture and Consumption: New Approaches to the Symbolic Character of Consumer Goods and Activities*. Bloomington and Indianopolis, IN: Indiana University Press.

Mackinnon, C. 1983: 'Feminism, Marxism, method and the state: an agenda for theory'. In E. Abel and E. K. Abel (eds), *The Signs Reader: Women, Gender and Scholarship*. Chicago, IL, and London: University of Chicago Press, 227–57.

Macpherson, C. B. 1962: *The Political Theory of Possessive Individualism: Hobbes to Locke*. London: Clarendon Press.

McRobbie, A. 1991: *Feminism and Youth Culture: From 'Jackie' to 'Just Seventeen'*. Basingstoke and London: Macmillan.

McRobbie, A. 1994: *Postmodernism and Popular Culture*. London: Routledge.

McRobbie, A. 2007: 'Top girls?', *Cultural Studies*, 21/4–5: 718–37.

McRobbie, A., and Nava, M. (eds) 1984: *Gender and Generation*. London: Macmillan.

McVeigh, 2000: 'How Hello Kitty commodifies the cute, cool and camp: "Consumutopia" versus "Control" in Japan', *Journal of Material Culture*, 5/2: 225–45.

Maffesoli, M. 1991: 'The ethic of aesthetics', *Theory, Culture and Society*, 8: 7–20.

Maffesoli, M. 1993: *The Shadow of Dionysus: A Contribution to the Sociology of the Orgy*. Albany, NY: State University of New York Press.

Mandel, R. E., and Humphrey, C. 2002: *Markets and Moralities: Ethnographies of Post-Socialism*. Oxford and New York: Berg.

Manovich, L. 2001: *The Language of New Media*. Cambridge, MA: MIT Press.

Manuelli, S. 2000: 'Searching for an identity', *Design Week* (14 January).

Marcuse, H. 1968: *One Dimensional Man*. London: Sphere.

Marres, N. 2009: 'Testing powers of engagement: green living experiments, the ontological turn and the undoability of involvement', *European Journal of Social Theory*, 12/1: 117–33.

Martin, B. 1981: *A Sociology of Contemporary Cultural Change*. Oxford: Blackwell.

Marx, K. 1967: *Capital, Volume 1*, trans. S. Moore and E. Aveling. New York: International Publishers.

Marzano, S. 2000: 'Branding=Distinctive authenticity'. In J. Pavitt (ed.), *Brand.New*. London: Victoria and Albert Museum, 58–9.

Mason, M. 2008: *The Pirate's Dilemma: How Hackers, Punk Capitalists, Graffiti Millionaires and Other Youth Movements are Remixing Our Culture and Changing Our World*. Harmondsworth: Penguin.

Mathur, P. 1989: 'An eighties alphabet', *Blitz: A Magazine of the Nineties* (December): 56–67.

Mauss, M. [1925] 1954, reprinted 1990: *The Gift: The Form and Reason for Exchange in Archaic Societies*. London: Routledge.

Mercer, K. 1994: *Welcome to the Jungle: New Positions in Black Cultural Studies*. New York and London: Routledge.

Meyers D. 2003: 'Whose brand is it anyway?' In N. Ind (ed.), *Beyond Branding: How the New Values of Transparency and Integrity are Changing the World of Brands*: London and Philadelphia, PA: Kogan Page, 21–35.

Michael, M. 2000: *Reconnecting Culture, Technology and Nature: From Society to Heterogeneity*. London: Routledge.

Miller, D. 1987: *Material Culture and Mass Consumption*. Oxford: Blackwell.

Miller, D. 1998: *A Theory of Shopping*. Ithaca, NY: Cornell University Press.

Miller, D. 2001: 'The poverty of theory', *Journal of Consumer Culture*, 1/2: 225–43.

Miller, D., Jackson, P., Thrift, N., Holbrook, B., and Rowlands, M. 1998: *Shopping, Place and Identity*. Abingdon and New York: Routledge.

Mitchell, A. 2001: *Right Side Up: Building Brands in the Age of the Organized Consumer*. London: HarperCollins Business.

Moi, T. 1991: 'Appropriating Bourdieu: feminist theory and Pierre Bourdieu's sociology of culture', *New Literary History*, 22: 1017–49.

Mollerup, P. 1997: *Marks of Excellence: The History and Taxonomy of Trademarks*. London: Phaidon Press.

Montgomerie, J. 2007: 'Financialization and consumption: an alternative account of rising consumer debt levels in Anglo-America', *CRESC Working Paper No.43*. Available at: <http://www.cresc.ac.uk/publications/papers.html>.

Moor, L. 2003: 'Branded spaces: the scope of "new marketing"', *Journal of Consumer Culture*, 3/1: 39–60.

Moor, L. 2007: *The Rise of Brands*. Oxford and New York: Berg.

Moor, L. 2008: 'Branding consultants as cultural intermediaries', *Sociological Review*, 56/3: 408–28.

Moor, L., and Littler, J. 2008: 'Fourth worlds and neo-Fordism: American Apparel and the cultural economy of consumer anxiety', *Cultural Studies*, 22/5: 700–23.

Mort, F. 1989: 'The writing on the wall', *New Statesman and Society*, 12 (May): 40–1.

Mukerji, C. 1983: *From Graven Images: Patterns of Modern Materialism*. New York: Columbia University Press.

Mulhern, F. 1974: *The Moment of 'Scrutiny'*. London: New Left Books.

Mulvey, L. 1975: 'Visual pleasure and narrative cinema', *Screen*, 16/3: 6–18.

Myers, K. 1986: *Understains: The Sense and Seduction of Advertising*. London: Pandora.

Naughton, J. 1992: 'Personal services', *Observer Magazine* (13 December): 68–9.

Nava, M. 1992: *Changing Cultures: Feminism, Youth and Consumerism.* London: Sage.

Nava, M. 1995: 'Modernity's disavowal: women, the city and the department store'. In M. Nava and A. O'Shea (eds), *Modern Times: Reflections on a Century of English Modernity.* London: Routledge: 38–76.

Ngai, S. 2006: 'Competitiveness: from "Sula" to "Tyra"', *Women's Studies Quarterly*, 34/3&4: 107–39.

Nicholls, A., and Opal, C. 2005: *Fair-Trade: Market-driven Ethical Consumption.* London: Sage.

Nicholson-Lord, D. 1992: 'In the consumer's cathedral', *The Independent on Sunday* (13 December): 3.

Nixon, S. 1996: *Hard Looks: Masculinities, the Visual and Practices of Consumption.* London: Routledge.

Nixon, S., and du Gay, P. 2002: 'Who needs cultural intermediaries', Special Issue, *Cultural Studies*, 16/4: 495–500.

Oakley, A. 1976: *Housewife.* Harmondsworth: Penguin.

Partington, A. 1991: 'Melodrama's gendered audience'. In S. Franklin, C. Lury and J. Stacey (eds), *Off-Centre: Feminism and Cultural Studies.* London: Harper Collins, 49–68.

Pateman, C. 1988: *The Sexual Contract.* Cambridge: Polity.

Pavitt, J. 2000: 'Branding the individual', in J. Pavitt (ed.), *Brand.new.* London: V&A Publications, 154–75.

Peters, T. 1999: *The Brand You 50: Fifty Ways to Transform Yourself from an 'Employee' into a Brand that Shouts Distinction, Commitment, and Passion!* New York: Alfred A. Knopf Inc.

Piore, M. J., and Sabel, C. 1984: *The Second Industrial Divide: Possibilities for Prosperity.* New York: Basic Books.

Polan, B. 1989: 'Buying and selling a new decade', *Weekend Guardian* (11 November): 9.

Poovey, M. 1998: *A History of the Modern Fact.* Chicago, IL: University of Chicago Press.

Pope, P. 1995: 'The premier league', *Melody Maker*, (14 January): 10–11.

Prahalad, C. K., and Ramaswamy, V. 2004: *The Future of Competition: Co-creating Unique Value with Customers.* Boston, MA: Harvard Business School Publishing.

Preteceille, E., and Terrail, J.-P. 1985: *Capitalism, Consumption and Needs.* Oxford: Blackwell.

Radner, H. 1995: *Shopping Around: Feminist Culture and the Pursuit of Pleasure.* New York: Routledge.

Rai, A. 1994: 'An American Raj in Filmistan: Images of Elvis in Indian Films', *Screen*, 35/1: 51–77.

Ramamurthy, A. 1991: *Black Markets: Images of Black People in Advertising and Packaging (1980–1990).* London: Cornerhouse and Arts Council.

Rheingold, H. 1994: *The Virtual Community: Finding Connection in a Computerized World.* London: Secker and Warburg.

Rich, A. 1981: *Compulsory Heterosexuality and Lesbian Existence*. London: Onlywomen Press.

Rifkin, J. 2001: *The Age of Access: How the Shift from Ownership to Access is Transforming Modern Life*. London: Penguin Books.

Ritzer, G., and Jurgenson, N. 2010: 'Production, consumption and pro-sumption: the nature of capitalism in the age of the digital "prosumer"', *Journal of Consumer Culture*, 10/1: 13–36.

Rogers, H. 2005: *Gone Tomorrow: The Hidden Life of Garbage*. London and New York: The New Press.

Ross, A. 1989: *No Respect: Intellectuals and Popular Culture*. New York and London: Routledge.

Sahlins, M. 1974: *Stone Age Economics*. London: Tavistock.

Sahlins, M. 1976: *Culture and Practical Reason*. Chicago, IL: Chicago University Press.

Sassatelli, R. 2007: *Consumer Culture: History, Theory and Politics*. London: Sage.

Saunders, P. 1990: *A Nation of Home Owners*. London: Unwin Hyman.

Saunders, P., and Harris, C. 1994: *Privatization and Popular Capitalism*. Milton Keynes: Open University Press.

Savage, J., and Frith, S. 1993: *Pearls and Swine: The Intellectuals and the Mass Media*. Manchester: Working Papers in Popular Cultural Studies, Manchester Institute for Popular Culture.

Savage, M. et al. 1992: *Property, Bureaucracy and Culture: Middle Class Formation in Contemporary Britain*. London: Routledge.

Schor, J. 1999: *The Overspent American: Upscaling, Downshifting and the New Consumer*. London: HarperCollins.

Scott, H. 1995: 'The new Chelsea girls', *Elle* (May): 27–8.

Sedgwick, E. Kosofsky. 1994: *Tendencies*. London: Routledge.

Seger, L. 1990: *Creating Unforgettable Characters*. New York: Henry Holt.

Seltzer, M. 1993: 'Serial killers (1)', *Differences: A Journal of Feminist Cultural Studies*, 5/1: 92–128.

Sennett, R. 2007: *The Culture of New Capitalism*. New Haven, CT: Yale University Press.

Seyfang, G. 2009: *The New Economies of Sustainable Consumption: Seeds of Change*. London: Palgrave Macmillan.

Shamir, R. 2008: 'The age of responsibilization: on market-embedded morality', *Economy and Society* 37/1: 1–19.

Sheller, M. 2003: *The Binding Mobilities of Transatlantic Consumption*. Lancaster: Department of Sociology, University of Lancaster; available at: <http://www.comp.lancs.ac.uk/sociology/soc123ms.html>.

Shove, E. 2007: *Comfort, Cleanliness and Convenience: The Social Organization of Normality*. London: Berg Publishers.

Simmel, G. 1971: 'Subjective culture'. In D. N. Levine (ed.), *Georg Simmel: On Individuality and Social Forms. Selected Writings*. Chicago, IL: University of Chicago Press, 227–34.

Simmel, G. 1990: *The Philosophy of Money*, ed. D. Frisby. London: Routledge.

Skeggs, B. 1997: *Becoming Respectable: An Ethnography of White, Working-class Women*. London: Sage.

Skeggs, B. 2005: 'The making of class and gender through visualizing moral subject formation', *Sociology*, 39/5: 965–82.

Skeggs, B., and Wood, H. 2004: 'Notes on ethical scenarios of self on British reality TV', *Feminist Media Studies*, 4/1: 205–8.

Slater, D. 1997: *Consumer Culture and Modernity*. Cambridge: Polity.

Slater, D., and Tonkiss, F. 2001: *Market Society: Markets and Modern Social Theory*. Cambridge. UK, and Malden, MA: Polity.

Sombart, W. 1967: *Luxury and Capitalism*. Michigan, MI: University of Michigan Press.

Stacey, J. 1994: *Stargazing: Hollywood Cinema and Female Spectatorship*. London and New York: Routledge.

Steedman, C. 1998: *Landscape for a Good Woman: A Story of Two Lives*. London: Virago.

Steedman, C. 2000: 'Enforced narratives: stories of another self'. In Cosslett, T., Lury, C. and P. Summerfield (eds), *Feminism and Autobiography: Texts, Theories, Methods*. London: Routledge, 25–40.

Sterling, B. 2005: *Shaping Things*, designed by L. Wild, Cambridge, MA: MIT Press.

Storper, M. 2001: 'Lived effects of the contemporary economy: globalization, inequality and consumer society'. In J. Comaroff and J. L. Comaroff (eds), *Millenial Capitalism and the Culture of Neoliberalism*, 88–124.

Strasser, S. 1999: *Waste and Want: A Social History of Trash*. New York: Metropolitan Books.

Strathern, M. 1994: 'Foreword: the mirror of technology'. In R. Silverstone and E. Hirsch (eds), *Consuming Technologies: Media and Information in Domestic Spaces*. London: Routledge, pp. vii–xiv.

Tapscott, D., and Williams, A. D. 2007: *Wikinomics: How Mass Collaboration Changes Everything*. London: Atlantic Books.

Terranova, T. 2004: *Network Culture: Politics for the Information Age*. London: Pluto.

Thaler, R. H., and Sunstein, C. R. 2008: *Nudge: Improving Decisions About Health, Wealth and Happiness*. New Haven, CT: Yale University Press.

Thompson, D. 2008: *The $12 Million Stuffed Shark: The Curious Economics of Contemporary Art*. London: Aurum Press.

Thompson, J. 1990: *Ideology and Modern Culture: Critical Social Theory in the Era of Mass Communication*. Cambridge: Polity.

Thrift, N. 2005: *Knowing Capitalism*. London: Sage.

Toffler, A. 1980: *The Third Wave*. New York: Bantam.

Travis, A. 2008: 'Revealed: Britain's secret propaganda war against al-Qaida', *Guardian*, (26 August): 1.

Trentmann, F. (ed.) 2006a: *The Making of the Consumer: Knowledge, Power and Identity in the Modern World*. Oxford and New York: Berg.

Trentmann, F. 2006b: 'Knowing consumers – histories, identities, practices: an introduction'. In F. Trentmann, ed., *The Making of the Consumer: Knowledge, Power and Identity in the Modern World*. Oxford and New York: Berg, 1–30.

Trentmann, F. 2009: 'Crossing divides: consumption and globalization in history'. In I. Rees Jones and D. J. Ekherdt, *Consumption and Generational Change: The Rise of Consumer Lifestyles*. New Brunswick, NJ: Transaction Publishers.

Trodre, R. 1993: 'Future chic', *The Observer Life* (10 October): 14.

Turkle, S. 1986: *The Second Self: Computers and the Human Spirit*. New York: Simon and Schuster.

Tyler, C.-A. 1991: 'Boys will be girls: the politics of gay drag'. In D. Fuss (ed.), *Inside/Out: Lesbian Theories, Gay Theories*. New York and London: Routledge, 32–70.

Urry, J. 1990: *The Tourist Gaze*. London: Sage.

Veblen, T. 1925: *The Theory of the Leisure Class: An Economic Study of Institutions*. London: Allen and Unwin.

Vidal, J. 2003: 'Retail therapy', *Guardian*, Society (26 February): 2–3.

Vidal, J. 2009: 'Plastic bag revolt halves nationwide use to 450m', *Guardian* (17 July): 9.

Virno, P. 2004: *A Grammar of the Multitude*. Los Angeles, CA, and New York: Semiotexte.

Vogel, D. 2006: *The Market for Virtue: The Potential and Limits of Corporate Social Responsibility*. Washington, DC: Brookings Institution.

Walby, S. 1990: *Theorizing Patriarchy*. Cambridge: Polity.

Walby, S. 1997: *Gender Transformations*. London: Routledge.

Wang, J. 2008: *Brand New China: Advertising, Media and Commercial Culture*. Cambridge, MA: Harvard University Press.

Warde, A. 1992: 'Notes on the relationship between production and consumption'. In R. Burrows and C. Marsh (eds), *Consumption and Class: Divisions and Change*. London: Macmillan, 15–31.

Warde, A. 1994: 'Consumers, identity and belonging: reflections on some themes of Zygmunt Bauman'. In R. Keat, N. Whiteley and N. Abercrombie (eds), *The Authority of the Consumer*. London: Routledge, 58–74.

Warde, A. 2005: 'Consumption and theories of practice', *Journal of Consumer Culture*, 5/2: 131–53.

Ware, V. 1992. *Beyond the Pale: White Women, Racism and History*. London: Verso.

Weber, M. 1930: *The Protestant Ethic and the Spirit of Capitalism*, trans. T. Parsons. London: Allen and Unwin.

Weedon, C., and Jordan, G. 1995: *Cultural Politics: Class, Gender, Race and the Postmodern World*. Oxford: Blackwell.

Weekes, D. 2002: 'Get your freak on: how black girls sexualise identity', *Sex Education*, 2/3: 251–62

Wernick, A. 1991: *Promotional Culture: Advertising, Ideology and Symbolic Expression*. London: Sage.

Wernick, A. 2006: 'Rebranding Harvard', *Theory, Culture and Society*, 23/2–3: 566–7.

West, C. 1990: 'The new cultural politics of difference'. In R. Ferguson, M. Gever, Trinh T. Min-ha and C. West (eds), *Out There: Marginalization and Contemporary Cultures*. Boston, MA: MIT/New Museum.

West, C. 1992: 'Nihilism in Black America'. In G. Dent (ed.), *Black Popular Culture*. Seattle, WA: Bay Press, 37–47.

Whiteley, N. 1994: 'High art and the high street: the "commerce-and-culture" debate'. In R. Keat, N. Whiteley and N. Abercrombie (eds), *The Authority of the Consumer*. London: Routledge, 119–38.

Williams, P. J. 1993: *The Alchemy of Race and Rights*. London: Virago.

Williams, R. 1974: *Television: Technology and Cultural Form*. London: Fontana.

Williams, R. 1980: 'Advertising: the magic system'. In R. Williams, *Problems in Materialism and Culture*. London: Verso, 170–95.

Williams, R. 1983: *Keywords: A Vocabulary of Culture and Society*. London: Fontana.

Williamson, J. 1986: 'Woman is an island: femininity and colonization'. In T. Modleski (ed.), *Studies in Entertainment: Critical Approaches to Mass Culture*. Bloomington and Indianapolis, IN: Indiana University Press, 119.

Willis, P. 1982: 'The motor-bike and motor-bike culture'. In B. Waites et al. (eds), *Popular Culture: Past and Present*. London: Croom Helm, 284–94.

Willis, P. 1990: *Common Culture*. Milton Keynes: Open University Press.

Willis, S. 1990: 'I want the Black one: is there a place for Afro-American culture in commodity culture?', *New Formations*, 10 (spring): 77–97.

Willis, S. 1993: 'Disney World: public use/private state', *The South Atlantic Quarterly*, 92/1: 119–37.

Wilmott, H. 2010: 'Creating "value" beyond the point of production: branding, financialization and market capitalization', *Organization*, 17/5: 517–42.

Willmott, P., and Young, M. 1973: *The Symmetrical Family: A Study of Work and Leisure in the London Region*. London: Routledge and Kegan Paul.

Winship, J. 1983: '"*Options* – for the way you want to live now", or a magazine for superwoman', *Theory, Culture and Society*, 1/3: 44–65.

Winship, J. 1987: *Inside Women's Magazines*. London: Pandora.

Winship, J. 2000: 'Culture of restraint: the British chain store 1920–39'. In P. Jackson, M. Lowe, D. Miller and F. Mort (eds), *Commercial Cultures: Economies, Practices, Spaces*. Oxford: Blackwell, 58–68.

Winward, J. 1994: 'The organized consumer and consumer information co-operatives'. In R. Keat et al. (eds), *The Authority of the Consumer*. London: Routledge, 75–90.

Yan, J. 2003: 'The brand manifesto: why brands must act now or alienate the future's primary consumer group'. In N. Ind (ed.), *Beyond Branding: How the New Values of Transparency and Integrity are Changing the World of Brands*. London, and Philadelphia, PA: Kogan Page, 199–221.

York, P. 1980: *Style Wars*. London: Sedgwick and Jackson.

York, P. 1994: 'The dead beat of the street', *The Independent on Sunday* (24 November): 24.

Young, M., and Willmott, P. 1957: *Family and Kinship in East London*. London: Routledge and Kegan Paul.

Zizek, S. 1999: 'You may!', *London Review of Books*, 21/6 (March): 3–6.

Zukin, S. 1988: *Loftliving: Culture and Capital in Urban Change*. London: Radius.

Zukin, S. 1991: *Landscapes of Power*. Berkeley and Los Angeles, CA: University of California Press.

Zukin, S. 1992: 'Postmodern urban landscapes: mapping culture and power'. In S. Lash and J. Friedman (eds), *Modernity and Identity*. Oxford: Blackwell, 221–48.

Zukin, S. 2004: *Point of Purchase: How Shopping Changed American Culture*. New York: Routledge.

Zwick, D., Bonsu, S. K., and Darmody. A. 2008: 'Putting consumers to work: "co-creation" and new marketing governmentality', *Journal of Consumer Culture*, 8/2: 163–93.

Index